FREE VIDEO

Essential Test Tips Video from Trivium Test Prep!

Thank you for purchasing from Trivium Test Prep!
We're honored to help you prepare for your exam.
To show our appreciation, we're offering a

FREE *Essential Test Tips* Video

Our video includes 35 test preparation strategies that will make you successful on your big exam. All we ask is that you email us your feedback and describe your experience with our product. Amazing, awful, or just so-so: we want to hear what you have to say!

> To receive your **FREE** *Essential Test Tips* **Video,** please email us at
> **5star@triviumtestprep.com.**

Include "Free 5 Star" in the subject line and the following information in your email:

1. The title of the product you purchased.
2. Your rating from 1 – 5 (with 5 being the best).
3. Your feedback about the product, including how our materials helped you meet your goals and ways in which we can improve our products.
4. Your full name and shipping address so we can send your **FREE** *Essential Test Tips* **Video**.

If you have any questions or concerns please feel free to contact us directly at:
5star@triviumtestprep.com.

Thank you!
– Trivium Test Prep Team

SIE Exam Prep 2023 and 2024:

2 Practice Tests and Study Guide for the FINRA Securities Industry Essentials

Elissa Simon

Copyright ©2023 by Trivium Test Prep

ISBN-13: 9781637984420

ALL RIGHTS RESERVED. By purchase of this book, you have been licensed one copy for personal use only. No part of this work may be reproduced, redistributed, or used in any form or by any means without prior written permission of the publisher and copyright owner. Trivium Test Prep; Accepted, Inc.; Cirrus Test Prep; and Ascencia Test Prep are all imprints of Trivium Test Prep, LLC.

DISCLAIMER: FINRA was not involved in the creation or production of this product, is not in any way affiliated with Trivium Test Prep, and does not sponsor or endorse this product.

Image(s) used under license from Shutterstock.com.

Table of Contents

Online Resources vii

Introduction ix

1 Regulatory Entities and Agencies — 1

Securities Regulation 1
The Securities and Exchange Commission 2
Registration of Security Issuers 10
Self-Regulatory Organizations (SROs) 16
Other Regulators and Agencies 20
Answer Key 23

2 SRO Regulatory Requirements for Associated Persons — 27

Employee Conduct and Reportable Events 34
Answer Key 43

3 Market Participants and Market Structure — 45

Market Participants and Their Roles 45
Other Participants 50
Depositories and Clearing Corporations 55
Market Structure 56
Offerings 59
Obligations of Market Participants 63
Answer Key 67

4 Economic Factors — 69

Economic Factors 69
Business Economic Factors 76
Answer Key 86

5 Financial Products — 89

Equity Securities 89
Financial Products 89
Debt Instruments 93
Options 100
Packaged Products 104
Municipal Fund Securities 106
Direct Participation Programs 108
Real Estate Investment Trusts (REITs) 109
Hedge Funds 111
Exchange-Traded Products 112
Answer Key 115

6 Investment Risks and Rules — 119

Investment Risks 119
Investment Rules 124
Answer Key 129

7 Trading, Settlement, and Corporate Actions — 131

Orders and Strategies 131
Investment Returns 136
Trade Settlement and Corporate Actions 142
Answer Key 148

v

8 Customer Accounts and Compliance Considerations — 149

Account Types and Characteristics............ 149
Customer Account Registrations................ 153
Anti-Money Laundering................................ 163
Answer Key 167

9 Prohibited Activities — 169

Market Manipulation 169
Prohibited Activities..................................... 169
Insider Trading 172
Other Prohibited Activities.......................... 174
Answer Key 180

10 SIE Practice Test — 183

Answer Key 193

Online Resources

To help you fully prepare for your SIE exam, Trivium includes online resources with the purchase of this study guide.

Practice Test

In addition to the practice test included in this book, we also offer an online exam. Since many exams today are computer based, getting to practice your test-taking skills on the computer is a great way to prepare.

From Stress to Success

Watch From Stress to Success, a brief but insightful YouTube video that offers the tips, tricks, and secrets experts use to score higher on the exam.

Reviews

Leave a review, send us helpful feedback, or sign up for Trivium promotions—including free books!

Access these materials at:
https://triviumtestprep.com/sie-online-resources

Introduction

Congratulations on choosing to take the Securities Industry Essentials (SIE) exam! By purchasing this book, you've taken the first step toward becoming a registered General Securities Representative.

This guide provides a detailed overview of the SIE, so you'll know exactly what to expect on test day. We'll take you through the concepts covered on the exam and give you the opportunity to test your knowledge with practice questions. Even if it's been a while since you last took a major test, don't worry; we'll make sure you're more than ready!

What is the SIE?

The Securities Industry Essentials (SIE) exam measures a candidate's competency to perform the duties of a General Securities Representative (GSR):

- To become a registered GSR, a candidate must pass both the SIE exam and the Series 7 exam.
- The SIE is administered by the Financial Industry Regulatory Authority (FINRA), Inc.

What's on the SIE?

The candidate must be familiar with the four major functions that make up the exam. The subject matter and percentages of the exam are as follows:

WHAT'S on the SIE?			
SECTION	DESCRIPTION	PERCENTAGE OF EXAM	NUMBER OF QUESTIONS
1	Knowledge of Capital Markets	16%	12
2	Understanding Products and Their Risks	44%	33
3	Understanding Trading, Customer Accounts and Prohibited Activities	31%	23
4	Overview of the Regulatory Framework	9%	7
TOTAL	1 hour and 45 minutes		75 (+10 pretest)

Questions on Section 1 (Knowledge of Capital Markets) test knowledge of the mission, purpose, and jurisdiction of the Securities and Exchange Commission (SEC), Self-Regulatory Organizations (SROs), and other agencies. An understanding of the definitions and roles of market participants (investors, broker-dealers, traders, etc.) is also tested. Expect questions on market structure and economic factors: the primary, secondary, third and fourth markets, monetary and fiscal policy, interest rates, business cycles, and more.

Section 2 (Understanding Products and Their Risks) comprises the bulk of the exam. Equities, debt instruments, options, and municipal fund securities are all covered. Candidates should be familiar with specialized products like direct participation programs (DPPs), real estate investment trusts (REITs), exchange traded products (ETPs), 529 plans, and more. The risks associated with these products are also addressed.

Questions on Section 3 (Understanding Trading, Customer Accounts and Prohibited Activities) delve into strategies, actions, and rules when transacting on the market. Expect questions on account types, compliance, and best practices. These questions will also cover prohibited activities, market manipulation, and anti-money laundering (AML). Candidates should know relevant laws and rules.

Section 4 (Overview of the Regulatory Framework) questions cover registration, conduct, and education requirements for GSRs and people associated with SROs. Again, it is essential to know the relevant laws and rules.

How Is the SIE Administered?

The SIE is a computer-based exam. Examinees have one hour and forty-five minutes to complete the exam. Each exam consists of 85 multiple-choice questions; 75 questions are scored. There are 10 pretest, unscored questions that are randomly distributed throughout the exam. Each question lists four possible answer choices. Only one answer choice is correct.

About This Guide

This guide will help you master the most important test topics and develop critical test-taking skills. We have built features into our books to prepare you for your exam and increase your score. Along with a detailed summary of the test's format, content, and scoring, we offer an in-depth overview of the content knowledge required to pass the test. Throughout the guide, you'll find sidebars that provide interesting information, highlight key concepts, and review content so that you can solidify your understanding. You can also test your knowledge with sample questions throughout the text as well as practice questions. We're pleased you've chosen Trivium to be a part of your professional journey!

1 Regulatory Entities and Agencies

Securities Regulation

History and Purpose of Securities Regulation

US **securities regulation** integrates federal laws (which represent the bulk of what finance professionals observe) and state statutes created and enforced by multiple agencies. Several regulatory agencies oversee securities regulation:

- The primary regulatory agency is the Securities and Exchange Commission (SEC).
- Stock exchanges, like the New York Stock Exchange (NYSE) and NASDAQ, have structured, stringent listing requirements based on industry regulations that members must meet.
- Self-regulatory organizations (SROs), such as the Financial Industry Regulatory Authority (FINRA) focus on futures and derivatives.

These agencies protect issuers' and stakeholders' interests in capital markets across a broad range of industries. Federal law and state statutes create fair, efficient, and transparent security transactions, which will be discussed at length in this chapter.

Security regulations embrace all and any transactions involving the following:

- stocks (equities)
- Treasury stocks
- notes
- debentures
- bonds
- swaps in any of the above
- futures and derivatives in any of the above

- notes, agreements, or certificates that reflect the following:
  - indebtedness
  - interest
  - profit-sharing
  - collateral trust
  - preorganization
  - subscription
  - transferable shares

Securities regulation made its mark in the early 1930s to remove obstructions in the transaction experience for investors and security issuers. From the security issuers' perspective, the removal of obstructions means protection from dubious or false stakeholder claims.

Securities regulation also provides peace of mind to stakeholders by protecting them from issuers' malpractice. With clear rules and guidelines, the capital markets can function with significantly improved efficiency and free-flowing liquidity. A regulation platform is meant to establish unsurpassed market integrity. Ideally, it gives all transactional parties confidence that the investment data submitted to the public by issuers is genuine and accurate.

Securities regulation started with the stock market crash of 1929, which exposed significant investment promoter transgressions that today's security laws would never tolerate. The Securities Act of 1933 was the first time the government applied its legal resources to quell misleading and overenthusiastic representations of primary market investment opportunities.

Before the act passed, the investment arena resembled the Wild West, where almost any outlandish action went unnoticed. Companies issued stocks unhindered by oversight bodies or committees, freely overstated forecasts, and paid scant attention to solidly verifying their predictions. Brokers promised their clients unrealistic profits that were, in some cases, entirely fraudulent. Thousands of investors fell for the hype, chasing rewards that were too good to be true.

These problems stayed hidden for years. Nobody saw a need to disrupt the system until it came crashing down in 1929—the start of the Great Depression. The Securities Act of 1933 (the Securities Act) and the Securities Exchange Act of 1934 (the Exchange Act, or SEA) offered some relief.

QUICK REVIEW QUESTION

1. What is the high-level purpose and mission of securities regulation?

The Securities and Exchange Commission

The Securities Exchange Act of 1934 created the **Securities and Exchange Commission (SEC)** with widespread authority to execute securities industry regulations. The SEC applies regulations to protect investors from fraud and manipulations in the US securities secondary markets. In addition, the SEC umbrella encompasses the following:

- corporate takeovers
- registration statements
- underwriting activities (otherwise known as book-runners)

The regulation protocols extend to two other government agencies:

- the Federal Reserve Board (FRB)
- the Federal Deposit Insurance Corporation (FDIC)

The president of the US appoints five commissioners to the SEC, each with a focused team who reports to them. One of the commissioners takes the chair, and each team has a five-year term with an eighteen-month extension to account for a handover. To guarantee nonpartisanship, the law stipulates that a maximum of three commissioners (60 percent) can belong to the same political party. The structure consists of the five divisions:

1. **Division of Trading and Markets:** This division ensures markets are fair, orderly, and efficient.
2. **Division of Corporate Finance (CF):** This division ensures investor information is accurate, comprehensive, and relevant as concerns whether to buy or sell stocks.
3. **Division of Investment Management (IM):** This division registers and regulates investment companies, variable insurance products, and federal investment advisors.
4. **Division of Enforcement (DE):** This division formulates and enforces SEC-structured guidelines and compliance for issuers and sellers and punishes rogue broker-dealers by doing the following:
   - investigating cases after receiving complaints or observing flagrant rule violations
   - initiating civil suit prosecutions and implementing administrative proceedings
5. **Division of Economic and Risk Analysis (ERA):** This is the analytics arm responsible for integrating economics and big data into the mission statement. It is where the SEC reconciles federal and state laws to help formulate the best investor protections and create maximum market efficiencies.

HELPFUL HINT

The Division of Trading and Markets is sometimes referred to as the Market Regulation Division.

QUICK REVIEW QUESTIONS

2. What asset categories do the SEC regulations cover?

   _____

3. How many SEC divisions are there?

   _____

SEC Rules

The SEC rule-setting process takes many opinions into account. The first step in making rules is the receipt of a proposal from three of the five commissions, Congress, another government agency, a private company, or anyone in the public domain. Once created, the draft rule may be circulated to the public with alternatives, detailed explanations, and a questionnaire for feedback. Alternatively, it may go to a roundtable discussion with commission members, who may request teams develop a more detailed proposal and present it to the full commission.

After a rule undergoes the process described above, the following takes place:

- The commission decides to accept or reject the draft rule.
- If accepted, the commission circulates the recrafted written rule to the public for feedback via the *Federal Register* and on the SEC website, where it remains—typically for one to two months.
- Finally, after considering outside commentary, the commission designates a team to structure the ultimate rule version, and the full commission votes on it. The SEC adopts it and adds it under the appropriate section if the majority agrees.

Rule generation inside the commission can only come from the Division of Trading and Markets, Corporate Finance, or Investment Management. However, when requested, numerous offices may offer advice and support. For example, a single rule proposal can initiate a sequence of checks within the following offices. Any one of these checkpoints can kill a proposal:

- the Office of the General Counsel (OGC)
- the Office of Management and Budget (OMB)
- the Office of the Secretary (OS)
- the Office of Information Technology (OIT)
- the Office of Filings and Information Services (OFIS)
- the Division of Economic and Risk Analysis (DERA)

Their contributions to rule finality cover the following:

- ranking the rule as major or minor
- cost-benefit analysis
- compliance or conflict with existing statutes, regulations, and mainstream SEC policies
- organizing communications to the public and between relevant offices
- monitoring the process through the different steps
- recording documentation
- assessing the rule's impact and flexibility
- evaluating economic ramifications
- the paperwork burdens under the Paperwork Reduction Act (PRA)

These are only a few of the extensive social, economic, and legislative considerations when establishing a new rule. Precise procedures must be followed for a rule to become part of the SEC protocols.

QUICK REVIEW QUESTIONS

4. Which three SEC divisions can propose rules?

_____

5. Who outside the SEC can propose new rules?

_____

SEC Investigations

Investigations by the SEC begin in any number of ways, the most common being

- routine clearinghouse and brokerage firm inspections by FINRA,
- scanning reports and schedules,
- alerts from whistleblowers and/or any other government agencies,
- news articles focusing on improprieties, and
- tips and complaints from investors that align with recent rule and regulation changes under the Dodd-Frank Act.

The irregularities that emerge relate to

- security offerings unregistered with the SEC,
- inexplicable accounting records,
- suspicious transaction patterns that may indicate insider trading,
- unscrupulous selling methods,
- inadequate supervision in all the places it is called for, and
- misleading content in publicly issued material.

The process kicks off with a formal **order of investigation** authorizing the Enforcement Division to call witnesses to provide testimony at a hearing. However, the submission of requested documents likely precedes any in-person interaction.

Most SEC investigations start informally as **Matters Under Inquiry (MUIs)**. The investigation may close or escalate to a formal affair. Since the SEC does not have subpoena power in MUI investigations, momentum in these situations relies on the cooperation of the targeted parties.

The **formal investigation stage** signifies that the investigation will intensify considerably. At this stage, the SEC can use subpoenas to compel witnesses to provide evidence under oath. The SEC subpoena powers can have a long reach, drawing in almost anyone the commission thinks can provide information on the issues under focus. Formal investigation orders, approved by the division heads, make the missteps of the subject of the investigation clear and spell out

> **HELPFUL HINT**
> The Divisions of Trading and Markets, Corporate Finance, and Investment Management are commonly referred to as the "rule makers."

> **HELPFUL HINT**
> The SEC can only institute civil actions, but it may recommend criminal investigations under the auspices of the US Attorney's Office. SEC collaboration with the attorney general to prove criminality is common. As a result, parties receiving an SEC subpoena should not assume that the investigation stops at a possible civil suit; it may extend to a criminal action.

the SEC regulations which have been violated. Summary conclusions without further action are possible in the formal stages but unlikely since the investigation is so advanced.

In rare cases, the SEC skips the step of recommending formal status and goes directly to an enforcement order. In each of these situations—no matter the level of investigation—the SEC keeps all details of proceedings confidential.

When an enforcement recommendation passes after going through the process described above, defendants may receive a Wells notice (named for the chairman who initiated it), first by phone, followed by a letter.

A **Wells notice** explains the SEC's intentions, provides reasons for the investigation, and gives the recipients a month to respond with counterarguments. Counterarguments, unless carefully worded, can further incriminate the defendants. As a result, their attorneys may advise them not to respond.

When individuals or companies violate SEC regulations, resulting in illegal gains, the SEC may seek civil financial penalties and disgorgement.

Disgorgement is a statute that deals with unjust enrichment by enforcing the return of all ill-gotten funds to the injured parties: anyone who makes money at the expense of others could face disgorgement penalties. These penalties cover insider trading, embezzlement, and a range of illegal actions under the **Foreign Corrupt Practices Act (FCPA)**. However, a five-year statute of limitations applies to any civil actions claiming disgorgement. Moreover, disgorgement does not apply to every case the SEC launches.

The **Enforcement Division (DE)** works with federal prosecutors in certain circumstances. Parallel criminal investigations are not unusual, and the commission staff have no obligation to divulge knowledge of legal actions outside the SEC case; however, there is a bit of a catch-22:

- Attorneys routinely advise defendant clients not to respond to SEC civil case prompts in case there is a criminal case in the wings they do not yet know about.
- Admissions to the SEC can infringe one's Fifth Amendment rights to protect against self-incrimination.
- Conversely, an inept response or nonresponse can signal the validity of the SEC's accusations, motivating the agency to press on.

SEC investigations and criminal investigations are different in many respects; however, the comingling of the two calls for legal counsel who can guide the defendant in navigating the tactics that both the SEC and US Attorney's Office will undoubtedly apply in unison.

QUICK REVIEW QUESTIONS

6. What is an MUI?

7. How are defendants notified of an enforcement recommendation?

8. What term describes the statute that attacks unjust enrichment when individuals or companies violate SEC regulations, resulting in illegal gains?

   _____

9. What is the difference between an SEC action and an attorney general action?

   _____

State Law (Blue Sky Laws)

When Congress created more regulation after the Great Depression, it did not do so in a vacuum. Many states in the 1920s had working compliance regulations (called **blue sky laws**), but they were state-centric and did not apply country-wide. Congress used relevant state law definitions and concepts to create more consistent, far-reaching, and overriding federal laws.

Ideally state laws kick in when there is no federal provision. Unfortunately, blue sky laws vary significantly from state to state based on

- products and transactions;
- registration requirements for brokers, dealers, and issuers; and
- definition and coverage of fraudulent actions.

After studying the differences, astute criminal minds may concentrate their activities in the states with the least punitive consequences and most glaring legal gaps.

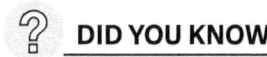

DID YOU KNOW?

The term *blue sky laws* refers to a quote from Supreme Court Justice Joseph McKenna that says in part "speculative schemes which have no more basis than so many feet of blue sky."

QUICK REVIEW QUESTIONS

10. What are blue sky laws?

    _____

11. When do state laws apply?

    _____

12. What is a major disadvantage of state laws?

    _____

Federal Law

The **Securities Act of 1933** is a set of laws, statutes, and regulations formulated after the 1929 stock market crash that contributed to the Great Depression. The goal was to prevent a similar catastrophe from occurring in the future. The Securities Act represented a significant attempt to stop misrepresentation in financial data when companies issue new shares. As a result, investors can rely on company information to make informed decisions.

Thanks to the Securities Act, corporate reporting became more transparent, and investors did not have to second-guess themselves. The act removed excessive hype from broker sales pitches and executive-level projections. Moreover, it

> **DID YOU KNOW?**
> The term *C-suite* is used to describe executive-level positions in an organization, notably those that begin with a *c*, such as *chief executive officer*.

imposed responsibility on stakeholders to represent their businesses in a realistic light—or face severe penalties.

The secondary market, which deals with security trading on public bourses like the NYSE and Nasdaq, has always greatly affected the US economy. Unlike trading on the primary market, investors publicly trade the shares from the launch, relying on current data and financial statements instead. Stockbrokers promote or recommend stocks to people who did not buy shares in the initial offering.

Because there is considerable opportunity for the misrepresentation of information outside of company reporting, the **Securities Exchange Act of 1934 (SEA)** focused on governing secondary market securities transactions. Like the 1933 act, the SEA aimed to suppress fraud or the manipulation of newly issued securities. The SEA created the SEC and its far-reaching powers to hold bad actors in the financial environment accountable for their actions.

QUICK REVIEW QUESTIONS

13. What was formulated after the 1929 stock market crash to prevent a similar catastrophe?

_____

14. Which legislation focuses on governing secondary market securities transactions?

_____

Definitions Under the Securities Exchange Act of 1934

Section 3(a) of the SEA covers several definitions, including the following:

- *facility* as it pertains to *exchange*
- *transaction* as it pertains to *exchange* and *facility*
- *member* as it pertains to *exchange*
- *broker* as it pertains to *exchange*

The term *exchange* must include marketplaces or facilities that connect buyers and sellers of securities to get the same results as commonly understood entities, such as recognized stock exchanges. These marketplaces/facilities can be an incorporated (or unincorporated) organization, association, group of persons, or de facto stock exchange.

Exchange refers to a marketplace or facility central to its functioning. A facility, when used, includes its premises and tangible or intangible assets (even if they are not held on the premises). However, it also extends to entities or people with the right to deploy the facility (its premises and assets) for exchange-like transactions. A facility **transaction** can be one or all of the following:

- completing it end to end
- reporting it on an exchange (see definition above)

- communicating it to and from the exchange via a ticker or any other mechanism as long as the transmitter/receiver has been maintained by or used with the consent of the exchange

A **member**, as it pertains to an exchange, refers to any natural person allowed to transact on an exchange without broker assistance, usually on the floor. Moreover, a member includes registered brokers or dealers who

- are connected to the natural person,
- are designated to represent natural persons, and
- agree to the exchange regulations while transacting on the exchange.

Alternatively, a member of a registered securities association is any broker or dealer who agrees to be regulated by such an association for as long as the association agrees to comply with the protocols and provisions of the SEA and aligns its own rules with those of the SEA. The term *member* applies to any person working within the exchange arena whom the SEC expects to comply with the rules and regulations discussed in the previous sections. The term also impacts other sections of the SEA, namely the following:

- Section 6(b) - (1), (4), (6), (7)
- Section 6(d), (f)
- Section 17(d)
- Section 19(d), (e), (g), (h)
- Section 21

The term *broker* defines anyone who transacts securities on an exchange for customer accounts or clients (natural persons or entities). There's one major exception: banks. Neither the bank nor a bank employee is considered a broker under this definition. This is because of third-party brokerage arrangements, which occur through a contractual written agreement.

The bank, if it wants to assist clients in the securities arena, allows a registered broker-dealer attached to an exchange to transact for its client either in the bank or elsewhere. In these cases, the bank should clarify certain details, such as credentials, compensation restrictions, and the fact that the bank's brokerage services are distinct from traditional bank services.

QUICK REVIEW QUESTIONS

15. What is an exchange according to the SEA?

16. What are the other crucial definitions under Section 3(a)?

Securities Investor Protection Act of 1970 (SIPA)

The **Securities Investor Protection Act (SIPA)** of 1970 is an amendment to the Securities and Exchange Act of 1934. It created a nonprofit company under the auspices of the US government—the **Securities Investor Protection Corporation (SIPC)**. SIPA made it compulsory for most registered brokers and dealers under the SEA to become members of the SIPC.

The single-minded purpose was to make good on investor losses resulting from proven broker incompetence or bankruptcy, thus creating confidence in the registered investment arena. Every member pays SIPC assessment fees that build a reserve fund to cover these losses. SIPC limits and restrictions include the following:

- The maximum single investor claim is $500,000 (or $250,000 if cash).
- The coverage has nothing to do with market volatility and losses incurred due to the volatility.

QUICK REVIEW QUESTIONS

17. What is the primary purpose of the Securities Investor Protection Act of 1970?

18. What is the maximum claim any investor can make under SIPA?

19. How is the SIPC funded?

20. Who are members of the SIPC?

Registration of Security Issuers

Registration Requirements

Section 5 of the Securities Act of 1933 requires that issuers register nonexempt securities with the SEC. A **registration statement** is a detailed summary of a security issuer's business operations and its intended equity offering. This information boosts investors' confidence and helps inform their investment decisions. This portion of the chapter will discuss relevant sections under the Securities Act of 1933 and the Securities and Exchange Act of 1934, including the following:

- Securities Act of 1933, Section 7 (information required in a registration statement)
- Securities Act of 1933, Section 8 (taking effect of registration statements and amendments thereto)
- Securities Act of 1933, Section 23 (unlawful representations)
- Securities and Exchange Act of 1934, Section 12 (registration requirements for securities)
- Securities and Exchange Act of 1934, Section 15A (registered securities associations)

Registration statements are covered under **Section 7** of the Securities Act of 1933 (information required in a registration statement). Rules in Section 7 compel fundraisers to provide sufficient and accurate information, thereby enabling investors to assess the opportunity without any data gaps. Section 7 explains what a registration form should contain and creates two primary drivers:

1. SEC authority and latitude to expand (or condense) the informational requirements
2. investors' realistic expectations that the registration statements provide the following:
   - reliable issuer details
   - itemized terms and conditions around the investment the issuer is seeking

For a registration statement to take effect, it must pass an SEC review under **Section 8** of the Securities Act of 1933 (taking effect of registration statements and amendments thereto). Section 8 ensures (to the satisfaction of the SEC) that all pertinent disclosures are clear and transparent.

Section 8 allows the registration statement to take effect within twenty days of submission to the SEC. However, the SEC has the power to speed up or delay the process if it detects information deficiencies or omissions.

The two big takeaways from Section 8 are the following:

1. Security issuers cannot raise funds without a registration statement green light from the SEC unless they are operating under an exemption (see Regulation D in the following section).
2. After passing registration, issuers are liable for misrepresentations or material omissions in such a statement.

When issuers have successfully complied with the provisions of Section 8, it signifies the following:

- The registration has passed SEC evaluation and is currently effective.
- The path forward should be clear of desist or stop orders that obstruct registration effectiveness.

Section 23 of the Securities Act of 1933 (unlawful representations) establishes that it is unlawful to make, intimate, or instigate any representations contrary to the effective registration statement.

Section 12 of the Securities Exchange Act of 1934 (registration requirements for securities) underscores that until the SEC has granted effectiveness to a security, that security is ineligible for the following:

- national securities exchange transactions
- transaction initiations by any exchange member, broker, or dealer

Section 15A of the Securities Exchange Act of 1934 (registered securities associations) mandates that brokers and dealers—the parties instrumental in processing and initiating effective registration statements—must be registered

DID YOU KNOW?

If information in the Registration Statement is unsatisfactory, the SEC will issue **deficiency letters** that suggest changes the security issuer must address. The SEC suggestions generally assist issuers rather than admonish them for incorrect original statement content and messaging. The goal is to meet investor needs without qualification.

HELPFUL HINT

Exempted securities (see Regulation D in the following section) can bypass qualifications laid out in Section 12.

with the SEC. This can take the form of an association of brokers and dealers registered under one of the following categories:

- a national securities association
- an affiliated securities association
- a grouping (not specifically an association) that abides by the association rules and other information the SEC deems relevant to the public interest or investor protection

QUICK REVIEW QUESTIONS

21. What document, which summarizes the details of a security issuer's business and intended equity offering, must pass SEC review before the issuer can offer the investment on any exchange?

22. Which section of the Securities Act of 1933 covers registration statements?

23. What is required for a registration statement to take effect?

24. When does registration take effect?

25. Which regulation stipulates that brokers and dealers—the parties instrumental in processing and initiating effective registration statements—must be registered with the SEC?

Registration Exemptions (Regulation D)

Regulation D (rules governing the limited offer and sale of securities without registration under the Securities Act of 1933, also known as Reg D) outlines several registration exemptions. In other words, Regulation D permits some companies to transact their securities (i.e., offer and sell) free from strict registration rules and protocols. The exemptions are detailed under **Rule 504** of Regulation D, which says that some companies can offer and sell securities for up to $5,000,000 over twelve months.

Rule 506 of Regulation D says that companies can issue securities without registration as long as the following occurs:

- They do not promote or advertise securities for sale.
- The buyers are accredited investors (with no limit on numbers) who meet SEC prescribed/recognized criteria (e.g., income, net worth, certifications, and reputation).

Nonaccredited investors or their purchasing representatives may buy securities under Reg D, but the issuers must vet them. Of course, the issuers' offers

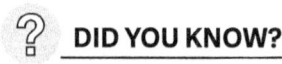

DID YOU KNOW?

Unless a company has a registration exemption, issuers must file Form D electronically with the SEC within fifteen days after selling the securities. Form D provides the SEC with stakeholder/sponsor details and information relating to the securities themselves.

to both accredited and nonaccredited investors must align with the rules in the acts, which broadly forbid material omissions and misrepresentations.

The SEC's default position is that offers and sales of securities can only go ahead if registered with the SEC. Exceptions are possible if the seller can demonstrate a valid exemption from the registration requirements.

According to **Rule 144** of Regulation D (persons deemed not to be engaged in a distribution and therefore not underwriters), one of these exemptions involves selling "restricted or controlled securities" in the marketplace without an underwriter. The process is challenging; for example, suppose someone owns restricted securities or holds control securities and wants to offer them to the public. A circumstance like this may involve proving such a sale is exempt from registration. Typical considerations that arise include the following:

- how long the securities have been in the person's (or elected entity's) name
- the method to be deployed in selling the securities
- the number of units the person intends to sell and a sales date (or dates if there are more than one selling tranche)

In addition to satisfying the above requirements, the seller must contract a transfer agent to remove the legend—a statement on a stock certificate that notes any restrictions pertaining to the transfer of the stock.

Relatedly, **Rule 144A** (private resales of securities to institutions) modifies the rules for transacting privately placed controlled or restricted securities (described under Rule 144) with qualified institutional buyers. It focuses on the fact that institutional investors are sophisticated, so all the protocols provided in Section 144 do not apply. As opposed to individuals, institutions do not require the following:

- full details
- long holding mandates

Also under Regulation D, **Rule 145** (reclassification of securities, mergers, consolidations, and acquisitions of assets) addresses any situation where one security replaces another resulting in a reclassification. When this occurs, the securities may have no SEC registration intact. Usually this is the consequence of a merger, consolidation, or acquisition.

In other words, Rule 145 covers activities that initiate the exchange of securities of one incorporated entity for those of a different company or organization. The Rule stipulates that if the security owners vote for reselling the securities, they must first register them.

Rule 147 ("Part of an Issue," "Person Resident," and "Doing Business Within") for the purposes of Section 3(a)(11) delineates intrastate offering exemptions. It also emphasizes how federal and state legislation work together for investors' benefit:

- The Rule and its related Sections focus on intrastate and smaller private securities offerings.

DID YOU KNOW?

Critics fear that the definition of *institution* in the Securities and Exchange Act is too broad, leading to possible abuse by unscrupulous overseas companies flying under the SEC's radar.

- The amendments define a new **safe harbor** for intrastate security offers (note *offers*, not *sales*) to purchasers residing out of state.
- Rule 147 increased the offering threshold governed by Rule 504 of Regulation D from $1 million to $5 million and simultaneously removed Rule 505.

The bottom line: Rule 147 created more viable capital-raising channels for smaller companies without upending the investor protections. Notably, it empowers state securities regulators to add extra investor protections they deem necessary for offerings within their states.

QUICK REVIEW QUESTIONS

26. Which regulation allows registration exemptions?

27. Which rule defines a safe harbor for intrastate security offers?

28. What are some advantages of selling unregistered securities?

Prospectuses

The prospectus is the first part of a registered statement and is covered under **Section 10** of the Securities Act of 1933 (information required in prospectus). A **prospectus** is at the core of an honest and transparent registration statement accessible to every prospective investor for a registered security. It must provide an audited rendition of the following:

- business operations of the holding company and subsidiaries, including results
- current and projected consolidated financial statements comprised of the following:
  - cash flows
  - profit and loss accounts
  - balance sheets
  - a summary of the company's financial condition
- competition and the risks involved in the investment, backed by statistics and data
- governance matters and structures providing the following:
  - explanation of the management culture in the business
  - management and board director resumes
  - conflicts of interest
  - any extraordinary legal proceedings in which the company is involved

- mainstream company advisors, such as lawyers, sponsoring brokers, auditing firm, registrar, and banks
- all aspects of the security itself

Rule 431 of the Securities Act of 1933 (summary prospectuses) addresses the **summary prospectus**, which is a condensed, plain-English version of the prospectus described above. Its goal is to communicate the pertinent aspects of the more comprehensive document to provide investors with the main takeaway from the Section 10 prospectus.

Any company issuing a summary prospectus alongside a comprehensive one should refer to **Schedule A** and **Schedule B** for the headings that the commission considers crucial to transparent and informative disclosure. These include details (to name a few) of the following:

- the issuer
- the underwriter
- advisors
- board of directors
- management
- the security, its classification, and interest rates/maturity dates (if applicable)
- strategic objectives
- fee and expense tables
- risk factors to consider
- subsidiaries
- financial assets and liabilities
- profit history
- projections with motivations

HELPFUL HINT

The summary prospectus is not intended to replace the prospectus. Most importantly, it cannot contain any information not included in the primary prospectus.

The prospectus is not a document that lends itself to "fluff"; instead, the Schedules in this section underline that facts rule. Any positivity injected into the content should not deviate from the relevant data and credentials of the parties involved in the registration.

The Securities Exchange Act of 1934 accounts for unique situations in **Part 164** of Regulation D (post-filing free writing prospectuses in connection with certain registered offerings). Specifically, it addresses the conditions under which an issuer's registered offering is a free writing prospectus. This means it is any written communication that the Act defines as an offer to sell or solicit an offer to buy a registered security where it complies with SEA acceptability outside of

- a prospectus that fulfills Section 10(a) requirements;
- communication defined by Rules 163B, 167, and 426 and Section 5(d) of the SEA; and
- prospectus definition exceptions as outlined in Clause (a) of Section 2(a)(10) of the SEA.

While Part 164 looks open-ended, anyone using it to evade Section 5 of the SEA will almost certainly find that such communications are unacceptable to the commission. On the other hand, deploying this section and other exemptions and exclusions for their intended purposes is perfectly acceptable.

QUICK REVIEW QUESTIONS

29. An audited, honest, transparent registration statement accessible to every prospective investor for a registered security is called what?

30. What is the term for a condensed version of a prospectus?

31. What guidance ensures that issuers building a registration statement cover all the relevant headings required in the prospectus/summary prospectus?

Self-Regulatory Organizations (SROs)

Defining SROs

Any entity with the authority to develop and enforce regulations/standards outside of government control for a stand-alone industry is a **self-regulatory organization (SRO)**. When an industry's leaders believe that unique circumstances are not covered adequately by legislation or SEC jurisdictions, they may form an SRO. An SRO serves as an extra "set of eyes" that assists the SEC and other government regulatory bodies in keeping a defined industry or profession on the straight and narrow:

- None of its power or reach arises from government accommodations.
- The government can still step in if any power excesses or abuses emerge.

The SEC amendment to its original **Rule 15b9-1** regarding SRO membership makes it mandatory for broker-dealers to join an SRO as members and abide by its regulations. Thus, it creates extraordinary oversight (over and above SEA guidelines) to ensure investor protection from every angle.

SROs frequently have the power to enforce standards on not only industry participants (members) but also over the entire industry. Noncompliance cannot result in criminal charges, but an arduous and often stressful process begins to convert behavior without being punitive. This may include confidential conversations with noncompliant members or even making violations public through various media and consumer alerts. The latter is generally a last resort to encourage uncooperative bad actors to behave acceptably. It may even report Section 5 violations (if apparent without a satisfactory response to the Federal Trade Commission [FTC]) for law enforcement action. Members are generally eager to comply with SRO regulations and rectify any noncompliance complaints for fear of exposure.

QUICK REVIEW QUESTIONS

32. What is the purpose of an SRO?

_____

33. Are SEA-registered dealers mostly members of SROs?

_____

34. Can SROs bring charges against their members?

_____

FINRA

The Financial Industry Regulatory Authority, better known as **FINRA**, is a de facto Congress-authorized SRO. **Article I** of its By-Laws states that FINRA exists to preserve the integrity of financial markets. It does this by ensuring there are basic investor protections behind every transaction:

- Misleading securities advertisements never air or, if they do, they are met with swift cease-and-desist orders.
- Nobody untested, unqualified, and unlicensed can transact securities on behalf of clients.
- Investment benefits and features accurately match investor needs.
- Fully transparent disclosures precede any investment transaction.

The primary goal of FINRA is to foster and grow investor confidence in the markets covered by the SEA and the SEC. As a result, it is arguably the most prominent and influential SRO, overlapping and coordinating with the NYSE and other relevant SRO regulations.

FINRA focuses on US broker-dealers and counts over 612,000 members (under the By-Laws of **Article IV**) involved in billions of market transactions daily. Per the By-Laws of **Article XV**, like every other SRO, FINRA does not have the power to bring charges against members (unlike the SEC). However, its rules are taken very seriously by all members because noncompliance can result in the following:

- persuasive actions to correct wrongdoings done to customers:
  - sanctions
  - levying fines
  - restitution orders
- suspensions or expulsion from FINRA, which often signals the beginning of the end of SEA registrations for noncompliant brokers

Fraud and other potentially criminal actions fall under FINRA. In these cases, FINRA can report the culprits to the SEC or the Federal Trade Commission to face more severe penalties.

REGULATORY ENTITIES AND AGENCIES 17

QUICK REVIEW QUESTIONS

35. What is FINRA?

_____

36. Who are members of FINRA?

_____

Other SROs

The **Municipal Securities Rulemaking Board (MSRB)** is an SRO that focuses on creating and monitoring rules and policies governing the activities of investment firms and banks involving the following:

- transactions connected to municipal securities, including bonds and notes
- states, cities, and counties issuing municipal securities
- anything related to municipal securities underwriting, trading, and selling to fund public projects

The MSRB covers the following actions:

- registered municipal advisor firms
- Series 50-qualified municipal advisor representatives
- Series 54-qualified municipal advisor principals

It also includes MSRB-registered dealers and executing brokers who have been issued an executing broker symbol (EBS), which permits them to enter municipal securities transactions. Finally, as an SRO, it has extensive powers to ensure consistent compliance with MSRB rules and regulations, extending to FTC reporting about criminal activity. Members generally avoid public communication about their noncompliant behavior as it may result in severe reputational consequences, among other liabilities.

All municipal securities dealers or municipal advisors who are FINRA members fall under FINRA's regulatory framework, which, in turn, enforces MSRB policies and rules. Close ties between the two SROs are evident.

Another SRO, the **New York Stock Exchange (NYSE)**, facilitates NYSE-registered securities transactions through registered broker-dealers to the public. The NYSE primarily facilitates the following:

- equities
- equity index funds
- debentures
- bonds

The NYSE is the biggest SRO of its kind globally, making it attractive to publicly traded companies and broker-dealers from all walks of life. However, the NYSE allows only SEA-registered members to apply for membership in

DID YOU KNOW?

FINRA also administers the professional qualifications program for the MSRB.

the exchange. It creates and governs the rules and regulations that members must follow.

Like FINRA, the NYSE can take meaningful action against noncompliant members to remedy deviations or escalate the remedies to include further investigation by the SEC or FTC and subsequent consequences. Suspension from trading on the NYSE for malpractice reasons can irreparably ruin a member's reputation. Consequently, high transactional standards are the expected and sustainable norm. FINRA integrates closely with the NYSE, including as follows:

- having many NYSE regulations in its rule book
- enforcing transactional standards on all FINRA members who also belong to the NYSE

In addition, the SEC approved a rule that requires all NYSE member entities to integrate under FINRA membership as well. As a result, there's little room in the two SROs for noncompliant broker-dealers to function without getting fined, sanctioned, or suspended.

The **Chicago Board Options Exchange (Cboe)** is the most significant options exchange. The Cboe transacts equity, index, and interest rate futures contracts globally.

Only SEA-registered broker-dealers qualify as **trading permit holders (TPHs)**. They are subject to the Cboe's comprehensive rules book that defines ethics and trading practices. As an SRO approved by Congress, the Cboe can penalize, sanction, suspend, and expel noncompliant traders depending on the degree of malpractice.

The Cboe is committed to taking swift action to curtail manipulative behavior on all the options exchanges that function under its umbrella. For example, the client suspension rule approved by the SEC in 2016 aims to quickly stop disruptive quoting and trading practices. In addition, the Cboe U.S. Regulatory Complaints, Tips and Referrals Form aims to regulate the trading patterns of member and TPH interactions, including day traders.

> **DID YOU KNOW?**
> The Cboe was founded in 1973 and rebranded in 2017 as Cboe Global Markets.

> **DID YOU KNOW?**
> One famous Cboe index is the VIX, recognized as the primary buffer against market volatility.

QUICK REVIEW QUESTIONS

37. What is the MSRB?

38. What is the NYSE?

39. What is the Cboe?

Other Regulators and Agencies

Federal Regulators and Agencies

The **Internal Revenue Service (IRS)** of the US Department of the Treasury plays an important role in securities regulation. If one owns securities for twelve months or less, the IRS regards it as a trading profit outside of the capital gains arena. Investors buying securities for a long-term hold qualify for capital gains tax exemptions.

For the purposes of tax rulings, Section 475(c)(2) of the Internal Revenue Code defines securities as the following:

- equities, exchange-traded funds (ETFs), indexes, real estate investment trusts (REITs), and mutual funds
- beneficial ownership interests in partnerships and trusts
- debt instruments
- certain notional principal contracts
- interest via derivative financial instruments in the above assets

Sometimes bad actors try to skirt the tax laws. For example, a bad actor might claim trading profits as capital gains or fail to declare gains altogether. As a result, the SEC and IRS can collaborate to identify manipulations and regulatory gaps to develop strategies that enhance their respective regulatory responsibilities.

The **Federal Reserve (FR)** is the single most significant force behind the money supply. The FR buys or sells bonds and other securities through open-market operations. It does this by interacting with banks via the **Federal Open Market Committee (FOMC)** policies. Indirectly, the FR's overall mission is to avert financial crises for investors by steadying volatile economic conditions.

The FOMC aligns with the regulations and rules of the SEC, FINRA, MSRB, and any other SRO entity drawn into these transactions. Accordingly, the FR does not regulate broker-dealers operating within SEA and SRO jurisdictions.

The Securities Investor Protection Corporation (SIPC) is not a government body or agency empowered by the Securities Investor Protection Act of 1970. As discussed in the SIPA section earlier in this chapter, it is an insurance fund for brokerage customers who fall victim to dysfunctional broker-dealers, including those going bankrupt or encountering financial hardship due to financial misconduct.

However, the SIPC does not cover losses from traditional market volatility and investors' transactions with broker-dealers who follow the SEA and relevant SRO rules and regulations. Also, SIPC does not get involved in fraud or securities crime investigations.

The **Federal Deposit Insurance Corporation (FDIC)** is an independent federal agency that functions to prevent "run-on-the-bank" situations, such as those that destroyed the wealth of millions and led to the Great Depression. The US

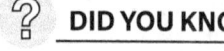

DID YOU KNOW?

Open-market operations substantially deflected the worst downturn effects during the 2008 Global Financial Crisis and the COVID-19 recession.

government created the FDIC in 1933 to rebuild the public's confidence in the country's financial institutions and banking practices. The FDIC insures bank deposits up to $250,000 per depositor for all banking entities that fall under its membership (most well-known commercial banks). Depositors should confirm their institutions are FDIC insured.

The FDIC backup offers peace of mind to anyone who has money in checking, savings, and bank money market accounts and CDs in an FDIC-insured bank. For banks to secure FDIC coverage for their customers, they must meet the FDIC financial ratios and strict terms and regulations. These terms align closely to relevant SRO rules and the Securities Act and the SEA (plus amendments) wherever applicable.

Both banking customers and institutions rely on the FDIC. Through training programs, the FDIC provides extensive guidance on laws and legislation insights.

QUICK REVIEW QUESTIONS

40. Who works to prevent bad actors from skirting tax laws regarding securities?
_____

41. Does the Federal Reserve have anything to do with regulating broker-dealers directly?
_____

42. What is the primary goal of the Federal Reserve?
_____

43. What does the FDIC do?
_____

State Regulators

The **North American Securities Administrators Association (NASAA)** is an association of state securities administrators responsible for protecting investors entering the securities markets based on receiving investment advice.

Unlike the federally focused SEC, NASAA is state-centric. Still, the two regulators work hand in hand. For example, NASAA's oversight includes licensing stockbrokers and investment advisor firms who manage under $100 million in a state. Also, it covers state-located securities firms.

NASAA members traditionally conduct collaborative training programs with relevant SROs. For example, the Uniform Securities Agent State Law Exam, or Series 63, was developed by NASAA, but the exam is administered by FINRA. NASAA members also
- participate in multi-state enforcement initiatives, and
- share securities-related information.

DID YOU KNOW?

NASAA has been operating since 1919—long before the Great Depression. It is the longest-standing international investor protection organization.

Notably, NASAA reviews the process relied on by companies using Regulation A of the Securities Act of 1933 to raise capital.

QUICK REVIEW QUESTIONS

44. What is NASAA?

_____

45. Which regulator is state-focused: NASAA or the SEC?

_____

Answer Key

1. The high-level purpose and mission of securities regulation is to protect issuers' and stakeholders' interests in capital markets across a broad range of industries and to create fair, efficient, and transparent security transactions.

2. Security regulations embrace all and any transactions involving stocks (equities), Treasury stocks, Treasury notes, debentures, bonds, swaps, futures and derivatives, certain notes, agreements, or certificates.

3. There are five SEC divisions: the Division of Trading and Markets (MR); Corporate Finance (CF); Investment Management (IM); the Division of Enforcement (DE); and the Division of Economic and Risk Analysis (ERA).

4. The Division of Trading and Markets (MR), Corporate Finance (CF), and Investment Management (IM) are the three SEC divisions that can propose rules.

5. Congress, another government agency, a private company, or anyone in the public domain can propose new rules.

6. An MUI is a Matter Under Inquiry—the informal start of an SEC investigation.

7. Defendants are notified of an enforcement recommendation through a Wells notice.

8. Disgorgement describes the statute that attacks unjust enrichment when individuals or companies violate SEC regulations, resulting in illegal gains.

9. SEC action is always civil; AG action is criminal.

10. Blue sky laws are state laws.

11. State laws apply when there are no federal provisions.

12. State laws vary from state to state.

13. The Securities Act of 1933 was created to prevent a catastrophe similar to that of the 1929 stock market crash.

14. The Securities Exchange Act of 1934 (SEA) focuses on governing secondary market securities transactions.

15. According to the SEA, an exchange is almost any location or place that transacts registered securities.

16. Other important definitions under Section 3(a) include those for the terms *exchange, facility, transaction, member, broker, banker.*

17. The primary purpose of the Securities Investor Protection Act of 1970 is to compensate for investor losses resulting from proven broker incompetence or bankruptcy and to create confidence in the registered investment arena.

18. The maximum claim any investor can make under the Securities Investor Protection Act (SIPA) is $500,000 (if cash, $250,000).

19. The Securities Investor Protection Corporation (SIPC) is funded by assessment fees paid by its members.

20. Members of the Securities Investor Protection Corporation (SIPC) are most registered brokers under the Securities and Exchange Act of 1934.

21. A registration statement is a document that summarizes a security issuer's business details as well as the issuer's intended equity offering. It must pass SEC review before the issuer can offer the equity on any exchange.

22. Section 7 of the Securities Act of 1933 covers registration statements.

23. For a registration statement to take effect, it must pass SEC review under Section 8.

24. Registration takes effect up to twenty days from submission to the SEC.

25. The Securities and Exchange Act of 1934, Section 15A (registered securities associations) stipulates that brokers and dealers must be registered with the SEC.

26. Regulation D allows registration exemptions.

27. Rule 147 defines a safe harbor for intrastate security offers.

28. Fewer protocols, saving considerable time, and far more operational flexibility are some advantages of selling unregistered securities.

29. A prospectus is an audited, honest, transparent registration statement accessible to every prospective investor for a registered security.

30. A summary prospectus is the term used to describe a condensed version of a prospectus.

31. Schedules A and B ensure that issuers building a registration statement cover all the relevant headings required in the prospectus/summary prospectus.

32. The purpose of an SRO is to create extra oversight of its members' activities.

33. Yes, the SEC requires entities and individuals under SEA regulations to be SRO members.

34. No, SROs cannot bring charges against their members, but they can—and do—have persuasive responses to noncompliance.

35. FINRA is the Financial Industry Regulatory Authority, which is a Congress-authorized self-regulatory organization (SRO).

36. Registered broker-dealers in the US (over 612,000 at last count) are members of the Financial Industry Regulatory Authority (FINRA).

37. The Municipal Securities Rulemaking Board (MSRB) is an SRO that creates and monitors rules and policies to guide the activities of investment firms and banks trading municipal securities.

38. The New York Stock Exchange (NYSE) is one of the largest SROs; it facilitates NYSE-registered securities transactions.

39. The Chicago Board Options Exchange (Cboe) is the most prominent options exchange.

40. The IRS and the SEC work to prevent bad actors from skirting securities-related tax laws.

41. No, the Federal Reserve does not have anything to do with directly regulating broker-dealers.

42. The primary goal of the Federal Reserve is to avert financial crises by steadying volatile economic conditions.

43. The FDIC insures bank deposits up to $250,000 per depositor for all banking entities that fall under its membership; it also offers guidance on laws, legislation insights, and training programs.

44. The North American Securities Administrators Association (NASAA) is an association of state securities administrators.

45. The North American Securities Administrators Association (NASAA) is a state-focused regulator.

2 SRO Regulatory Requirements for Associated Persons

SRO Qualification and Registration Requirements

Definitions and Registration

A **self-regulating organization (SRO)** refers to FINRA and stock exchanges like the NYSE. The rules and regulations of SROs align with those of the SEC but relate more specifically to the entity's member activities. The SEC effectively lets individuals operate legally in the investment arena as long as they are SEC-registered broker-dealers and registered with at least one SRO.

An SRO will only admit members who are SEC-registered broker-dealers. In other words, it is impossible to function on a trading platform without at least a dual membership: SEC and SRO registration.

- From the SEC's viewpoint, if someone successfully applies for SEC registration as a broker-dealer but does not follow through with an SRO membership, that person is considered nonregistered.
- Likewise, an SRO considers anyone applying for SRO membership without having SEC registration as nonregistered.

Article V of FINRA's By-Laws (registered representatives and associated persons) lays out the definitions of registered representatives (RRs) and associated persons. A **FINRA registered representative** is

- licensed by the SEC to buy and sell securities for others, and
- sponsored by a firm that itself is registered with FINRA.

FINRA associated persons include

- member firm sole proprietors,
- partners,
- officers,
- directors,

HELPFUL HINT

When SEC/FINRA-registered persons or entities fail to adhere to the rules and, as a result, become disqualified, they simultaneously become nonregistered.

- branch managers, and
- anyone who can demonstrate the ability to fulfill a similar function.

In other words, associated persons include anyone directly or indirectly controlling a FINRA member firm or entity controlled by a FINRA broker-dealer, even individuals who are not (or who are exempt from being) registered SEC/SRO broker-dealers.

FINRA-associated persons also include

- entities (not people) that control or are controlled by a member firm, such as a company, government/political subdivision, or agency;
- anyone regarded as a registered representative;
- all employees of the member firm; and
- any of the above who is not an associated person but expects to become one shortly.

> **DID YOU KNOW?**
> Some member firms may have clerical and ministerial personnel who are not considered FINRA-associated persons.

Rules for FINRA membership are laid out in the **FINRA By-Laws, Article VI** (dues, assessments, and other charges) and in the **FINRA 1000 Series** (member application and associated person registration). Applying for FINRA membership requires filing **Form BD**, the Uniform Application for Broker-Dealer Registration. Form BD is filed with the SEC, FINRA, and other relevant SROs. The application process comprises eight steps:

1. reserving the firm's name
2. signing up to obtain system access
3. submitting the application fee
4. confirming that the applicant meets FINRA's admission criteria
5. submitting Form BD online
6. submitting a hard copy of Form BD
7. submitting all additional required forms
8. submitting fingerprints

Fees start at $75 for each member. Depending on the firm size and complexity, discounts and additional fees apply.

Per **FINRA Rule 1122** (filing of misleading information as to membership or registration) FINRA has zero tolerance for deliberately providing misleading or inaccurate information for its membership application:

- Registered representatives and associated persons should not contemplate filing any information that, by omission or inclusion, creates a different impression from what exists in reality.
- Even in cases where the misleading content is innocent, if the member fails to correct it, FINRA will consider the information definitively dishonest.
- Failing to register an associated person in a member firm (even though the majority are on the register) is a material omission under the protocols mentioned above.

FINRA Rule 2010 punishes unethical behavior. According to "the 2010 rule," FINRA can levy fines

- ranging from $5,000 to $146,000 against any entity (e.g., a firm) as a registered representative or associated person that misleads in the manner described above; and
- ranging from $2,500 to $37,000 for any individual who provides misleading information as described above.

FINRA can add a suspension ranging from five days to a month for mild infringements and up to two years for reckless behavior. For numerous violations, disqualification and expulsion are possible. All of these consequences apply to both individuals and entities.

The **Municipal Securities Rulemaking Board (MSRB)** is an SRO focused on regulating trade in municipal securities. It develops rules, policies, standards, and best practices for trading municipal bonds, notes, and other municipal securities. (See chapter 1 for more details on the MSRB.)

Like other SROs, the MSRB aligns its rules and regulations with FINRA and the SEC. According to **MSRB Rule G-7**, member dealers must show that their associated persons possess the requisite qualifications to transact municipal securities and file that information with the appropriate regulatory agency.

QUICK REVIEW QUESTIONS

1. What is a FINRA-registered representative?

   _____

2. Are all FINRA-associated persons registered representatives?

   _____

Eligibility

Eligibility for FINRA membership as a registered representative is defined by **Section 1** of the **FINRA 0100 Series**. Section 1 covers the following designations, all of which carry SEC authorization to transact securities for clients as a regular business:

- registered broker-dealers
- municipal securities broker-dealers
- government securities broker-dealers
- any entity or individual in any investment banking/securities branch in the US with SEC approval

Anyone who cannot comply with FINRA's eight application steps listed above cannot qualify as a FINRA member and, therefore, cannot qualify as an employee of such an entity. In addition, the following registered individuals or entities would no longer qualify for membership or associated person status:

- Excluded membership plus excluded associated-person status covers any FINRA entity or individual member currently under FINRA suspension or disqualification.
- Excluded associated-person status covers any employee of a FINRA entity or individual member, thus qualifying as a FINRA-associated person, working for the same entity or individual currently under FINRA suspension or disqualification.

Sections 2 and 3 of the FINRA 1000 Series address the specific rules/regulations covering suspension/disqualification, such as board hearings, appeals, SEC involvement, and other protocols.

MSRB rules and regulations align closely with those of the SEC and FINRA. **MSRB Rule G-2** (standards of professional qualifications) addresses, as the name would suggest, professional qualification standards. Rule G-2 emphasizes that MSRB rules are the only acceptable guidelines for any transaction in municipal securities. From start to finish, the MSRB rules govern registered broker-dealer behavior and that of their associated persons.

MSRB Rule G-3 (professional qualification requirements) defines the requirements for first-time applicants. Anyone who wants to qualify for the first time as a **municipal securities representative (MSR)** and be a member of the SRO must pass two entry exams:

- the Securities Industry Essentials Examination (SIE)
- the Municipal Securities Representative Qualification Examination (Series 52)

Some candidates are exempt from the entry exams:

- general securities representatives and municipal securities sales limited representatives who have already passed the Series 7 exam
- limited representatives for investment companies and variable contracts products who have passed the Series 6 exam

However, the MSRB Rule G-3 has a proviso applicable to all of the above parties. Those who are inactive in municipal securities transactional business for two years or more must requalify and retake the entry exams—regardless of previous qualifications.

The MSRB defines an MSR as anyone involved with brokering, dealing, underwriting, and transacting municipal securities. The definition also includes the following:

- employees acting as a municipal securities advisor, consultant, and/or promoter (i.e., communicator to the public), where the ultimate goal is to influence municipal security transactions
- individuals involved in research and/or investment advice if their work relates to transactions

Clerical and ministerial employees are not considered MSRs; otherwise, the definition is broad with few exceptions, which should give anyone operating in the municipal securities arena reason to pause before working with clients.

Unfortunately, bad actors can seek to manipulate records and steal value from investors. To protect the industry, all partners, directors, officers, and employees must submit fingerprints under the Rules of **Section 17(f)(2) of the Securities Exchange Act of 1934**, with only a few exceptions. Other employees, like bookkeepers and accountants, must submit fingerprints if their work involves issuing and receiving checks and/or entering general ledgers and other record books.

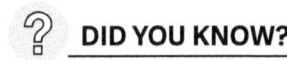

DID YOU KNOW?
As a safety precaution, most firms ensure everyone submits fingerprints.

The Chicago Board Options Exchange (Cboe) arguably exercises the most stringent crime prevention measures of all SROs in the US. Under **Cboe Rule 7.10** (fingerprint-based background checks of exchange directors, officers, employees, and others) the exchange must obtain the fingerprints and criminal background checks of the following people:

- Cboe directors, officers, and exchange employees
- temporary workers on the exchange
- independent workers who function as contractors, consultants, vendors, and service providers for the exchange
- anyone with access to Cboe facilities and records
- candidates for exchange directorship
- prospective exchange employees who are in the interviewing stages

All the data received goes to the US Attorney General for scrutiny and review. As a rule, people with undisclosed criminal histories are unlikely to become Cboe members.

FINRA's 2015 regulatory notice that revises **FINRA Rule 3110(e)** (responsibility of member to investigate applicants for registration) places the onus on broker-dealer members to conduct background checks on all relevant associated persons. "Relevant" means every name the member wants registered with FINRA via Form U4. **Form U4** focuses on the following:

- good character references
- reputation in business
- qualification pertinent to the envisioned job
- experience

Form U4 must be reviewed by the firm's counsel and compliance officer before it is submitted to FINRA. In general, the submission must meet the revised Rule's protocols that now require details regarding the following:

- background check processes (including the scanning of public records)
- the member's supervisory policies and processes
- applicant data about past employment
- any fingerprint results mandated under Exchange Act Rule 17(f)(2)

Form U4 is covered in more detail later in this chapter.

QUICK REVIEW QUESTIONS

3. Who must submit fingerprints under Section 17(f)(2) of the Securities Exchange Act of 1934?

4. What law deals with FINRA disqualification and suspension protocols?

Statutory Disqualification

According to the FINRA By-Laws, Article III (qualifications of members and associated persons), if a registered FINRA member suffers **statutory disqualification**, that person or entity will lose FINRA eligibility:

- Any registered associated persons who do not or cannot terminate their relationship with the ineligible member will likewise lose eligibility.
- Under the Securities Exchange Act of 1934, FINRA can cancel registrations connected to a disqualified member.

Disqualification under FINRA aligns with SEA definitions and coverage. In other words, FINRA and the SEC are on the same page when it comes to dealing with disqualifications.

Section 3(a)(39) of the SEA (definitions and application of title [statutory disqualification]) lists the same disqualification definitions as FINRA. Disqualification situations include the following:

- specified misdemeanors and all felony criminal convictions (spanning ten years)
- any valid court injunctions (regardless of their age) connected to numerous illegal investment banking or securities activities
- associations with disqualified individuals or entities if not addressed as prescribed (see above)
- certain rulings from SROs, regulatory bodies, and other authorities showing deception or malfeasance

HELPFUL HINT

Associated persons must terminate all links to disqualified entities/individuals. Still, in some cases, FINRA may allow eligibility to continue despite the disqualification. FINRA Rule 9520 lays out the exemptions.

QUICK REVIEW QUESTIONS

5. What is the term used to describe when a person or entity loses continued FINRA eligibility?

6. Can associated persons maintain ties to a disqualified person?

Permitted Activities and Communications

FINRA Rule 3270 (outside business activities of registered persons) regulates the activities of registered persons:

- Registered persons can only work for their member firms; typically, they may not work for other firms—even as independent contractors, directors, or partners.
- Registered persons may not receive any form of compensation for any business activity outside the membership firm's work definition.
- A few exceptions exist relating to conflicts of interest.

Registered persons who do not follow this guidance risk losing registration status, therefore becoming nonregistered under FINRA disqualification or suspension penalties.

FINRA Rule 3280 (private securities transactions of an associated person) discusses permissible activities relating to personal securities trades. The Rule defines *private securities* as any securities transaction outside an associated person's job description as an employee of the member. This includes transactions in registered securities and those categories exempt from SEC registration. Excluded transactions

- fall under Rule 3210 requirements, involving immediate family members (and where there is no associated person selling compensation), and
- are personal in private equity and variable annuity securities.

Rule 3280 defines *selling compensation* as receiving paid compensation—directly or indirectly—for a private securities purchase or sale. It includes the following:

- receiving commissions, finder's fees, or securities
- rights given to acquire securities or participate in profits
- access to tax benefits and dissolution proceeds
- reimbursement of expenses

According to Rule 3280, associated persons cannot transact private securities in any way unless they provide written notice to the member describing the following in detail:

- the proposed transaction
- the associated person's role in the transaction
- the selling compensation earned for fulfilling the role

Whenever selling compensation is above zero, the member firm must respond in writing. The response includes the following information:

- whether the transaction was approved or disapproved
- an acknowledgement of receipt of the associated person's written notice
- whether it has offered directional advice on the associated person's expected behavior in the defined role

QUICK REVIEW QUESTIONS

7. Can registered persons work for entities outside of their member firms?

8. Under Rule 3280, can associated persons transact private securities?

Employee Conduct and Reportable Events

Reporting Requirements

Per **FINRA Rule 4530** (quarterly reporting requirements), certain activities are **reportable**. Member firms must report on specified events quarterly, statistically, and in summary. Any member actions related to the following would be considered **specified events**:

1. outside business activities (according to Rule 3270)
2. unresolved judgments or liens
3. bankruptcy filings
4. creditor compromises
5. address changes and keeping address history current
6. criminal convictions (past and current)
7. customer complaints

Outside business activities are defined in Rule 3270, which is discussed in the previous section. Essentially, registered persons may only work for their member firms and, with few exceptions, may not receive outside compensation.

Permissible **private securities transactions** are defined by FINRA Rule 3280 and discussed in detail in the previous section. These apply, with few exceptions, to any securities transaction outside an associated person's job description as an employee of the member.

QUICK REVIEW QUESTIONS

9. What are TWO reportable events for a FINRA member?

10. What is generally considered "outside business activity" for a registered person?

Contributions, Gifts, and Compensation

Registered persons must follow regulations when it comes to political contributions. **MSRB Rule G-37** (political contributions and prohibitions on municipal securities business) prohibits registered persons/entities from underwriting, advising, or providing any financial service to a municipal issuer for two years after making a political contribution to that entity. Rule G-37 applies to the following registered persons:

- municipal securities dealers and finance professionals
- political action committees (PACs) connected to dealers or municipal finance professionals

DID YOU KNOW?

Certain exemptions apply to Rule G-37, such as contributions of no more than $250.

Non-cash compensation (NCC) refers to nonmonetary rewards from direct participation in securities sale and distribution. Several FINRA rules cover NCC:

- FINRA Rule 2310(c)—non-cash compensation
- FINRA Rule 2320(g)(4)—non-cash compensation
- FINRA Rule 2341(l)(5)—non-cash compensation (limits on from whom compensation may be accepted)
- FINRA Rule 5110(h)—non-cash compensation

Items that fall under NCC rules include the following, among others:

- merchandise
- nonmonetary gifts
- travel expenses

No member firm or associated member can accept (or deliver) NCC directly or indirectly from (or to) anyone, except for the following:

- values no higher than $100 per person
- a qualified occasional/infrequent event (like a meal or entertainment ticket)
- if the NCC arises from training or education sessions with location specifications and has nothing to do with influencing attendance
- if the NCC is classified as an internal reward based on total production and the equal weighting of product sales (i.e., unspecified sales/production segments that are part of the total)

FINRA Rule 3220 (influencing or rewarding the employees of others) sets a $100 limit for the total value of annual gifts and gratuities that are given by a FINRA member to an individual with whom the member conducts business.

HELPFUL HINT

Permissible NCC must not be connected to reaching sales targets.

No registered or associated persons in a FINRA member firm can receive cash or NCC of more than $100 annually that is related to the business. Exceptions include cases of pre-employment written agreements for services rendered that reflect the following:

- the compensation value
- the services it connects to
- the employer's acquiescence

Moreover, the member firm (the employer) must retain detailed written records of all executed compensation described above under the Rule and its exceptions (SEA Rule 17a-4).

MSRB Rule G-20 (gifts, gratuities and non-cash compensation [e.g., limited to less than $100]) provides similar guidance as do the FINRA regulations for registered persons. This Rule prevents dealers and advisors in the municipal securities arena from entering into NCC over $100 with any person or entity involved in similar activities.

Like other Rules, there are exceptions to Rule G-20. A gift range is permitted for the following purposes:

- decorative gifts linked to achievement, such as a plaque or trophy
- promotional/thank-you gifts valued below $100 per item, such as picture calendars, pens, and notebooks
- gifts for bereavement, such as flowers
- certain personal gifts, such as those for weddings, births, and seasonal holidays

QUICK REVIEW QUESTIONS

11. What is the maximum political contribution a municipal securities dealer can make to someone in a municipal securities–issuing capacity?

12. Under FINRA Rule 3220, FINRA members may give gifts to an individual with whom they conduct business. What is the annual maximum monetary limit for the value of these gifts?

Employee Conduct

Broker-dealer representatives, investment advisors, and securities issuers fall under the heading of registered persons with relevant jurisdictions and SROs, like FINRA. Numerous employee designations in SRO member firms must also register as associated persons. **Form U4** (uniform application for securities industry registration or transfer) establishes registration of an associated person:

- Member firms have thirty days to amend Form U4.
- When a statutory disqualification is involved, that period is shortened to ten days.
- Form U4 includes vital data to signify if applicants are suitable candidates for registration.

There are numerous pages of guidance related to Form U4. **FINRA Rule 2263** (arbitration disclosure to associated persons signing or acknowledging Form U4) focuses on changes to the behavior codes required for arbitrating customer and industry disputes:

- Member firms must provide their associated persons with the new arbitration disclosures whenever these individuals sign a new or amended Form U4.

- Thus, associated persons cannot claim they were unaware of the amendments to the form.

Form U5 is the official uniform termination notice for securities industry registration. The document serves notice of the termination to the appropriate jurisdictions and/or SROs. The member firm must submit Form U5 electronically within one month of the individual's last day at work. It is advisable to provide reasons for the termination. Penalty fees may ensue for missing the thirty-day deadline.

FINRA Rule 2060 (use of information obtained in fiduciary capacity) pertains to confidentiality. It prevents members from taking advantage of inside information by acting in the following capacities:

- paying agent
- transfer agent
- a trustee or otherwise

Rule 2060 addresses leveraging early knowledge about securities ownership for profit. Members may not execute securities purchases, sales, or exchanges based on early knowledge of securities ownership.

FINRA's formal disciplinary actions are laid out in **FINRA By-Laws, Article XII** (disciplinary proceedings). Article XII focuses on alleged member and associated-person violations of the following:

- FINRA Rules
- the Securities and Exchange Act
- MSRB Rules

Disciplinary action begins with FINRA Enforcement (led by a team of attorneys), which is the internal division that officially files a complaint with the Office of Hearing Officers. From there, the process falls under FINRA's Procedure Code contained in Article XII of FINRA's By-Laws (Rules 9110 and 9211).

Under Article XII, FINRA can

- impose fines,
- suspend membership, and
- disqualify members and associated members from FINRA (effectively terminating their registrations).

FINRA jurisdiction is broad. All felony criminal convictions close the guilty member's registration for ten years. FINRA has zero tolerance for the following situations, which result in membership disqualification:

- when a member is under a court's injunction concerning illegal banking/securities activities
- when a member is expelled from or denied registration by the SEC, CFTC, state commission, another SRO, or equivalent foreign agency/authority
- when a member deliberately provides false information or omissions on Form U4

> **HELPFUL HINT**
> FINRA Rule 2263 doesn't significantly alter essential arbitration disclosures; it updates the language in this narrow arena.

> **DID YOU KNOW?**
> FINRA cannot proceed with criminal actions against the parties; however, it can refer the case to the SEC to consider such measures.

If the SEC, Commodity Futures Trading Commission (CFTC), or an SRO discovers and proves after a hearing that an associated person deliberately violated SEA, commodity trading, or MSRB regulations, disqualification is possible. Moreover, it is a violation to aid, abet, counsel, command, induce, or procure a violation described above. Even failing to supervise someone who commits a violation is cause for disqualification.

Bankruptcy and liens, however, are not a cause for disqualification as long as the member reports the situation in a timely and compliant fashion. Bankruptcy or liens could cause a member to be expelled only if the member

- lied on the bankruptcy documents,
- hid assets, or
- criminally defrauded creditors (like the IRS), resulting in adverse judgments, liens, and other charges.

A lien or bankruptcy investigation generally arises from member or customer complaints; however, it doesn't automatically result in any penalties because failing to pay creditors (even the government) is not necessarily fraudulent or criminal. Such situations may hurt a member's reputation but are not grounds for disbarment. On the other hand, skewing the truth when reporting liens or bankruptcy to FINRA, or failing to report these entirely, can result in severe penalties and possible disqualification.

QUICK REVIEW QUESTIONS

13. What form is used when a registration reaches the point of termination?

14. Do bankruptcy and liens cause disqualification?

Customer Complaints

FINRA protects investment clients by requiring a level of transparency from all registered FINRA members. **FINRA Rule 2267** (investor education and protection) requires members to annually communicate with customers by providing them with the following:

- FINRA hotline (reserved for discussing urgent matters)
- FINRA website
- the availability of the FINRA BrokerCheck brochure

FINRA members who do not record transactions, handle customer accounts, or hold securities only need to provide the above information once. Several other categories of associated persons in a member firm are exempt from updating these details.

BrokerCheck is FINRA's primary online resource for investors. It covers the more than 820,000 currently active SRO members and thousands of previously registered members. BrokerCheck, a transparency tool, is a central repository of the following member information:

- employment history
- registration exam history
- disciplinary actions

FINRA Rule 8312 (FINRA's BrokerCheck disclosure) requires FINRA to release information on registered members and/or associated persons upon request. Any customer requesting information on a FINRA member by phone (toll free) or online is therefore eligible to receive FINRA BrokerCheck information about the following:

- current (or former) FINRA members of any other recognized SRO exchange and the BrokerCheck firms for which they work (or worked)
- associated persons who are (or were) FINRA members or members of any other recognized SRO exchange and the BrokerCheck firms for which they work (or worked)

Accessible data includes the most recent content on the FINRA registration forms (U4, U5, U6, Form BD, and Form BDW) in addition to the following:

- confirmation of current registrations
- historic customer complaints (settled and unsettled) with set dollar limits
- any arbitrations between the member and customers (with awards)
- applicable penalties (past and current) that stand against the members' names or titles
- the latest comment by the member to FINRA (if any) if requested by FINRA under its protocols
- member qualification details (not including test scores)
- past convictions, misdemeanors, liens, bankruptcies, or record blemishes reported on the registration forms

HELPFUL HINT

When an associated person leaves employment with a member, information reported in Section 3 (reason for termination) of Form U5 is NOT disclosed through BrokerCheck.

In some cases, the member must follow FINRA Rule 3170 (tape recording of registered persons by certain firms). The **Taping Rule** mandates that designated member firms record all telephone conversations between specified registered persons and their prospects or clients, review the conversations, and report the information to FINRA. The taping rule aims to do the following:

- monitor the behavior patterns of registered persons working for firms with spotty regulation histories (i.e., taping firms)
- detect fraudulent and improper practices in selling pitches

According to FINRA Rule 3110(a)(3), firms must establish an **office of supervisory jurisdiction (OSJ)** to ensure compliance. An OSJ exists where there is considerable transactional activity, including order execution, developing public offerings, and organizing private placements.

Complaints are primary member considerations. FINRA requires members to maintain a separate record of written customer complaints in each OSJ of their company. **FINRA Rule 4513** (written customer complaints) requires that written customer complaint records be preserved for at least four years:

- The definition of the term *complaint* covers practically all member actions regarding clients, not only in the OSJ arena.
- Firms must preserve complaints connected to all members and associated persons working in the company offices (even those outside the OSJ definition).
- In each case, the recording member OSJ should add the action it took (if any) regarding the complaint.

SRO enforcement divisions can impose and record the following:

- penalties
- suspensions
- disqualifications

Through SEC collaboration, SRO enforcement divisions can escalate misconduct to criminal consideration. Almost all misconduct cases emerge from client or other member complaints. Investors should be aware of potential **red flags** regarding FINRA members. Customers can request information from FINRA, state regulators, or the SEC to check the background and integrity of any broker-dealer. Investors can overview and assess the following:

- SEC, state, or SRO disciplinary actions
- lawsuits involving questionable transactions
- arbitration claims (and their magnitude) brought by customers
- "taped" protocols impacting a firm and its employees (see Taping Rule information above)
- current registration status

HELPFUL HINT

Even if broker-dealers do not have a record of client accusations, they may still be employed by a firm that has a record of severe misconduct; this is also a warning signal.

Borrowing and lending against the asset value of securities is more complex. The potential exists for investor abuse scenarios not seen in traditional markets. **FINRA Rule 4330** (customer protection—permissible use of customers' securities) applies unique guidelines and regulations in these cases.

Lending/borrowing arrangements using customers' "on margin" securities is known as leveraging. Leveraging is illegal without written client authorization. Moreover, in complying with **SEA Rule 15c3-3**, which is known as the "Customer Protection Rule," a member can only create borrowing structures with customers' fully paid or excess margin securities.

The Customer Protection Rule addresses custodial protocols that brokerages must adhere to when leveraging customer-owned securities. The member must do the following:

- physically hold the securities in a safe place
- create and maintain detailed records of all items listed above and below under SEA Rule 17a-4(a)

- provide certified ratings to support any related security due diligence
- provide at least one month's notice to FINRA of intention to enter a borrowing arrangement
- verify that the perceived borrowings are appropriate given the customer's circumstances
- deliver a written agreement and disclosure for customer consideration that covers crucial aspects, including
  - loss of voting rights and restrictions on selling the securities while in the arrangement,
  - expected compensation,
  - provisions of the Securities Investor Protection Act of 1970 that may no longer apply if the borrower fails to return the security,
  - tax implications,
  - other risks,
  - the collateral involved in the deal and the basis of valuation,
  - broker-dealer and associated member fees from the arrangement.

QUICK REVIEW QUESTIONS

15. What is FINRA's primary online research resource for investors?

_____

16. For how long must written customer complaint records be preserved?

_____

Continuing Education (CE) Requirements

Continuing education (CE) is a critical component of FINRA membership. Registered and associated persons cannot sustain a long-standing FINRA relationship or retain SEC recognition without participating in the CE program.

FINRA Rule 1250 (continuing education requirements) requires all registered persons to adhere to their CE protocols, schedules, and overall CE requirements. Every member firm must submit a comprehensive CE needs analysis that aligns with the company's size and addresses the following:

- organizational structure
- the scale of business activities
- the current regulatory performance of registered members
- envisioned regulatory improvement
- the expected level of regulatory supervision and supervisory training
- similar analysis on securities knowledge, talents, and skills as described in items 3 – 5 above

CE focuses on two primary education areas: the regulatory element and the firm element. The **regulatory element** of CE covers what registered members are required to know. At the start of the second year after acceptance into FINRA, every registered member must complete a training session. Registered representatives must do the following:

- complete training between twenty-four and twenty-eight months after the member's registration date
- complete a similar FINRA course every three years

Training focuses on the following issues:

- compliant practices
- understanding regulations
- ethical sales practices

The **firm element** of CE allows members to demonstrate expertise in the products, brands, planning methods, and advice FINRA communicates to customers. The investment arena is vast, and member firms must determine how much of it falls within their professional capabilities and staff resources. Once the firm has defined its activity boundaries, each member in its specialized channel should possess the skills and talents to offer clients the best solutions. The needs analysis determines the scope and content of the firm element training and the modules that go into it.

> **HELPFUL HINT**
>
> FINRA publishes and distributes a Firm Element Advisory and a Guide to Firm Element Needs Analysis and Training Plan Development. In addition, numerous FINRA e-learning courses supplement the CE program.

QUICK REVIEW QUESTIONS

17. What TWO CE channels does FINRA follow with its members?

18. What is the primary guideline for the firm element part of CE education?

Answer Key

1. A FINRA-registered representative is an SEC-registered broker-dealer with FINRA dual membership.

2. No. Associated persons include those who are connected to a FINRA member firm who are not (or who are exempt from being) registered with the SEC as broker-dealers.

3. Under Section 17(f)(2) of the Securities Exchange Act of 1934, partners, directors, officers, and employees—especially those who issue checks and/or maintain record books—must submit fingerprints.

4. Section 3 of the Securities Exchange Act of 1934 deals with FINRA disqualification and suspension protocols.

5. The term *statutory disqualification* describes when a person or entity loses continued FINRA eligibility.

6. No, aside from certain exemptions, associated persons cannot maintain ties to a disqualified person.

7. No, unless the exceptions under Rule 3270 apply, registered persons cannot work for entities outside of their member firms.

8. Yes, associated persons can transact private securities if they provide written notice to the member.

9. Any of the following are considered reportable events for a FINRA member: outside business activities (according to Rule 3270), unresolved judgments or liens, bankruptcy filings, creditor compromises, address changes, criminal convictions, or customer complaints.

10. Any work outside of a registered person's member firm is considered "outside business activity."

11. The maximum political contribution a municipal securities dealer can make to someone in a municipal securities–issuing capacity is $250.

12. The annual maximum monetary limit for the value of gifts to an individual with whom a FINRA member conducts business is $100.

13. Form U5 is used when a registration reaches the point of termination.

14. No, unless the member fails to report bankruptcy and liens properly, these are not grounds for disqualification.

15. BrokerCheck is FINRA's primary online research resource for investors.

CONTINUE

16. Written customer complaint records must be preserved for four years.

17. The regulatory element and the firm element are the two continuing education (CE) channels FINRA follows with its members.

18. The needs analysis that FINRA requires every member firm to complete is the primary guideline for the firm element part of continuing education (CE).

3. Market Participants and Market Structure

Market Participants and Their Roles

Investors

An **accredited investor** is a person or entity qualified to invest in unregistered private securities. Traditional regulators regard this investor category as financially sophisticated. Examples of unregistered securities include the following:

- hedge funds
- private equity pools
- a range of real estate fund options (excluding publicly traded real estate investment trusts [REITs])

Accredited investors who commit funds to unregistered assets cannot rely on the same SEC/SRO monitoring and abuse remedies enjoyed by those entering registered investment categories. Still, these investments do have some SEC oversight under Regulation D.

The **Dodd-Frank Wall Street Reform and Consumer Protection Act** helps the SEC decide which people or institutions have the financial insight to evaluate private funds and the ability to address uncertainties and complex situations the SEC routinely regulates.

Rule 215 of the Securities and Exchange Act of 1933 (and some tributary sections and rules) lays out the requirements to be an accredited investor.

CONTINUE

TABLE 3.1. Types of Accredited Investors

TYPE OF INVESTOR	EXAMPLES
Individual investors	• registered broker-dealers • executives, directors, and board members of sponsoring companies (insiders) • holders of certain professional qualifications (e.g., Series 7, 62, or 82 certifications) • individuals with an annual income of $200,000 (for couples, $300,000) • individuals/couples with a net worth of $1 million (excluding primary residence)
Institutional investors (entities)	• savings and loan associations/commercial banks • state employee benefit plans (e.g., pension funds) • private business development companies • REITs • insurance companies • hedge funds • corporations/partnerships valued at least $5 million • any recognized entity where all the equity owners can prove that they are accredited investors

 DID YOU KNOW?

Today, most individuals and couples choosing the net worth option simply have a registered broker-dealer, attorney, or licensed accountant sign a third-party letter confirming that the individual or couple qualifies as accredited.

Some major investors are referred to as *qualified purchasers*. **Qualified purchaser** is an SEA classification for investors with a value of at least $5 million. Both qualified purchasers and accredited investors can invest in Regulation D unregistered securities.

Retail investors are not professionally qualified to evaluate the risks of the financial arena. Retail investors typically

- invest relatively small amounts of money at a time in exchange-traded funds (ETFs), mutual funds, pension funds, etc.,
- rely on SEC-registered persons to guide their decisions,
- conclude most of their transactions and deals via online brokerage firms, and
- can also buy certain securities through registered brokers.

Many in the industry see retail investors as the opposite of institutional investors and, therefore, most in need of protection. The Securities Act of 1933 and the Securities Exchange Act (SEA) of 1934 emerged to end dishonest dealings that exploited retail investors.

Retail investors sometimes meet accredited investor benchmarks, which means they can make their own decisions regarding unregistered securities. There are approximately 13.5 million accredited investors in the US (family households)—a small portion of the retail body of investors.

QUICK REVIEW QUESTIONS

1. Which type of investor is qualified to invest in unregistered private securities?
   _____

2. Which types of investors generally rely on professionals to guide their decisions?
   _____

Broker-Dealers

This content will distinguish between three different types of broker-dealers:

- introducing broker-dealers
- clearing broker-dealers
- prime brokers

Section 15 of the Securities Exchange Act of 1934 **(registration and regulation of brokers and dealers)** defines the basic requirements no matter which type of broker-dealer is involved.

- Section 15 clarifies that anyone calling themselves a broker-dealer must comply with all Section (b) Rules, resulting in registration.
- Without an official registration, anyone or any entity cannot promote, influence, or induce registered securities transactions, such as assets bought and sold through national exchanges.

Section 15(b) describes how to obtain broker-dealer registration. Applicants are scrutinized and can expect further scrutiny after successfully registering. A single disruptive touchpoint may be enough to cause the registration to fall through. Some examples of disruptive touchpoints include

- failing to secure a FINRA membership or that of another recognized SRO;
- client or peer complaints that ultimately lead to suspension or disqualification;
- ignoring the required continuous education that is integral to the job;
- lapses in reporting misdemeanors that break the law, especially if these fracture fiduciary confidentiality;
- tardy recording of client asset placement and transactions contrary to SEA and SRO protocols;
- being associated with misconduct by another broker in the same firm.

Finally, the SEC can partially or entirely exempt a transaction intermediary from participating in a deal. Such cases generally involve private Regulation D categories under accredited status conditions.

DID YOU KNOW?

Even an isolated complaint can damage a registered dealer's career if it leads to an investigation. A dealer's record is open to the public and all investigations are included in the record.

QUICK REVIEW QUESTIONS

3. What law defines the basic requirements for broker-dealers?

4. What section of the Securities Exchange Act of 1934 lists the many requirements a candidate must meet to become a broker-dealer?

Introducing Brokers

Introducing brokers choose to provide investment advice only. They connect their clients to other registered dealers who handle the details required to complete securities transactions.

A set of unique skills is required to engage with the public in an advisory capacity, create interest in different assets, and hand over the process from there. Introducing brokers fulfill a vital function in the investment process as long as they

- act with integrity and rely on verifiable information that companies circulate with SEC sanction, and
- stay within the bounds of their SRO regulations.

Introducing brokers have no participation in arranging payments to or from the client, record-keeping, or any aspect of managing securities as a clearinghouse. Instead, this broker category splits commissions and fees on an agreed-upon basis without being involved in a significant portion of the transaction process.

Introducing brokers take orders for commodities and futures markets, but these orders are executed by **futures commission merchants (FCMs)**.

QUICK REVIEW QUESTIONS

5. Which type of broker-dealer provides investment advice only?

6. Do introducing brokers arrange payments to or from clients?

Clearing Brokers

Clearing brokers connect introducing brokers to clearinghouses. They focus on the smooth transition of buy and sell orders involving the movement of payments and securities custody. (Self-clearing brokers are authorized to perform both functions themselves and do not need clearing brokers.) The responsibilities of a clearing broker include

- tracing the process to ensure that trades settle in the prescribed manner,
- performing research and due diligence to ensure the legitimacy of transactions,
- engaging with the clearinghouses to handle fund transfers,
- completing continuing education,
- handling trades where fund and equity asset custodial segregation are expected.

The clearing broker role resonates throughout the financial system and carries significant financial and legal responsibilities for registered securities transactions. As a result, all clearing brokers—or the firms they work for—must be registered with FINRA. Most states insist that clearing brokers hold advanced certifications, including Series 7 and Series 63 with continuing education.

QUICK REVIEW QUESTIONS

7. Which kind of broker connects introducing broker-dealers to clearinghouses?

_____

8. Do clearing brokers need to be FINRA-registered?

_____

Prime Brokers

Prime brokers offer services crucial to the functioning of investment banks, hedge funds, and institutional investors. They deal with complex transactions that leverage cash or securities arrangements and must take advantage of trading opportunities that yield substantial returns at this level. The best examples of these are

- hedging,
- negotiating interest rates,
- taking timed positions.

Major financial services firms, such as Goldman Sachs, UBS, and Morgan Stanley, commonly offer prime brokerage services to their clients. These brokerages work on a much larger scale of operations than traditional brokers, and fees and remuneration are subject to negotiation (typically $50 million – $200 million starting points).

Prime brokers are institutions serving other institutions and can eventually expand to include thousands of banking clients. Clients with diverse portfolios may work with more than one prime broker, each performing on different platforms.

The SEA and FINRA have detailed regulations about asset custody and due diligence in managing hedge funds, pension funds, and private equity pools.

Mega-fund clients who prefer outsourcing the service rather than conducting operations in-house commonly use prime broker services. Prime broker concierge services include

- risk management,
- introducing capital,
- securities and cash financing,
- secondary market operations,
- real estate acquisitions,
- currency and asset hedging,
- arbitration, and
- structuring collateral for lending arrangements.

QUICK REVIEW QUESTIONS

9. Which type of brokers deal with complex transactions that leverage cash or securities arrangements?

10. Which types of trading opportunities are characteristic of prime brokers?

Other Participants

Investment Advisors

The term *investment advisor* seems general—a catchall for anyone offering advice to someone who wants to commit funds to an asset class. However, to avoid exploitation and conflicts of interest, there are legal limitations on who may influence others.

There is a difference between a broker and an investment advisor, although the lines are blurred. Many brokers are also investment advisors, but as brokers, their aim is to sell a proposition. They act as a broker if, when they give clients their "advice," they impart it as a registered FINRA member following SEA protocols to complete a sale.

According to FINRA, the purist definition of a financial advisor or an investment advisor's representative embraces the following:

- an SEA registered individual or entity who earns a living by providing advice on a range of securities for client benefit
- other titles that signify an investment advisor
- asset manager
- investment counselor
- portfolio manager

HELPFUL HINT

The debate around what constitutes investment advisor qualifications triggered the Securities Act of 1933 and the SEA of 1934, leading to the SEC, FINRA, and other SROs.

SEC regulations focus on all investment advisors responsible for managing $110 million or more of client assets. Although there is significant alignment, state securities regulators cover investment advisors with less than $110 million under management.

Assets under management (AUM) is the metric that determines regulatory oversight. As the AUM shifts, advisors must keep track of their registrations to stay compliant. Clients should know a registered FINRA member's category when they engage to consider investments. For example:

- A fixed fee for investment advice is enough to make the distinction: the advisor gets paid whether the client transacts the securities in question or not.
- On the other hand, the investment advisor role is questionable if commissions are conditional on client action.

If the client has already committed the funds to a firm for investment and all the firm's representative does is advise on the placement of the funds, the investment advisor function is more definitive. The individual providing the most impact is possibly a FINRA member who is not directly communicating with the client but rather is behind the scenes doing the essential research. Registered individuals and entities are legally permitted to provide the following in combination or individually:

- customized investment advice
- managed investment portfolios
- financial planning services
- brokerage services

As discussed in Chapter 2, SEC- and state-registered investment advisors are listed in FINRA's BrokerCheck. In addition, the SEC's Investment Adviser Public Disclosure Database (adviserinfo.sec.gov) contains data on registered investment advisors and their representatives with over $110 million funds under management.

QUICK REVIEW QUESTIONS

11. Which type of investment advisor does the SEC focus on?

12. What does AUM stand for?

Municipal Advisors, Issuers, and Underwriters

According to Section 15(b) of the Securities Exchange Act, a **municipal advisor** is a person who can help interested parties understand municipal financial products, including

- the issuance of municipal securities, and
- the structure and timing of the investment opportunities.

A municipal advisor may also solicit on behalf of the municipal entity or an obligated person (all issuers of municipal securities or bodies positioned to facilitate payments for municipal securities on offer).

FINRA extends the definition of municipal advisor to cover any persons representing themselves who engage in advisory services around municipal securities. The used titles include

- financial advisors,
- guaranteed investment contract brokers,
- third-party marketers,
- placement agents,
- solicitors,
- finders,
- swap advisors.

An **issuer** is a legal entity that conceives and structures registered securities specifically to help fund its business. Issuers are recognized when new bonds, equities, or warranties (the most common types of securities) come to market for the first time.

Typical issuers include

- corporations,
- investment trusts, and
- government bodies (domestic and foreign).

An **underwriter** takes on insurance or someone else's risk surrounding issued securities in return for a fee. Moreover, the underwriter, as part of its responsibilities in the securities arena, may

- purchase securities from an issuer outright for further distribution to the public, thereby orchestrating the entire primary offering;
- promote, market, and sell the securities on behalf of the issuer without initially purchasing them while still underwriting the offer directly or indirectly;
- assess market interest, thus establishing a viable offering price that aligns with a successful launch.

The specific role of underwriting syndicates in IPOs is discussed in depth later in this chapter.

QUICK REVIEW QUESTIONS

13. Who helps people understand municipal financial products?

_____

14. A legal entity that conceives and structures registered securities specifically to help fund its business is called what?

_____

15. What term describes the entity that takes on insurance or someone else's risk surrounding issued securities in return for a fee?

_____

Traders and Market Makers

Market makers are registered persons or firms and SRO members transacting securities—mainly on secondary markets—for their own accounts and clients. Their activities provide market liquidity and volume in an attempt to profit from bid-ask spreads.

The most common in this category are **brokerage houses** that are compensated for taking on the risk of holding securities (on their own accounts) between purchase and sale and providing transactional solutions for investors. Accurate reporting is a crucial ingredient in this.

Generally, **traders** refers to anyone who buys and sells assets for profit. In the financial markets the term relates to securities. Securities traders traditionally hold the assets for short durations, moving in and out of their positions frequently:

- Day traders can buy and sell a single asset many times in twenty-four hours.
- Investors (distinct from traders) hold assets for a longer term—generally more than a year.

Because the term *trader* covers such a broad arena, it is split into those who do it for self-gain and those who act for others:

- Broker-dealers (individuals) or broker-dealer firms representing clients in trading transactions conceivably fall under the trader heading. Thus, they are all registered SEC traders under FINRA or other recognized SRO regulations.
- Day-trading firms that promote their services to day traders must be registered.
- Not all individual traders transacting for their own accounts must be registered; however, when high margins exist to leverage trader activities, FINRA may require the traders to pass specific tests.

QUICK REVIEW QUESTIONS

16. What are common market makers?

_____

17. Which type of traders buy and sell an asset many times in twenty-four hours?

_____

Custodians, Trustees, and Transfer Agents

There are situations in which brokers obtain investors' express permission to transact securities by accessing a safe box and return cash or securities from the transactions back to the safe box after completion.

In these cases, the "safe box" is a stand-alone account. The situation described above is a frequent occurrence since many high-net-worth clients require that their securities be held separately in an account under their name (or nominee name). High-net-worth investors use custodians to provide an extra layer of security. They often do so by keeping the securities holdings separate from the brokerage (under a nominee's name).

Custodians are responsible for the safekeeping of investors' assets that usually require a significant staff complement to administer accounts according to SEA regulations. As a result, most custodian companies are institutional. On the other hand, brokers who transact clients' securities without custodians legally commingle client assets in their activities. They also function with fewer SEA protocols.

Clients who insist on custodial accounts need a manager to connect the custodian to the broker, which can be expensive. Larger broker firms have moved toward brokering under one division and offering custodial services under another at a lower cost than working with two independent entities.

Similar to custodians, a **trustee** is a person or an entity that holds and administers assets on behalf of the asset's owner (the trustor) for the advantage of a third party (the trust beneficiary). Trustees hold assets in terms of a trust (a document describing the relationships and role of the trustee).

The trustees have full asset control and understand the trust's guidelines. Trustees are appointed because the trustor trusts them to do the right thing. In other words, trustees carry a fiduciary responsibility which means

- they must make decisions that favor the beneficiaries,
- they do not act on their personal goals and preferences, and
- the assets are safe.

Trustees must maintain a transparent record of all transactions, financial statements, and tax returns. The trust protocol recommends regular meetings with the beneficiaries to keep them updated.

Shareholders expect accurate investment information at all fundamental levels. In some cases, member firms incorporate a transfer agent division, though many shareholders prefer third-party transfer agents based on a fee arrangement.

A **transfer agent** is a trust company, bank, or similar institution that a company assigns to maintain investors' financial records and account balances as follows:

- collaborating with registrars of securities to ensure investors receive their interest/dividends on time
- tracking and recording transactions
- validating issued certificates or canceling them

- administering investor mailings (including monthly statements to mutual fund shareholders)
- dealing with issues such as lost or stolen certificates
- monitoring interest and dividend payments to meet schedules
- facilitating voting on securities motions by controlling the flow of proxies

QUICK REVIEW QUESTIONS

18. What term refers to those responsible for the safekeeping of investors' assets?

_____

19. A person or an entity that holds and administers assets on behalf of the asset's owner for the advantage of a third party is called what?

_____

20. What is a trust company, bank, or similar institution that a company assigns to maintain investors' financial records and account balances?

_____

Depositories and Clearing Corporations

Depository Trust and Clearing Corporation

Launched in 1999, the **Depository Trust and Clearing Corporation (DTCC)** is a US financial services company that provides clearing and settlement services for the financial markets. The DTCC functions as a global centralized clearinghouse for securities platforms (exchanges). Its work includes

- streamlining and completing transactions for buyers and sellers (trillions of dollars daily),
- connecting all brokers involved in each transaction,
- processing the data through the NSCC, and
- generating a report for all relevant brokers in the trade that reflects the net securities positions and money required to settle the deal.

Upon receiving settlement instructions from its subsidiary, the DTCC complies by transferring securities ownership from the selling broker's account to the purchasing broker's payments in the other direction.

After completing the steps described above, the participating brokers are responsible for adjusting their client accounts to align with the DTCC process and reports. Typically, the process is completed the same day for institutional and retail investors. This results in less risk for investors and more confidence in the system.

DID YOU KNOW?

The DTCC came about from the merger of the DTC (Depository Trust Company) and the National Securities Clearing Corporation (NSCC). With the restructuring the NSCC is a DTCC subsidiary.

QUICK REVIEW QUESTIONS

21. What is the primary purpose of the DTCC?

_____

22. What is a subsidiary of the DTCC?

_____

The Options Clearing Corporation

Founded in 1973, the **Options Clearing Corporation (OCC)** operates as a central clearinghouse and regulator representing the SEC and the Commodities Futures Trading Commission (CFTC) in the US derivatives markets. The OCC is responsible for clearing transactions through exchanges that involve

- future contracts,
- options on futures contracts,
- interest rate composites,
- single-stock futures,
- securities lending contracts.

In addition, the OCC provides significant added value to investors and intermediaries in the form of

- research services,
- investor education,
- technical support,
- marketing outreach.

The OCC's mission is to help market participants control risk and manage transactions with support and backup.

QUICK REVIEW QUESTIONS

23. What is the primary purpose of the OCC?

_____

24. Who does the OCC represent in the US derivatives markets?

_____

Market Structure

There is a strong divide between primary and secondary markets. A primary market deals exclusively with first-time fundraising. The secondary market deals with trading financial instruments after the primary launch. The secondary market accommodates trading in securities only after the company has raised capital for the first time.

The Primary Market

The **primary market** is where private entities become eligible to solicit investments from the public. An initial fundraiser is exclusive to primary markets.

An **initial public offering (IPO)** describes all new issues of equity. An IPO deals only with new issues or primary offerings and does not cover debt and treasury issues; these are offered under different formats. The goal of every IPO is for a company's private owners to raise capital for their business via equity (by separating pieces of the shareholding).

The term *new issue* embraces any equity IPO defined by the Securities and Exchange Act:

- Some entities prefer to raise debt versus equity via bonds, preferred instruments, and convertibles.
- Governments also get involved in primary offerings, generally in the form of Treasury certificates.

Once the securities launch in this manner, they enter secondary markets, where the original public investors sell them to others (see below). Established public companies offering more equity for additional equity sales also make secondary offerings.

Primary offerings/new issues via IPOs require protocols and disclosures. Detailed documentation must be submitted to the SEC to be scrutinized for accuracy, integrity, and transparency. Once listed as a security and trading openly on exchanges, there are no overly onerous disclosures per trade; primary market scrutiny is considered sufficient.

HELPFUL HINT

An IPO is also known as a first public offering.

QUICK REVIEW QUESTIONS

25. Where do private entities become eligible to solicit investments from the public?

26. What term describes new issues of equity?

The Secondary Market

Any financial market that legally allows securities owners to transact with others is a **secondary market**. Typically, national stock exchanges like the New York Stock Exchange (NYSE) and the Nasdaq Stock Market fall into this category.

The secondary market is a step away from the original transaction that created the publicly accessible asset. Secondary markets can take on different shapes.

Over-the-counter (OTC) markets are sometimes called "dealer markets." A subsection of the secondary market, OTCs are decentralized locations where FINRA and other SRO members can trade with each other and rely on **electronic** market systems.

Over-the-counter markets imply massive volumes and profiting from slight price differences and astute timing. Brokers and dealers deal directly one-to-one. They understand that the counterparty risk is significantly higher than in traditional exchanges, where counterparty risk is practically zero thanks to strict regulations and the fact that exchanges are guarantors behind every transaction. More than 12,000 securities trade on the OTC market, including

- stocks,
- ETFs,
- foreign exchange trades (forex or FX),
- bonds,
- commodities, and
- futures.

OTC participants include investment banks transacting ETFs and mutual funds. Real estate lending entities like Fannie Mae and Freddie Mac also transact mortgage parcels through a secondary market.

Electronic decentralized markets broaden the securities landscape because asset classes not listed on traditional exchanges can be traded on the OTC with a unique ticker symbol. Moreover, online brokers help smooth the electronic processes; otherwise, buying and selling function the same way for both exchanges and OTC markets.

Auctions on secondary markets (electronic or physical) are where buyers enter the transaction by publicly announcing bid prices for securities. Sellers announce offer prices (the prices they are ready to sell at). Then, the parties negotiate, trying to get the other participant to compromise and agree to their bids/offers or meet in the middle.

Bargaining and negotiating energize the process through a middle broker to close the transactions. In volatile markets, the opening bids or offers seldom hold for long, depending on supply and demand conditions. In addition to the primary and secondary markets, third and fourth markets exist for certain transactions:

- Broker-dealers and members of FINRA transact with massive institutions through **third markets**.
- Institutions transact among themselves through **fourth market** transactions.

HELPFUL HINT

There is always a risk that one party in an OTC transaction will default wholly or partially in meeting its contractual obligations.

QUICK REVIEW QUESTIONS

27. OTCs rely on what kind of market systems?

28. Institutions transact among themselves in which market?

Offerings

Types of Offerings

Private companies have two main ways to raise capital: public offerings and private offerings. **Public offerings** allow companies to offer shares or other securities for sale to the public via a recognized stock exchange. Public securities offerings become available for the first time in an IPO, generally underwritten by an investment bank.

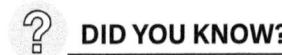

DID YOU KNOW?

Securities sales to more than thirty-five people are considered public offerings.

After the IPO (which takes place on the primary market) the securities are open for public subscription on the secondary market. The shareholders and their investment bank agree on a price that they believe will gain market traction.

Every company going for an IPO wants assurance that investors will subscribe all the stock on offer. Investment banks support the launch and partner with companies in three ways:

1. **With full commitment:** The investment bank buys the entire subscription and then sells it to the market. (The underwriter owns the balance if the public fails to absorb all the stock; the investment bank takes on the risk of unsold shares.)
2. **In best efforts:** The investment bank acts as the company's agent, promotes the IPO, and sells as many shares as possible. If some of the equity eligible for subscription remains unsold, the bank does not take on the risk.
3. **All-or-none agreement:** Investors and the investment bank must absorb the entire subscription, none are available, and the IPO aborts.

In each case, the company arranges a compensation package with the investment bank commensurate with the work involved and the risk accepted by the bank. In practice, a public offering is always an IPO under SEA and FINRA regulations.

In a **private securities offering**, a company can sell the stock privately—not through a recognized public exchange. Private offerings fall under Regulation D and SEA sections covering transactions with accredited investors. SEA vigilance is significantly less stringent than for an IPO, and investors must do their own due diligence:

- The SEC has strict guidelines regarding accredited investor qualifications. The sponsor should ensure that the subscribers meet these specifications.
- Sponsors do not have to register privately placed equities with the SEC or report back to any government body on approved accredited investors.

In summary, a public offering and an IPO are the same. A private offering has some SEA protection but significantly less than subscribing under an IPO.

Any offering that takes place *after* the IPO falls under the general heading of **follow-on public offerings (FPOs)**, in which the company sells new shares on the market. A **secondary offering** is a type of FPO and may refer to investors who:

- have acquired assets on the primary offering (e.g., the IPO); and
- enter exchanges that allow them to transact those assets with other investors.

Selling securities in a secondary offering allows revenue from the sale to go directly to the seller. The company that secured funds from the primary offering does not get involved or benefit from these secondary offerings.

A secondary offering occurs when companies want to raise additional capital after their introductory offer. But when they do so, the extra stock can dilute the current investors' holdings if it only goes to new investors.

For example, if a company issues 1 million shares to Group A investors in its primary offer, then a secondary offering of 500,000 shares to new investors (Group B) reduces Group A's holdings from 100% of the equity (owning all 1 million shares) to 67% (owning 1 million of 1.5 million shares) after the secondary issue.

On the other hand, if the secondary offer goes to Group A in total AND proportionately to their members' current holdings, the secondary offer is **non-dilutive**. In other words, an investor in Group A who held 100,000 of the 1 million shares before the secondary offer owns 10% of the equity. After a non-dilutive secondary offering, that same investor will own 150,000 shares of the 1.5 million (which is still 10%) after the secondary offer.

Dilutive secondary offers occur, for example, when debtors convert their loans to stock on a conversion agreement. A non-dilutive example could be an issue of shares to existing shareholders based on their current holdings—often called a **rights issue** (see chapter 7 for more on rights issues).

If existing shareholders do not want to take up their rights, they have two options:

- sell their rights to another investor
- dilute their shares down, but gain compensation from selling the rights

Companies can initiate IPOs, FPOs, and private offerings in two ways:

- through conventional registrations dictated by the SEC
- shelf registration procedures

In a **shelf registration**, the company submits a statement detailing the stock eligible for subscription for some time in the future. It requires the same declarations and adherence to strict protocols of traditional present-day SEC registrations, except the issue date is not set. If accepted by the commission as a shelf registration, it gives the company the right to sell the "shelf stock" anytime within two years. There are several advantages to shelf registration:

- The company can select the right moment to raise funds (i.e., it can use timing to obtain the best price).

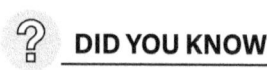

DID YOU KNOW?

Secondary offerings can significantly impact stock prices, so investors should look at the ramifications when they occur.

- It is much more economical for companies anticipating numerous fund injections in the future. One shelf registration prepares for that instead of a separate registration each time the need arises.
- One approval at the best time is better than possibly falling short on multiple registrations.

In summary, a shelf registration creates flexibility, removes time pressures, and prevents considerable process frustration and aggravation.

QUICK REVIEW QUESTIONS

29. What are the two main types of offerings?

___

30. What is the risk of a secondary offering?

___

Roles of Participants

Investment bankers manage the process that takes young companies to the launch stage on recognized stock exchanges. An investment banker's main function is to spearhead young companies' launches on public exchanges in IPOs and help them navigate any follow-up FPOs.

Any business that is focused on raising funds via a stock issue, floating a bond, merging with another business, buying a competitor outright, or selling itself to interested parties will call for an investment banker's support.

Investment banking expertise stretches further into the private company arena, where entities raise funds beyond appealing to the public. So, investment bankers help clients

- float bonds,
- instigate and control mergers,
- acquire competitors to benefit from the resultant synergy, and
- assess offers from parties interested in buying them out.

Investment bankers support their clients to raise funds for business expansion and profit enhancement. The profession covers public and private financing with stock issues, loans, acquisitions, and mergers.

Investment bankers and broker-dealers come together in an **underwriting syndicate** for scaled-up investment banking projects. A syndicate's reward connects to the underwriting spread (investors' price on the securities launch less the price agreed on and paid to the issuer). A lead underwriter usually guides the process. Once the project is completed, underwriting syndicates typically disband.

HELPFUL HINT

Underwriting syndicates are also known as underwriting groups, banking syndicates, or investment banking syndicates.

An underwriter syndicate spreads the risk when a project is too large for one advisor to manage. Examples include:

- an IPO or FPO
- private fundraising
- a merger, acquisition, or bond issue

QUICK REVIEW QUESTIONS

31. Investment bankers primarily focus on what?

32. Investment bankers and broker-dealers who come together specifically for scaled-up investment banking projects are called what?

Documents, Delivery Requirements, and Regulatory Requirements

A disclosure document refers to any filing with the SEC to facilitate account holder or investor transparency and maintain public disclosure obligations. A **program disclosure document** focuses on contractors when they expand projects into programs. Program disclosure documents connect to SEC-filed statements that describe the program and divulge all the relevant financial information. Program disclosure documents should be made available to

- all investors with (or planning to open new) accounts to participate in the program, and
- individuals or entities with an indirect interest in the program.

HELPFUL HINT

See Chapter 1 for more information on prospectuses.

A **prospectus** is a document in the registration statement that potential investors rely on to disclose the securities on offer alongside data covering the issuing company's financials and operations.

Not all securities offerings are SEC-registered. Therefore, they are **exempt** from providing investors with prospectuses. These are

- private offerings to accredited investors as contained in Rule 506 of Regulation D. (see above in this chapter in the section "Market Participants and Their Roles");
- limited size offerings; and
- intrastate, municipal, state, and federal government offerings.

Despite exemptions, many private offerings on a reputable platform provide investors with extensive information that parallels registered investment prospectuses.

Municipal securities issuers must prepare an **official statement** as a precursor to any primary offering. The official statement functions as the principal disclosure document for municipal bond issuers. Disclosures include

- the purpose of the bond,

- early redemption conditions, and
- redemption of interest and capital.

Finally, investors should be aware of state regulator blue sky laws, endorsed by the SEC. **Blue sky laws** are specific to states and supplement SEC regulations. They are covered in depth in Chapter 1.

Certain types of securities, known as **covered securities**, are exempt from blue sky laws. Covered securities

- meet SEC listing approval on the NYSE, NYSE American, and Nasdaq, including ETFs and mutual funds (essentially all registered securities);
- emerge from the same issuer with equal or higher rank versus securities already listed;
- are sold to accredited investors in compliance with Rule 506 of Regulation D; and
- can be issued without prospectuses under SEC prospectus exemptions.

Considering all the exemptions connected to covered securities, blue sky laws may seem to apply to only a tiny segment of private offerings. Still, these laws allow legal authorities and investors to sue issuers if they fail to meet their undertakings.

HELPFUL HINT

Each state has different filing requirements for securities issuers, alongside a process of merit reviews by appointed state agents. State agents adjudicate filings to ensure balanced and fair disclosures to investors.

QUICK REVIEW QUESTIONS

33. An official statement functions as the principal disclosure document for which issuers?

_____

34. Which type of securities are exempt from blue sky laws?

_____

Obligations of Market Participants

Market participants must follow certain rules. FINRA and Municipal Securities Rulemaking Board (MSRB) rules restrict compensation and require that certain information be made available to customers.

FINRA Rules Relating to Members

FINRA Rule 5250 (payments for market making) restricts compensation. Specifically, Rule 5250 states that when FINRA members or associated persons act as market makers or publish a quotation, they may not receive compensation of any kind, directly or indirectly, from an issuer and/or an issuer's affiliates and promoters. The same applies to any applications to get involved in market making. The following are exceptions to Rule 5250:

- bona fide services, such as investment banking (and, along with it, underwriting fees)
- reimbursement of SEC and SRO listing fees where they apply
- any compensation allowed by national securities exchanges after an SEC filing and approval

Rule 5250 ensures that members act independently when performing market-making actions or publishing quotations. FINRA aims to prevent any payments to members that signify a possible conflict of interest.

FINRA Rule 2266 (Securities Investor Protection Corporation [SIPC] information) requires all FINRA members (with some exceptions) to provide extensive information to new customers about SIPC. This way, customers can

- contact SIPC directly (i.e., by having FINRA members publicize its phone number and site URL);
- access its brochure; and
- understand the available protections if acting members compromise the customers' securities because of compliance issues or financial troubles.

Compliant members must repeat the same notifications in writing at least annually. When a broker and clearinghouse are involved in transactions for a client, only one (by mutual agreement) needs to take on the responsibility of creating SIPC awareness. Exceptions to Rule 2266 include:

- members covered by Section 3(a)(2)(A) (i) – (iii) of the Securities Investor Protection Act of 1970 (SIPA), which also excludes them from SIPC membership
- any individual members or member firms whose business falls outside SIPC protections

FINRA Rule 2269 (disclosure of participation or interest in primary or secondary distribution) states that FINRA members must provide customers with written notifications detailing the nature of their compensation. Rule 2269 applies to FINRA members acting as brokers or dealers who assist customers with primary or secondary market investment transactions for compensation. The goal is to create maximum client transparency.

QUICK REVIEW QUESTIONS

35. Which rule restricts compensation for FINRA members or associated persons who act as market makers or publish a quotation?

36. Which rule ensures that consumers are notified in writing of broker-dealer compensation?

MSRB Rules Relating to Members

Like FINRA, the **Municipal Securities Rulemaking Board (MSRB)** also has rules that members must follow. **MSRB Rule G-11** (primary offering practices) requires syndicates to list priorities for order categories surrounding a primary offering with flexible pricing:

- Once done, syndicates inform the syndicate members in writing that allocations align with the set priorities and explain them.
- Rule G-11 is essentially a "disclosure rule" to acquaint new issue participants with how syndicate practices work.

However, there is nothing in the Rule to guide priority structuring or direct syndicate boards on what to do. As a result, the offering price of new issue municipal securities can fluctuate between the start and end of the underwriting period.

Although fixed-price offerings were under consideration when G-11 was created, regulators decided it was not wise to restrict pricing for municipal securities because it may increase borrowing costs. However, disclosure of priorities sets the stage for understanding the flexible pricing system so that all issue participants are on the same page.

MSRB Rule G-32 (disclosures in connection with primary offerings) requires broker-dealers participating in municipal securities to disclose vital information to new issue buyers. The disclosure must occur before bond delivery and appear on a recognized internet portal linked to the MSRB (for investors to look up details).

Amendments to Rule G-32 establish that website publication also applies to advance refunding. Access to the refunding information must be simultaneous with the announcement. Ultimately, Rule G-32 keeps insiders from knowing information before the broader audience.

MSRB Rule G-34 (CUSIP numbers, new issue, and market information requirements) requires the assignment of Committee on Uniform Securities Identification Procedures (CUSIP) numbers to new municipal securities. A CUSIP number

- is a unique ID number that attaches itself to every publicly traded security,
- facilitates the settlement and clearance of stocks, and
- is found in computerized trading record-keeping systems at all relevant securities firms.

Recent amendments to MSRB Rule G-34 require all municipal advisors to ensure the bonds are allocated a CUSIP number within a specified period when interacting with clients in new and competitive municipal securities transactions. Still, advisors and their firms complain that the amendment is impractical because

- it does not enhance safety in securities transactions, and
- municipal bonds cannot trade publicly in any event without a CUSIP number, allotted in due course.

HELPFUL HINT

CUSIP is short for the "Committee on Uniform Securities Identification Procedures," which interested parties can obtain through the MSRB after entry into the Electronic Municipal Market Access (EMMA) system.

As a result, these concerns are currently under MSRB consideration.

QUICK REVIEW QUESTIONS

37. Which rule requires broker-dealers participating in municipal securities to disclose vital information to new issue buyers?

38. What is the number attached to every publicly traded security that facilitates the settlement and clearance of stocks?

Answer Key

1. Accredited investors are qualified to invest in unregistered private securities.

2. Retail investors generally rely on professionals to guide their decisions.

3. Section 15 of the Securities Exchange Act of 1934 defines the basic requirements for broker-dealers.

4. Section 15(b) lists the many requirements a candidate must meet to become a broker-dealer.

5. Introducing broker-dealers provide investment advice only.

6. No, introducing brokers do not arrange payments to or from clients.

7. Clearing brokers connect introducing broker-dealers to clearinghouses.

8. Yes, clearing brokers—or the firms they work for—must be registered with FINRA.

9. Prime brokers deal with complex transactions that leverage cash or securities arrangements.

10. Hedging, negotiating interest rates, and taking timed positions are trading opportunities characteristic of prime brokers.

11. The SEC focuses on investment advisors responsible for managing $110 million or more of client assets.

12. AUM stands for <u>a</u>ssets <u>u</u>nder <u>m</u>anagement.

13. Municipal advisors help people understand financial products.

14. An issuer conceives and structures registered securities specifically to help fund its business.

15. An underwriter takes on insurance or someone else's risk surrounding issued securities in return for a fee.

16. Brokerage houses are common market makers.

17. Day traders buy and sell an asset many times in twenty-four hours.

18. The term *custodians* refers to those who are responsible for the safekeeping of investors' assets.

19. A trustee holds and administers assets on behalf of the asset's owner for the advantage of a third party.

20. A transfer agent is assigned to maintain investors' financial records and account balances.

21. The primary purpose of the Depository Trust and Clearing Corporation (DTCC) is to provide clearing and settlement services for the financial markets.

22. The National Securities Clearing Corporation (NSCC) is a subsidiary of the Depository Trust and Clearing Corporation (DTCC).

23. The primary purpose of the Options Clearing Corporation (OCC) is to clear transactions through exchanges that involve futures contracts, options on futures contracts, interest rate composites, single-stock futures, and securities lending contracts.

24. The Options Clearing Corporation (OCC) represents the SEC and the Commodities Futures Trading Commission (CFTC) in the US derivatives markets.

25. Private entities become eligible to solicit investments from the public on the primary market.

26. An initial public offering (IPO) describes new issues of equity.

27. Over-the-counter (OTC) markets rely on electronic market systems.

28. Institutions transact among themselves in the fourth market.

29. The two main types of offerings are public and private.

30. The risk of a secondary offering is that the extra stock can dilute the current investors' holdings if it goes only to new investors.

31. Investment bankers primarily focus on initial public offerings (IPOs).

32. Investment bankers and broker-dealers come together specifically for scaled-up investment banking projects in an underwriting syndicate.

33. An official statement functions as the principal disclosure document for municipal bond issuers.

34. Covered securities are exempt from blue sky laws.

35. FINRA Rule 5250 restricts compensation for FINRA members or associated persons who act as market makers or publish a quotation.

36. FINRA Rule 2269 ensures that consumers are notified in writing of broker-dealer compensation.

37. Municipal Securities Rulemaking Board (MSRB) Rule G-32 requires broker-dealers participating in municipal securities to disclose vital information to new issue buyers.

38. A Committee on Uniform Securities Identification Procedures (CUSIP) number is attached to every publicly traded security and facilitates the settlement and clearance of stocks.

4 | Economic Factors

Economic Factors

Macroeconomic Equilibrium

Aggregate supply (AS) is the relationship between the total of all domestic output produced and the average price level. Essentially, AS is the sum of all of the microeconomic supply curves in an economy.

The **long-run aggregate supply (LRAS)** assumes that input prices have had enough time to adjust to changes in the various product markets. All markets—product and input—are at equilibrium, and there is full employment. This means that output does not change, regardless of price, creating a vertical curve.

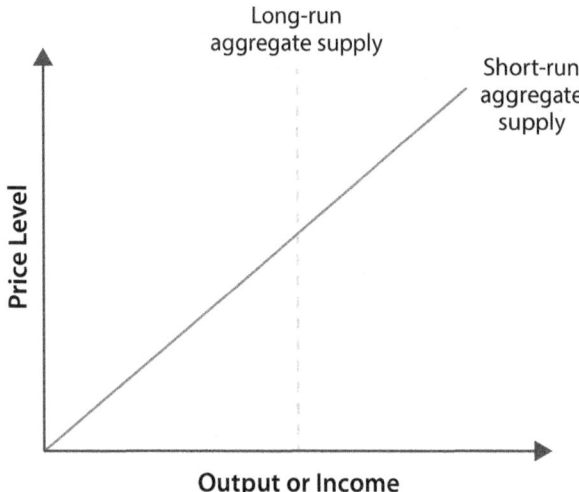

Figure 4.1. Aggregate Supply

Short-run aggregate supply (SRAS) curves fluctuate without impacting employment; however, if the LRAS curve shifts, there must be a change in the output level at full employment. These shifts result from a change in technology, productivity, and the availability of resources, both of which could alter a nation's output when working at full employment. In this way LRAS can be used as a measure of economic growth.

An economy is in **macroeconomic equilibrium** when the quantity of output demanded in an economy (as shown by aggregate demand—the sum of all demand curves in an economy), is equal to the quantity of output supplied.

This equilibrium does not always occur at full employment, though. If it does not, the economy is either experiencing inflation or recession—an aggregate supply and demand graph will reveal this information.

QUICK REVIEW QUESTIONS

1. What term describes the sum of all of the microeconomic supply curves in an economy (e.g., all domestic output × the average price level)?

2. What term describes when the output quantity demanded equals the quantity of output supplied?

Inflationary and Recessionary Gaps

An **inflationary gap** occurs when the intersection point between **aggregate demand (AD)** and SRAS is at a higher output level than the LRAS curve.

The LRAS curve represents the output level of full employment, so if the SRAS curve and the aggregate demand curve intersect at an output level beyond the LRAS curve, the economy is producing at an output level that is higher than full employment. Full employment describes when all labor resources available—skilled and unskilled—are being used to the utmost efficiency. This usually happens when the quantity demanded is suddenly increased through foreign or government spending, or even just very active consumers.

> **DID YOU KNOW?**
> In the New Deal, the government created jobs for people to counteract the recession (the Great Depression). These jobs created new demands for labor, which increased aggregate demand and shifted the equilibrium point closer to LRAS, which is at full employment.

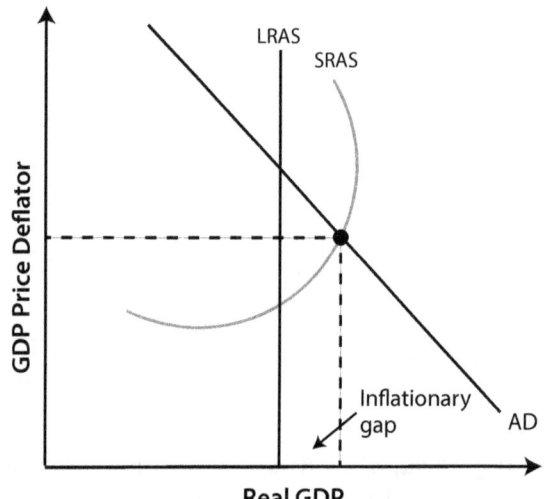

Figure 4.2. Inflationary Gap

On the other hand, if the equilibrium point is lower than the LRAS, a **recessionary gap** exists. This indicates that the nation is experiencing high levels of unemployment.

QUICK REVIEW QUESTIONS

3. When the AD and the SRAS intersect at a point higher than the LRAS, what can be expected to occur?

   _____

4. When the AD and the SRAS intersect at a point lower than the LRAS, what can be expected to occur?

   _____

Business Activity and Market Stability

The Federal Reserve (the Fed) behaves as a central bank of the United States and ensures the safety of the American monetary system. In the century since its inception, the role of the Fed has expanded:

- Its primary role is to maximize employment and stabilize prices in the United States.
- It was created in 1913 to thwart the economic "panics" that seized the nation every few years.
- The Fed is meant to stabilize the US money supply and moderate interest rates.
- Its duties have expanded to include monitoring and maintaining reserves for US banks.

The Federal Reserve is among the most important components of the US federal government and even has its own seal and flag. Still, it is decentralized. Rather than be considered a central bank, the US federal reserve is considered a banking system. The system is structured around three main bodies:

- the Board of Governors
- the Federal Open Market Committee (FOMC)
- twelve Federal Reserve Banks across the United States, based in the following cities:
  - Boston
  - New York
  - Philadelphia
  - Cleveland
  - Richmond
  - Atlanta
  - Chicago
  - St. Louis

- Minneapolis
- Kansas City
- Dallas
- San Francisco

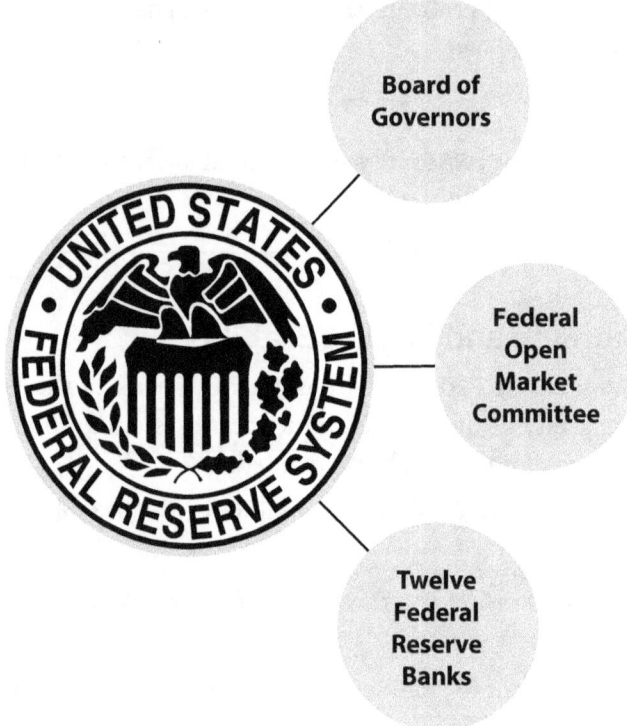

Figure 4.3. The Federal Reserve

The Federal Reserve also monitors **monetary stabilization**. Monetary stabilization

- includes efforts to keep prices, unemployment, and the money supply relatively stable; and
- helps prevent the economy from oscillating between inflation and recession.

The **Federal Reserve Board (FRB)** affects business activity and market stability through the discount rate. The **discount rate**, also known as the **Federal Funds Rate (FFR)**, affects credit availability in the economy. Essentially, the FFR is the specific rate of interest that banks pay for overnight borrowing in the federal funds market:

- Fluctuations in the FFR have a domino effect on other interest rates (e.g., mortgage rates).
- In this way, the FFR spreads to broad capital availability.
- The FFR stimulates (or reduces) business activity and household spending.

The FRB can adjust the FFR to make it easier—or harder—for businesses and individuals to access credit. For example, increasing the FFR puts pressure on firms and individuals to qualify for a loan given the adjusted repayment schedules. The opposite is true when the FFR moves down under FRB directives.

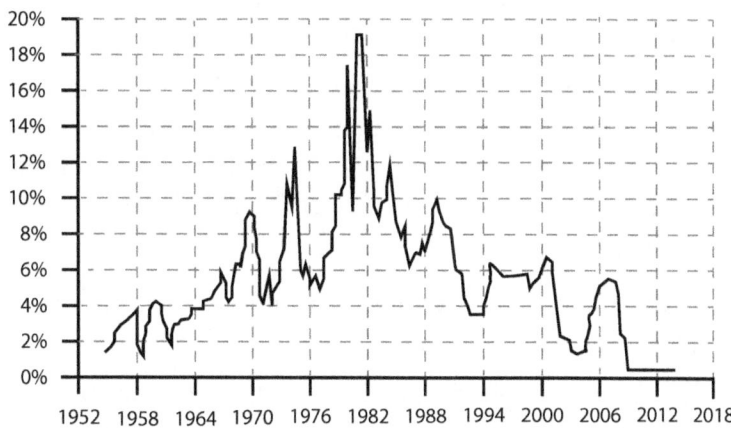

Figure 4.4. Federal Funds Rate

In this way, the FFR affects **business activity**. A low rate means easy credit terms, which allow businesses to expand and invest in more projects. Conversely, companies restrict borrowing and spending when credit tightens since they are less willing to take risks. In short, the FRB's use of FFR

- offers signals on how to behave in the marketplace, and
- creates attitudinal shifts that suppress or accelerate demand.

The FFR is a powerful tool. Raising the FFR can encourage less spending in inflationary times, thereby reducing inflation. A higher FFR can bring demand down to align with an overwhelmed supply. Similarly, when spending is low and markets experience excess supply, a lower FFR means more accessible credit. That gets people back in a spending mood. The FFR enables the FRB to balance supply and demand for output, avoid recessions, and control inflation.

QUICK REVIEW QUESTIONS

5. What is the Federal Reserve Board's most powerful tool for regulating business activity and stabilizing markets?

6. What is the Federal Reserve's primary function?

Monetary and Fiscal Policy

Fiscal policy is an approach to economic management in which the government is deeply involved in managing the economy:

- To counteract a recession, the government uses **expansionary fiscal policy**—either increasing spending or decreasing taxes.
- The government uses **contractionary fiscal policy** to combat inflation by reducing government spending or increasing taxes.

> **DID YOU KNOW?**
> Expansionary fiscal policy increases the aggregate demand curve.

The government consensus is that the Fed should be an independent entity that structures monetary policy without political interference. **Monetary policy** refers to controlling the money supply in a country. The actions of central banks (like the Fed) define monetary policy. The primary goals are

- stabilizing prices, and
- meeting balanced macroeconomic conditions (e.g., optimal employment and GDP growth).

Fiscal and monetary policy are different. Unlike monetary policy, **fiscal policy** converges on federal taxation and spending, and the protocols and limitations of these. Congress determines the latter, passing it down to the Fed, which must follow Congressional guidance. In practice, the **Federal Open Market Committee (FOMC)** develops monetary policy. The FOMC consists of

- the Board of Governors of the Federal Reserve,
- the president of the Federal Reserve Bank of New York, and
- four other Reserve Bank presidents on a rotating basis.

Since the FOMC uses fiscal policy projections and current implications, Congress indirectly influences macroeconomic issues:

- When governments make changes to spending and taxes, it affects their budget.
- When revenue (primarily money from taxes) exceeds spending, the government has a **surplus**.
- When spending exceeds revenues, the government has a **deficit**.

A deficit is not the same thing as a debt. A deficit is the gap between what the government has spent and what it has earned. To cover that deficit, the government must borrow money, which generates government debt.

> **DID YOU KNOW?**
> National debt develops over years of deficits.

Changes in **currency** are caused by—and impact—the strength of a nation's economy. **Currency appreciation** occurs when a country's money gains value in national and international markets. This increases foreign investment, as other countries gain more value for their money. However, a strong currency makes that nation's exports more expensive, which can affect trade.

Currency depreciation occurs when a country's money loses value in national and international markets and may point to instabilities in the nation's economy (such as high rates of inflation). When conducted in an intentional and orderly manner, however, currency depreciation can increase a nation's global competitiveness by lowering the cost of its exports. For example, China has used intentional currency depreciation to build a strong export-based economy and foster economic growth.

Open market activities, commonly referred to as **open market operations (OMOs)**, involve central banks (e.g., the Federal Reserve). In OMOs, the Fed buys and sells government securities as a monetary policy tool that impacts the ruling interest rate. The OMOs regulate the money supply. There are two scenarios that describe how this works in practice:

1. Bringing interest rates down involves buying bonds. When government bond prices go up in these moves, interest rates go down. So, when the Fed enters the open market to buy securities, it automatically creates reserves accessible to commercial banks at lower interest rates. In turn, the banks can use the relatively inexpensive funds to leverage more loans and investment capital for their clients.

2. Conversely, selling government securities decreases their prices and reduces reserves, thus pushing interest rates up. As a result, banks lend less and create more expensive debt for those they approve. The bottom line is that the money supply decreases to quell inflation.

QUICK REVIEW QUESTIONS

7. The government is combating inflation by reducing government spending or increasing taxes. What type of policy is this?

    _____

8. Which committee is responsible for developing monetary policy?

    _____

Different Rates

The Federal Reserve is the arbiter of interest rates for mortgages, the stock market, and any other monetary policy involving interest (e.g., money markets).

Lenders charge a percentage of the capital principal per month, day, or year until the borrower returns the funds. This percentage charge is an **interest rate**. Interest rates vary depending on the risk involved and the security behind the loan. Generally, the Fed's discount rate is used by commercial lenders as a minimum when structuring their interest rate tables. Furthermore, there are simple interest rates and compound interest rates.

Simple interest rates connect—in terms of percentage—to the loan's original capital. In **compound interest** rate calculations, the unpaid interest is added to the initial capital to derive a percentage rate. For example, compound interest works as follows:

- Interest of 8% on $100,000 accumulates to $108,000 after a year.
- It transitions to 8% on $108,000 in year two if the borrower does not pay out the 8% for the first year.

The discount rate aligns with the percentage the Federal Reserve charges commercial banks and depository institutions when allocating overnight loans to them. The Fed focuses on setting an independent rate through OMOs (see above), so the discount rate, or FFR, remains uninfluenced by the market's prevailing interest rates.

To avoid confusion, the term *discount rate* has a different meaning for financial advisors. They regard the discount rate as the percentage used for calculating the present value of future net cash inflows or outflows. Accordingly, they often refer to it as the **internal rate of return (IRR)**. In this capacity, the discount rate critically provides a time value of money and is vital for presenting projections to investors in an understandable manner. Insurance and pension institutions also deploy the discount rate to assess liabilities.

> **HELPFUL HINT**
>
> **Equilibrium interest rates**, regulated by the Fed, occur only when interest rates and the money supply are roughly equivalent.

QUICK REVIEW QUESTIONS

9. Who decides what the discount rate should be?

10. Which type of rates connect in percentage terms to the loan's original capital?

Business Economic Factors

Financial Statements

A **balance sheet** reflects the assets and liabilities of a business at a particular point in time—not over time. Assets are typically fixed (long term) and current (short term). Table 4.1 provides examples of fixed and current assets that companies typically hold.

TABLE 4.1. Asset Types and Common Examples

FIXED ASSETS	CURRENT ASSETS
• real estate holdings	• accounts receivable
• automobiles	• inventory
• equipment	• cash in the bank

Liabilities are debts a company owes. There are outsider liabilities and insider liabilities. The owners' equity and accumulated profits on the balance sheet on a certain date are known as the **balancing items**:

- A balancing item is considered an insider liability: the business owes this to shareholders.
- Outsider liabilities are those which pertain to outside creditors.

Table 4.2 contains typical examples of outsider and insider liabilities.

TABLE 4.2. Liability Types and Common Examples

OUTSIDER LIABILITIES	INSIDER LIABILITIES
• accounts payable • mortgages • bank loans	• shareholders' loan account • stock (at the issued value) • accumulated net income (after taxation and declaring dividends)

- In a successful company, the gap between assets and liabilities grows larger every year. Delivering more insider liability to the owners—growing their net worth—is the central objective of every enterprise.
- Conversely, if there are losses, the gap between assets and liabilities narrows, reducing net worth. (Management and CEOs are paid to avoid this!)

 DID YOU KNOW?

Also known as the balancing number, the balancing item metric makes liabilities equal to assets.

To review assets and liabilities over time, the reviewer must look at the balance sheets corresponding to different dates. The more dated observations involved in the analysis are, the easier it is to see the variations in asset ownership and debts emerging from operations.

Unlike a balance sheet, an **income statement** reflects business revenue minus expenses over time. Income statements show revenues from the sale of products or services and gross profit after deducting the **cost of sales (COS)**. In other words, COS tells businesses how much it cost them to produce the product they sold over the period under review. Common formulas for COS are found in Table 4.3.

Any inventory shrinkage is accounted for when counting the opening and closing inventory. Shrinkage is therefore an expense that automatically inserts itself into the cost of sales.

TABLE 4.3. Formulas for Cost of Sales

TRADER FORMULA	MANUFACTURER FORMULA
• COS = opening inventory + purchases - closing inventory	• COS = opening inventory + factory operational cost - closing inventory

Service businesses do not reflect the cost of goods sold. Their only concern is general expenses (called overhead). **Overhead** covers any costs not directly connected to creating a product (or providing a service) and includes

- administrative staff salaries,
- management compensation,
- IT expenses,
- travel,
- office utilities,
- interest on loans, and
- contributions to health plans.

 HELPFUL HINT

Factory operational cost includes the purchase of raw or semifinished materials.

Service, manufacturer, and product-selling businesses likewise focus on overhead that slots into the income statement under **gross profit**, which is calculated by subtracting COS from revenue.

The **gross margin** earned by the company is the gross profit as a percentage of revenue. For example, a 30% gross margin means that every dollar of revenue leaves thirty cents in the business after accounting for COS. Further steps are required to determine how much shareholders receive:

- On the income statement, gross profit minus total overhead equals net profit or **net income before taxation (NIBT)**.
- The bottom line is net profit, or **net income after taxes (NIAT)**. As the name suggests, NIAT equals NIBT minus taxes (NIBT − taxes = NIAT).

A company may distribute part or all of NIAT to the shareholders as a dividend. This bottom-most number on the income statement is called **retained income**, which is the quantity added to insider liability. Therefore, between the opening date of the income statement and its closing date, the following should be clear:

- Retained income added to the shareholders' funds (on top of the same balance sheet item coinciding with the opening date on the income statement).

OR

- If COS + overheads exceed top-line revenue, shareholders' net worth will reduce by the net loss.

QUICK REVIEW QUESTIONS

11. A statement of a business's assets and liabilities at a particular point in time is called what?

12. A document that reflects business revenue less expenses performance over time is called what?

Business Cycles

Business cycles describe volatility movements in economic activity in a region or country and are generally measured by changes in **gross domestic product (GDP)**. GDP is one of many indicators used to measure a nation's productivity and output. Indicators trend up or down over a specified period; therefore, a business cycle represents a GDP trend—contraction or expansion—over months or years.

A sustainable downward trend reflects a **contraction** in the business cycle. A contraction ends when it reaches a low point, called a **trough**. Enduring troughs reflect recessions.

Conversely, a sustainable upward trend amounts to an **expansion** in the business cycle. Expansions end in **peaks**, when GDP growth stops accelerating.

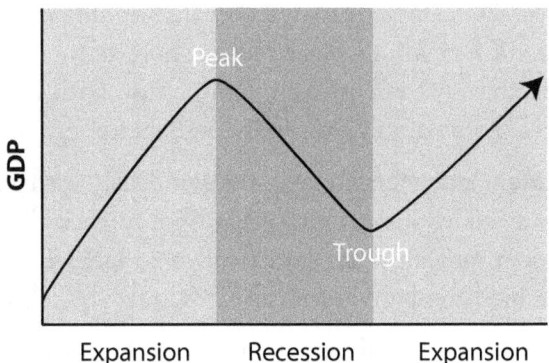

Figure 4.5. Business Cycles

QUICK REVIEW QUESTIONS

13. The low point of a contracting business cycle is called what?

14. The high point of an expansionary business cycle is called what?

Economic Indicators

Economic indicators are key performance indicators (KPIs) that relate to the economy's health and are based on data observation. **Leading indicators** are crucial, measurable variables driving the economy that offer clues as to the economy's direction:

- Examples of leading indicators include data from respected sources, like retail sales, stock indices, and the Purchasing Managers' Index (PMI).
- Leading indicators help the Fed and policymakers react appropriately to reverse disadvantageous occurrences (such as a full-blown recession) before they hit.

Lagging indicators are observable or measurable KPIs that alter after showing themselves in relevant economic, financial, or business data:

- They generally confirm a trend and indicate how it has changed.
- They do not predict future changes.
- Examples include the unemployment rate, corporate profits, and labor cost per unit.

 DID YOU KNOW?

PMI measures trends in manufacturing by surveying supply chains in nineteen industries every month.

ECONOMIC FACTORS

HELPFUL HINT

Coincident indicators are more similar to lagging indicators, but they are more current.

Observed over time, lagging indicators provide business and policy leaders with accurate guidance of entrenched trends in real time. In other words, a lagging indicator resembles a financial signal that appears only after a seismic trend shift.

Lagging indicators are vital to analysis because leading indicators invariably miss long-term trend formations obscured by short-term volatility. Therefore, leading indicators are most effective in conjunction with lagging indicators. Evaluating these KPIs in combination provides a better economic picture.

Finally, **coincident indicators** change simultaneously with general economic conditions to provide added insight into the current financial health of a country or region. Coincident indicators are statistically verifiable. Examples of coincident indicators include company turnover KPIs and production indices.

Inflation is a measurement of national price increases over time. Inflation is measured in percentages after overviewing a broad spectrum of leading/mainstream industry prices. To better understand the circumstances, economists can

HELPFUL HINT

The inflation index is another way of understanding the cost of living for the citizens of a country.

- extract inflationary indexes for subsections, like food, energy, and building materials; and
- analyze which price increases contributed most to the universal KPI—the official inflation number periodically announced by the Fed—that combines all of them.

QUICK REVIEW QUESTIONS

15. Which indicators do economists use to predict trends?

16. Which economic phenomenon is driven by rising price levels in a country?

Effects on Bond and Equity Markets

Business cycles and other economic factors have an impact on securities markets. Investors cannot influence economic cycles, but they can redirect their stock selections to avoid sharp drops in value.

Cyclical equities (also known as cyclical stocks or cyclical companies) react strongly to economic volatility:

- Cyclical stocks perform exceedingly well when the economy is booming; they crash when it recedes.
- Assessing cyclical stock movements and projecting them is as tricky as monitoring and forecasting economic cycles.

Conversely, **noncyclical equities** remain on an even keel in a fluctuating economy:

- Typical noncyclical equities include household necessities one must buy, regardless of economic conditions.

- Noncyclical shares attract investment in volatile times, generally outperforming cyclical stocks in a downturn.

In summary, cyclical shares follow economic trends; noncyclical shares are more stable. Table 4.4. shows some examples of common cyclical and noncyclical equities.

TABLE 4.4. Examples of Cyclical and Noncyclical Equities

CYCLICAL EQUITIES	NONCYCLICAL EQUITIES
• high-fashion brands • entertainment • fine dining • hospitality • vacations • airline travel • premium automobiles	• utilities (electric, water) • soaps • toothpaste • health care

In volatile times, noncyclical stocks represent a robust defense strategy to protect against portfolio volatility. These assets are often called **defensive stocks** because investors use them to defend their portfolios against economic disruption. During volatility, a defensive strategy means taking a noncyclical approach.

Defensive stocks offer stability to investors, but they will not skyrocket when market growth trends reoccur. To ensure portfolio growth, it is best to combine growth stocks with noncyclical equities.

Growth stocks feed on a vibrant economy. Noncyclical stocks are typically not growth stocks; however, if their projections indicate faster profit acceleration than average expectations, noncyclical stocks may fall into the category of growth stocks:

- Investors in growth stocks will expect the company to reinvest its profits; thus, investors will accept low—or even zero—dividends.
- Instead, the rewards come from capital gains rather than a steady cash inflow as the stock value climbs.

Examples of growth stocks include immature markets with significant growth potential and start-ups entering established markets with disruptive business models (e.g., Uber).

QUICK REVIEW QUESTIONS

17. Which type of stocks would investors seek in an economic downturn?

18. Noncyclical stocks are also known as what?

Principal Economic Theories

An understanding of principal economic theories is necessary for any investor. Major theories include Keynesian economics, supply-side economics, and monetarism.

The English economist John Maynard Keynes (1883 – 1946) revolutionized macroeconomic thought. According to **Keynesian theories**, the economy is in perfect balance when

- total market demand equals aggregate supply (i.e., total output); and
- consumers can easily pay the average pricing of that production.

However, Keynes believed that imbalance occurs frequently. For example, demand exceeds output, and pricing cannot remedy the gap. Similarly, he projected cases where output capacity exceeds demand for production and, again, pricing reaction does not help reduce the supply. Given specific imbalances, Keynes focused on the employment effect and inflation consequences.

According to Keynesian economists, central banks and government policymakers accept periodic disruptions to a balanced economy that will grow severe if left unchecked. To reset equilibrium, fiscal and monetary policy tools should be deployed.

In short, Keynes advocated a market economy left to the private sector—with one vital condition: the government and central bank can step in to regulate things in a measured manner when equilibrium is lost.

On the other hand, economists deploying **monetarist theories** see a central bank's ability to control the money supply as the be-all and end-all of economic stability. To Keynes, it was one tool used when needed. To monetarists, it is the only tool.

Monetarists contend that too much money in the system results in economic ills, starting with overspending and feeding inflation. By keeping the supply in check, imbalance never becomes an issue.

Instead of applying central bank power only to remedy economic downturns, monetarists support using it appropriately and actively to prevent the problem from occurring in the first place. So how do monetarists see the printing of money as the crux of the matter? It boils down to a basic formula that the monetarist theory follows: **$M \times V = P \times Q$**:

- M = total dollars circulating in the economy
- V = the velocity at which money circulates in the economy (the speed of transacting the money from entity to entity)
- P = price
- Q = output

When M increases, P, Q, or both increase (as long as V remains constant). Determining the value of V is the main question.

Nonetheless, like Keynes, monetarists believe that the variable with the most power to control the money supply is the Central Bank's control over M, with help from Congressional fiscal laws.

Finally, **supply-side economics** depends on the following strategies that put more money into the pockets of wealthy entities and individuals:

- applying tax cuts or cutting interest rates to promote more borrowing
- beneficiaries finding compelling ways to invest their extra wealth
  - employing more people who, in turn, spend more with their newfound salaries
  - creating economic stimulation while cutting unemployment

Supply-side economics relies on

- enacting tax cuts through fiscal policy,
- decreasing interest rates through the Fed's monetary policy and OMOs, and
- relaxing regulations by structuring laws and rules that promote more robust business practices.

QUICK REVIEW QUESTIONS

19. Who or what is central to Keynesian theory working to balance the economy?

20. Which economic theory supports putting more money into the pockets of wealthy entities and individuals?

International Economic Factors

Gross domestic product (GDP) is the total value of domestic production—the market value of all the final goods and services produced within a nation in one year:

- Final goods are those that are ready for consumption.
- Intermediate goods—ones that still require more processing—are not counted. (For example, tomatoes are intermediate goods, but jarred tomato sauce is a final good.)
- To avoid **double counting**, the count takes place at the final sale.

The GDP focuses on what was actually produced within a country, regardless of where it is headquartered. So if a shoe company is headquartered in California, but its production takes place in Vietnam, the total production of shoes would contribute to Vietnam's GDP, not that of the United States.

Secondhand sales, nonmarket transactions, and underground economies are all excluded from GDP. Countries where these play a stronger role—usually developing countries—have relatively weak GDPs.

The GDP should not be confused with the **gross national product (GNP)**. The GNP is the value of goods and services owned and produced by citizens of a country, regardless of where those goods and services are produced.

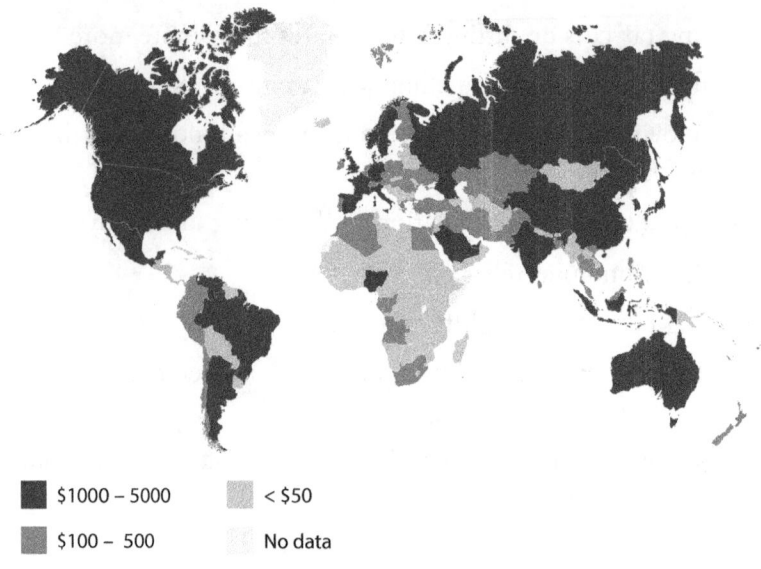

Figure 4.6. 2014 World Economies Map

The US **balance of payments (BOP)** revolves around all the transactions between US entities (e.g., individuals, government, and businesses) and the same in other countries globally for a defined period. The BOP includes current and capital accounts, each with a different focus:

- The **current account** covers the net bottom-line position (surplus or deficit) after accounting for transacting goods and services (e.g., imports and exports), cross-border investments, and net transfer payments.
- The **capital account** is the net position after accounting for financial instruments and central bank reserve transactions to settle current account imbalances.

As a result, after combining the capital and current accounts, the total transactions recorded in the balance of payments should be zero. This does not always happen because exchange rate variability and diverse accounting practices hinder tying up all the loose ends.

An **exchange rate** addresses converting currencies. Exchange rates guide transactions when one country's currency interacts with another country's currency. For example, when a business imports goods from Australia to the United States, US dollars (USD) must interact with Australian dollars (AUD). The exchange rate determines how many USD the Australian product is worth. Once they agree on the US price, the next step is getting down to exchange calculations:

- An Australian dollar may exchange for 0.70 USD on a specific day.
- Therefore, if the US product sells at 70 USD, the Australian buyer must pay 100 AUD on that date.

Exchange rates do not necessarily remain constant. In the above example, the rate could move up to 72 cents or, on other days, drop below 70 cents:

- Because of rate changes, trading parties should conclude the transaction immediately and not risk disadvantageous currency movements in the days ahead.
- The rate on the day applies to all transactions between Australia and the US on that date. Still, volatility may move the currency up or down, even on the same day.

Every country transacting internationally brings its exchange rate into the picture. Every trade (import and export) and money transfer connects to the exchange rates at the moment of the transaction. As a result, there are two crucial considerations:

- the timing of international deals
- hedging against exchange rate variability in the future (e.g., when foreign loans are repayable, or an order for delivery is firm on the price but only transacts at exchange rates down the line)

Considering there are trillions of international transactions daily, the accounting processes offered by banks acting as middlemen must be accurate, seamless, and fast. To add more complexity, there is seldom certainty on exchange rates, most of which fluctuate based on supply and demand in the currency markets:

- Some countries peg their currency to another because the trade volume is massive. This removes unnecessary volatility and creates more certainty when negotiating across borders.
- When a country's currency weakens, it assists exporters since the goods and services are less expensive to their trading partners.
- Conversely, a strengthening currency entices importers to buy more from foreign trading partners using the same logic.

QUICK REVIEW QUESTIONS

21. What are the two accounts in the US balance of payments?

22. What is the term that describes the basis of accounting that guides transactions when one country's currency interacts with another's?

Answer Key

1. Aggregate supply (AS) describes the sum of all of the microeconomic supply curves in an economy.

2. Macroeconomic equilibrium describes when the output quantity demanded equals the quantity of output supplied.

3. An inflationary gap can be expected to occur when the aggregate demand (AD) and the short-run aggregate supply (SRAS) intersect at a point higher than the long-run aggregate supply (LRAS).

4. A recessionary gap can be expected to occur when the aggregate demand (AD) and the short-run aggregate supply (SRAS) intersect at a point lower than the long-run aggregate supply (LRAS).

5. The Federal Funds Rate (FFR) is the Federal Reserve Board's most powerful tool for regulating business activity and stabilizing markets.

6. The Federal Reserve's primary function is to ensure the safety of the American monetary system.

7. Contractionary fiscal policy describes when the government combats inflation by reducing government spending or increasing taxes.

8. The Federal Open Market Committee (FOMC) is responsible for developing monetary policy.

9. The Federal Reserve decides what the discount rate should be.

10. Simple interest rates connect in percentage terms to the loan's original capital.

11. A balance sheet is a statement of a business's assets and liabilities at a particular point in time.

12. An income statement is a document that reflects business revenue less expenses performance over time.

13. A trough is the low point of a contracting business cycle.

14. A peak is the high point of an expansionary business cycle.

15. Economists use leading indicators to predict trends.

16. Rising price levels in a country drive inflation.

17. Investors would seek noncyclical stocks in an economic downturn.

18. Noncyclical stocks are also known as defensive stocks.

19. The Central Bank (monetary policy) and Congress (fiscal policy) are central to Keynesian theory working to balance the economy.

20. Supply-side economics is the economic theory that supports putting more money into the pockets of wealthy entities and individuals.

21. Current accounts and capital accounts make up the US balance of payments (BOP).

22. An exchange rate guides transactions when one country's currency interacts with another country's currency.

5 Financial Products

Equity Securities

An **equity security**, also called a **stock**, represents an ownership stake in the issuing company. Equity securities are issued by companies to raise funds:

- The buyer of an equity security seeks to benefit from the future prosperity of the company as the price of the stock appreciates.
- Buyers may also wish to collect dividend income.

Equity holders are the true owners of a company and are generally empowered to select the company's leadership and vote on major decisions the company makes.

Types of Equities

Common stock represents an ownership stake in the issuing company. Common stock

- is the most standard form of equity issued by companies,
- makes up most of the stock market,
- allows the shareholder to receive a pro rata share of dividends if distributed,
- typically includes the right to vote for members of the board of directors,
- is junior to debt, and
- is the primary stock in the capital structure of a company.

The authorized stock of the corporation is the total number of shares allowed to be issued, as defined in the corporation's charter.

Preferred stock offers certain rights that exceed those of common stock. Preferred stock

- is senior to common stock in the capital structure, and
- may or may not provide a dividend.

 DID YOU KNOW?

If a company goes into liquidation, holders of its common stock are typically last in line to get paid from the company's liquidated assets.

When dividends are distributed to preferred stockholders, they are based on a fixed (stated) rate and take precedence over dividends paid to holders of common stock.

Preferred stock has some characteristics of debt: it may provide fixed income from dividends and is senior to common stock in the capital structure. The issuer, however, does not default in the event of failure to pay a preferred stock dividend. In fact, for **cumulative preferred stock**, that unpaid dividend is deferred until a future time when the company can afford to pay it in arrears, and no other shareholder can receive a dividend payment until that happens.

Preferred stock is junior to debt in the capital structure. In the event of liquidation, **participating preferred stock** also gets a share of the common stock equity payout. If there is no money left over for common shareholders after liquidation, there may be no difference between the value of participating and nonparticipating preferred shares.

Both participating and nonparticipating preferred stock entitle the shareholder to a liquidation payment that takes priority over common stock.

Warrants represent a right—not an obligation—to purchase shares of the underlying stock directly from the issuer. Until the warrant is exercised, the stock has not been purchased, therefore no dividends are paid to the holder of a warrant.

Warrants are often structured like options, but they generally have a longer time to maturity. The number of shares addressed by each warrant can vary; an investor may need several warrants to purchase one share.

Like warrants, **rights** permit the holder to purchase shares for a set price. The difference between rights and warrants is largely a matter of terminology. Rights tend to be much shorter-dated than warrants, with a lower exercise price. In general, both rights and warrants can be thought of as call options.

An **American Depositary Receipt (ADR)** is US-issued stock in a foreign-listed company. This is accomplished when an affiliate of a US bank purchases shares of the company in the country where its equity is listed. The US bank issues stock that represents ownership of those shares held abroad. Local investors purchase shares of the ADR as an easier way to gain exposure to the equity of a foreign company in domestic accounts.

QUICK REVIEW QUESTIONS

1. What type of stock allows the shareholder to vote and receive dividends?

2. What kind of stock must receive all past unpaid dividend payments before a new dividend can be distributed to common stockholders?

3. Where is an ADR listed?

Ownership of Equities

Order of liquidation reflects the priority of payment for expenses and creditor claims in the event of bankruptcy. According to the absolute priority rule, liquidation proceeds must be paid to all parties in each tier of the liquidation order before the next tier can receive any disbursement.

The order of liquidation is inextricably related to the capital structure of a company. The hierarchy of payments in a liquidation will depend almost entirely on the way that a company has been financed. Absent any special circumstances, secured creditors have first priority. Within each tier of creditor claims, the general rule of priority is that the earliest to secure is paid first in the event of liquidation. Common stock usually takes last priority, meaning that those shareholders receive a payout only when all creditors and preferred shareholders have been paid in full. Preferred stock is senior to common stock but junior to debt. Holders of common stock may not receive any liquidation proceeds because their claims are in the lowest tiers of the liquidation order.

Limited liability describes a legal protection whereby the private assets of a company's investors and owners are not at risk in the event a company's debts or obligations exceed the company's liquidation value. This is an attractive feature for investors because it prevents them from being personally responsible for bad outcomes when they invest in companies without being directly involved in the management of day-to-day operations.

Voting rights allow shareholders to influence corporate decisions and board leadership in a manner proportional to their holdings of the corporation's equity. Certain classes of equity may offer greater voting power than other classes. Some classes of equity (usually, preferred stock) offer lesser voting power or no voting rights at all.

Convertible equity is preferred stock that can be exchanged for common stock. **Convertible preferred stock** offers investors the possibility of the equity upside if the common stock rallies far beyond the conversion price while providing a fixed dividend and a higher claim on assets in the interim.

QUICK REVIEW QUESTIONS

4. Who is last in line to receive a payout when a company goes bankrupt and is liquidated?

5. Who is first in line to receive a payout when a company goes bankrupt and is liquidated?

6. What kind of stock is convertible equity?

Control and Restrictions

Certain kinds of transactions produce **restricted securities**. Private placements, Regulation D offerings, employee stock, equity given in lieu of cash compensation, and stock granted in exchange for seed capital are all examples of situations that can result in a restricted holding.

SEC Rule 144 provides a safe harbor for the public sale of restricted and control securities. The safe harbor is based on five conditions that apply only to affiliates of the issuer and support the removal of the restrictive legend on the certificate of the securities (or the book entry that tracks their ownership). Those five conditions are as follows:

1. Holding period
   - Depending on the nature of the issuer, a restricted security exempted under Rule 144 must be held for at least six months prior to resale if the issuer is a reporting company under the Securities Exchange Act of 1934, or at least one year before resale if the issuer is a non-reporting company.

2. Current public information
   - Market participants must have access to adequate public information about the issuer. In the case of a reporting company, this means periodic disclosure in accordance with the filing requirements of the Securities Exchange Act of 1934.
   - In the case of a non-reporting company, publicly available information must satisfy specific rules about the business, leadership, and finances of the firm.

3. Trading volume formula
   - Rule 144 transactions within any three-month period must be smaller than a threshold of 1% of the outstanding shares of the same class, or one week's worth of trading volume if the security is listed on a stock exchange and heavily traded.

4. Ordinary brokerage transactions
   - Rule 144 transactions must be executed in a routine manner.

5. Filing a notice of proposed sale with the SEC
   - If all of these conditions are met, the issuer can be asked to remove the restrictive legend and permit public sale of the securities.

QUICK REVIEW QUESTIONS

7. When can an affiliate of the issuer make a sale of more than 1% of the outstanding shares of a restricted stock that does not trade on any exchange?

8. How long must a restricted security from a company that is not subject to the reporting requirements of the Securities Exchange Act of 1934 be held before it can be sold?

　

9. Who decides whether a restrictive legend can be removed?

　

Debt Instruments

Debt instruments are generally categorized with fixed-income securities. Debt is attractive to investors who seek a regular interest payment. These securities usually (but not always) involve a fixed maturity date, though there are certain cases where they may be prepaid by the debtor or called by the issuer.

Several different kinds of debt are widely traded in US markets. Among the most frequent are

- the government bond market,
- the corporate credit market,
- the municipal securities market, and
- the mortgage debt market.

Collectively, these and associated other markets are referred to as the **fixed income market.**

Treasury Securities

Bonds are the most common type of debt securities. Some bonds pay the holder a regular interest payment, known as a coupon. Other bonds, referred to as "zero-coupon bonds," provide no coupon payments.

- A **premium bond** is a bond trading above its face value.
- A **discount bond** is a bond trading below its face value.
- A **par bond** is bond trading at its face value.

Yield is a measure of the return on a bond investment. Price and yield have an inverse relationship: yield increases when bond price goes down and decreases when bond price goes up. Yield can be expressed in several ways:

- **Current yield** is the bond's annual interest (coupon) divided by the bond's market price.
- **Nominal yield** is the bond's annual interest payment divided by the bond's face value.

The nominal yield of a bond may provide an indication of the quality of the bond at the time of issuance, but it does not reflect changes in bond quality the way current yield does. The US Treasury issues certain securities ("Treasurys"):

- **Treasury bills (T-bills)** are United States government bonds issued with a maturity of one year or less. T-bills pay no coupons and are issued at a discount to par.
- **Treasury notes (T-notes)** are United States government bonds issued with a maturity of two to ten years. Their coupon yield is determined by auction.
- **Treasury bonds (T-bonds)** are United States government bonds issued with a maturity of thirty years. They are also referred to as "long bonds." Their coupon yield is determined by auction.
- **Treasury receipts** are zero-coupon bonds created by brokerage firms and collateralized with Treasury bonds.

The US Treasury holds auctions to issue new government bonds several times a year. The frequency of these issuances depends on the **tenor** (maturity) of the bond. Shorter-dated Treasurys are auctioned more frequently. The most recently auctioned Treasury debt securities are known as **on-the-run** Treasurys, and they tend to be more liquid than their preceding, off-the-run counterparts.

Treasury auctions function by accepting bids from potential buyers and setting the coupon payment (or in the case of T-bills, the discount rate) equal to the lowest-bid interest rate at which the entire issue can be placed. This optimal interest rate is called the "stop." All winning bidders for a given issue receive the Treasury security at the stop rate. Bids at the stop are allocated on a pro rata basis if their demand exceeds the issue size, and no single bidder is permitted to bid for more than 35% of the offering.

The US government also sells bonds whose principal amount is adjusted when consumer prices change. These bonds are known as **Treasury Inflation Protected Securities (TIPS)**.

> **DID YOU KNOW?**
> Treasurys have been issued via **single-price auction** since 1992.

QUICK REVIEW QUESTIONS

10. A bond with a 4% annual coupon is trading at half of its face value. What is its current yield?

11. An on-the-run Treasury security matures in seven years. What kind of issue is it?

12. A bond trades at a price of $90 with a current yield of 3%. If the current yield later rises to 3.8%, does the market price of the bond go up or down?

Other Securities

An **asset-backed security (ABS)** is a debt product that is backed by a pool of assets, such as credit cards or auto loans. These securitized products are often originated by major banks, so their credit quality can be very high as a result.

That said, the risk characteristics of ABSs can be quite different compared to bonds issued by the same banks. Trillions of dollars of ABSs have been issued since they were first issued in 1985. The assets bundled into these securities may lack a fixed maturity, their interest rates may float, and they may be subject to prepayment.

A **residential mortgage-backed security (RMBS)** is a securitized debt product whose interest payments come from home loans. As with asset-backed securities, prepayment of mortgage principal affects these securitized products.

Most RMBSs are issued by government agencies, but some are issued by third-party "private label" issuers. This market serves the public interest by making it easier for homebuyers to receive residential mortgage loans. Several corporations securitize and/or guarantee agency mortgage-backed securities:

- Federal National Mortgage Association (FNMA)—Fannie Mae
- Federal Home Loan Mortgage Corporation (Freddie Mac)
- Federal Agricultural Mortgage Corporation (Farmer Mac)

Fannie Mae and Freddie Mac are government-sponsored enterprises and publicly traded companies that were established by Congress. The Federal Agricultural Mortgage Corporation (Farmer Mac) works with agricultural mortgage-backed securities.

The Government National Mortgage Association (GNMA)—Ginnie Mae—is wholly owned by the federal government as part of the US Department of Housing and Urban Development. It is backed by the full faith and credit of the US government.

Residential mortgage loans are securitized in a variety of ways. The most basic way to create a security from mortgages is to bundle them and directly disburse the home loan payments to the holders of the RMBSs. This is called a **mortgage pass-through** because the loan interest payments from a pool of mortgages are passed through to the holder of the securitized product.

More complicated products, like **collateralized mortgage obligations (CMOs)**, allocate loan interest payments across tranches rather than passing them through. The simplest of these is a sequential-pay CMO that makes interest payments to all tranches but directs principal repayments to tranches one by one, starting with the most senior, until all tranches have been retired in order.

QUICK REVIEW QUESTIONS

13. What kind of securitized product is backed by credit card receivables?

14. Which kind of securitized product groups mortgage principal repayments by tranche?

15. Who owns the Ginnie Mae corporation?

Corporate Bonds and Municipal Securities

Corporate bonds are a means for companies to borrow money from investors. They represent debt of the issuer and may be secured by a mortgage on assets of the corporation. Corporate bonds that are issued without the backing of any specific assets are backed instead by the general credit of the issuer and are referred to in the US as **debentures**.

Corporate bonds trade in an over-the-counter market; there is no exchange that lists a bid and offer for each corporate bond. Electronic trading platforms allow market participants to request quotations for securities and transact those quotations, without the benefit of a continuous double auction with two-way live quotations. As with many other fixed-income securities, corporate bond trades are reported to FINRA's Trade Reporting and Compliance Engine within fifteen minutes of transaction:

HELPFUL HINT

Municipal bonds are often exempt from federal and state taxation.

- **Municipal bonds** are issued by state and local governments to raise funds for operations as well as schools, bridges, roads, and other capital projects.
- **General obligation bonds** are a common municipal debt instrument that is backed by the full faith and credit of the issuer.
- **Revenue bonds** are backed by cash flows from a specific project or activity.
- **Moral obligation bonds** are not backed by anything other than the issuer's full faith and credit—in other words, the issuer's desire to maintain its credit quality.
- **Special tax bonds** have features of both revenue and moral obligation bonds.
  - They are backed by the full faith and credit of the issuer.
  - Their repayment is financed by specific taxes (e.g., an excise tax on a particular kind of product or service).

Municipal bonds are offered to investors in one of two ways:

- With a **negotiated offering**, the issuer selects an underwriter who then works with both the issuer and the investors to raise the funds sought by the issuer while permitting investors to influence the terms of the bond deal.
- In a **competitive offering**, the issuer establishes terms for the bond and advertises it for sale.

Prospective buyers bid for the bonds and the bonds are sold to the buyer who bids the lowest yield. From the issuer's perspective, the decision between these two offering methods hinges upon several factors, including

- the issuer's credit quality,
- the amount of bond notional being issued, and
- market conditions.

Issuers can structure municipal bonds to be federally taxable, federally tax-exempt, or subject to the federal alternative minimum tax (AMT) that applies to high-income individuals under certain circumstances. These definitions are not strict; for example, interest income from tax-exempt municipal bonds would not be taxed at the federal level, but that interest income would affect the calculation of modified adjusted gross income to determine Medicare premiums and taxes on social security benefits; capital gains from a sale of those bonds would be taxable as income.

That said, tax-exempt municipal bonds have a higher effective yield than taxable instruments paying the same nominal coupon rate. Municipal issuers almost always save money by issuing tax-exempt bonds rather than taxable bonds; this is because investors will accept a lower-yielding bond when interest income is not taxed.

State or local governments may use short-term municipal obligations to remain liquid when they expect to receive funds within a few months but want to use the funds sooner than that;

- If the funds they expect to receive come from taxes, they may issue a **tax anticipation note** that will be repaid with the tax revenue when received.
- If they are waiting for a federal grant (e.g., for a transit project), the issuer may use a **grant anticipation note** to begin work on the project rather than waiting for the grant money to arrive.

New issuances of municipal bonds tend to have a settlement period between two days and two weeks. A municipal bond with a long settlement date of six weeks or more is called a **forward-delivery municipal bond**. Its buyer locks in a price, but neither the issuer nor the buyer receives interest accrual or makes a cash outlay until settlement occurs.

Issuers may prefer a forward-delivery municipal issuance because they can establish a future loan using currently prevailing interest rates and credit quality. This kind of transaction may be useful for issuers who wish to refinance existing debt at a lower interest rate but find themselves subject to IRS restrictions that prevent **advance refunding**, defined as issuing a new bond to refinance an existing bond more than 90 days before the existing bond is scheduled to mature.

QUICK REVIEW QUESTIONS

16. A state government issues a bond to build a suspension bridge and intends to repay the debt with tolls paid by motorists. What kind of bond is this?

17. What part of a tax-exempt municipal bond is exempt from federal tax?

18. What kind of short-term municipal obligation can a city use when it is expecting federal grant money?

Other Debt Instruments

The **money market** is characterized by the trading of extremely liquid short-term debt with minimal credit risk. Most transactions in the money market take place between institutions that exchange cash for instruments that are, like money, secure and fungible. These include Treasury bills as well as instruments issued by private institutions:

- **Commercial paper**, or unsecured short-term promissory notes issued by corporations, represents one example of a money market security.
  - Commercial paper is usually issued in denominations of $100,000 or more, with a maturity of 270 days or fewer.
- **Banker's acceptances** are promises of future payment with a time span of six months or less, issued by financial institutions and transferable prior to maturity.
- Like T-bills, neither commercial paper nor banker's acceptances pay coupons; they are sold at a discount of their face value.

Sometimes, institutions make a contractual agreement to sell a government security today and buy it back after a term of a few days (or even overnight) at a slightly higher price. This is called a **repurchase agreement**, or repo.

Money market yields tend to be low because these instruments do not carry much credit risk and are short-term investments that reside at the front of the yield curve. The money market is useful because it allows large institutions with excellent credit who need overnight cash to access it by issuing short-term debt or selling existing short-term debt holdings. It also allows those who have cash to generate a return by using it to buy cash-like instruments that yield interest.

Not all money market participants are institutions. Money market deposit accounts are insured by the Federal Deposit Insurance Corporation (FDIC) for up to $250,000 dollars. However, money market mutual funds held by a broker are not insured in this way.

Certificates of Deposit (CDs) provide a similar function for individual investors as they do in the money market. CDs provide a fixed interest rate and a set maturity date, and they are insured by the FDIC. Early withdrawal of funds from a CD results in penalty fees.

QUICK REVIEW QUESTIONS

19. Assuming an investment greater than what the FDIC will insure, what is the least risky instrument traded in the money market?

20. What is the maximum time to maturity for most commercial paper?

21. What is the maximum time to maturity for most banker's acceptances?

Service and Concepts

Credit ratings measure the default risk of a bond issue or issuer. They are established by credit rating agencies. The following are considered the "big three" credit rating agencies:

- Moody's Investors Service
- S&P Global Ratings
- Fitch Ratings

Of the three major rating agencies, S&P and Fitch use a rating scale that categorizes issues from AAA to D; Moody's uses a scale from Aaa to C.

TABLE 5.1. Types of Credit Ratings

BOND TYPE	S&P AND FITCH RATING	MOODY'S RATING
Investment grade bonds	AAA to BBB-	Aaa to Baa3
High-yield bonds	BB+ to D	Ba1 to C

In the US corporate credit market, investment-grade bonds are quoted in basis points as a yield spread to a benchmark Treasury security. High-yield bonds are quoted as a dollar price, with par being quoted as $100.

Rising stars are bonds issued at a high yield that subsequently become lower-yielding investments as credit quality improves and the market price of the bond rises. **Fallen angels** are bonds issued at a low yield that become riskier investments with higher yield as the issuer encounters problems and the bond price goes down.

A given issuer may have a variety of bonds outstanding, and these bonds may have unique features, varying maturities, and trade in the market at a different current yield. If an issuer has multiple similar outstanding bonds with varying maturities, their yields together characterize a **yield curve** that shows how the interest rate of the issuer's debt varies over time.

Yield curves are a basic aspect of debt markets and not specific to corporate issuers. Fixed income traders watch the US Treasury yield curve as a benchmark measure of risk-free interest rates and the cost of money. The difference between a corporate bond yield and the interpolated Treasury yield of the same maturity is known as the **G-spread**.

A yield curve where short-term rates are lower than long-term rates is often taken as a sign of a healthy economy. Under normal circumstances, short-term debt trades at a lower yield than long-term debt. Many theories can be proposed for why this is the case:

- Lenders charge more for long-term loans to compensate for uncertainty about future interest rate volatility.
- Long-term debt is more likely to experience default because it spans a greater time to maturity.
- Better liquidity of short-term debt means that investors and institutions who wish to keep their cash invested in interest-bearing assets can easily use short-term debt (i.e., the money market) instead of long-term debt to do so.

A bond's features and characteristics are described in its **bond indenture**, the legal document that describes the rights and responsibilities established between the issuer and the bondholder. This document may describe provisions that materially affect the market value of the bond. One such provision is a **call feature** that gives the issuer a right to pay a lump sum and retire the bond prior to maturity. The result is an effective lower bond for the market yield of the bond because if prevailing interest rates decrease past a certain point, the issuer can issue a new bond at a lower rate and call the existing bond to reduce interest costs.

Since yield and price have an inverse relationship, we can also think about the impact of a call feature in terms of price. Callable bonds typically trade at a slightly lower price than noncallable bonds to compensate for the bondholder's risk of losing future interest payments in the event the bond is called. Some callable bonds include a make-whole provision to reduce the call risk for the bondholder.

Convertible bonds, in their "vanilla" form, provide the bondholder with the option to relinquish the bond and receive shares of stock instead. As a result, convertible bond prices can fluctuate with the price of the issuer's equity. If the equity value moves higher, convertible bondholders can profit from the share price appreciation even if the issuer's credit quality and nonconvertible bonds have not changed. Other conversion types exist, but this is the simplest.

QUICK REVIEW QUESTIONS

22. If a bond is rated BB- by Fitch, is it a high-yield bond or an investment-grade bond?

23. All else being equal, which is worth more to a bondholder: a callable bond or a noncallable bond?

24. What happens to the bond yield of a rising star?

Options

Types of Options

Options represent the right—but not the obligation—for the option holder to buy (or sell) the underlying asset at a particular price. If the option is exercised, the **strike price** is the price at which the underlier would transact. As can be expected for any derivative contract, an option's value is based in large part on the underlying asset.

The price (also known as the **premium**) of an option, however, varies with other characteristics of the contract, such as its **expiration date**. Options do not last forever; their value increases when they allow more time for the option holder to make a decision. Option holders are not required to exercise an option, but their right to do so lapses when the expiration date passes.

Call options give the holder a right (but not an obligation) *to buy* the underlying asset for the strike price. Similarly, **put options** give the holder a right *to sell* the underlying asset at the strike price.

The underlying asset of the option can be just about anything with a price: agricultural products, petroleum, equities, stock market indices, currencies, bonds, or even other options.

> **HELPFUL HINT**
>
> **FINRA Rule 2360** defines and addresses options in detail.

QUICK REVIEW QUESTIONS

25. A 50-strike call option is offered at a price of $2. The underlying stock is trading at $49. What is its premium?

26. What kind of option gives the holder a right to sell the underlying asset at the strike price?

27. Which option is worth more: an ABC Feb 45-strike put or an ABC May 45-strike put?

Options Actions

Options can be used by traders and investors for a variety of purposes. Their nonlinear risk profiles are useful for **hedging** positions in the underlier. For example, investors who own long stock in XYZ Corporation can reduce downside risk by buying at-the-money put option contracts on XYZ stock:

- If the price of XYZ drops precipitously, some of the loss from the long shares will likely be canceled out by a gain on the put options.
- If XYZ stock rallies, the investors would make money on their long XYZ stock while losing only the amount paid for the puts.

Options are also a useful instrument for **speculation** because options strategies allow the trader to isolate very specific risk exposures. For example, a trader who predicts that ABC stock (currently trading at $50) will close at $65 on June options expiry can buy an ABC June 60/65/70 call butterfly, whose maximum payout of $5 would occur if the trader's prediction comes to fruition.

Dollar for dollar, options carry greater risks than a similarly capitalized investment in the underlying stock. A trader can express a view about the future state of the market more capital-efficiently with options than with stock, but it is far easier to lose money through buying options than through buying the underlying stock.

An option is "**at-the-money**" when the spot price of the underlier (i.e., where the underlier is trading in the market) is equal to the strike price. A put option is

FINANCIAL PRODUCTS

considered "**in-the-money**" when the market price of the underlier (also known as its spot price) is trading below the strike price, and "**out-of-the-money**" when the spot price exceeds the strike price. The inverse is true for call options.

When an option is in-the-money, the difference between its strike price and its spot price is its intrinsic value. The amount of premium that exceeds intrinsic value is known as the **time value**. If XYZ stock is trading at $26, a 25-strike call worth $3 has an intrinsic value of $1 and a time value of $2.

The maximum potential loss for an option buyer is the premium paid. Options can also be sold short, referred to as **writing** an option. The maximum potential loss for a put writer is the strike price minus the premium received. The maximum potential loss for a call writer is unlimited in theory because the underlying asset's value has no upper bound. When an option is written without being hedged by other options or shares of the underlying stock, it is said to be **naked**. This is due to the risk of outsized losses in case the market moves against the position.

Writing an option against the underlying stock is a common way to enhance the yield of a position. A **covered call** is one such strategy. Equity options listed in the US have a built-in multiplier of 100, so a covered call writer would buy 100 shares and sell one call contract. In contrast to a naked short call, the payoff profile of a covered call strategy is conservative.

Consider a buy-write strategy where an option trader writes a TUV September 30 call at $2 and simultaneously buys 100 shares of TUV for $25. This strategy improves the trader's profit if TUV stock remains stable and gives up some of the potential upside from TUV shares in exchange for a lower break-even price for the strategy:

- If TUV remains at $25 from now to the September options expiration, the trader has no profit or loss on the shares but will make $200 in premium from the call.
- If TUV drops to $23, there is no net profit or loss because the trader's $200 profit from the call premium cancels out the $200 loss on the TUV shares.
- However, if TUV rallies to $35, the trader still collects $200 in option premium but expects to be assigned to sell his shares at $30 due to the short call.
  - In such a case, the trader's overall $700 profit is the same as if TUV had only rallied to the short strike of $30.

Options holders are not obligated to **exercise** their option to transact the underlying security at the strike price. They sometimes choose to let options lapse unexercised, even when the options are in-the-money:

- A **European-style option** allows the long holder to make an exercise decision only at maturity.
- An **American-style option** allows the long holder to make an exercise decision either at maturity or, irreversibly, upon any business day before maturity.

- An American-style option that expires in September can be exercised in September, and it can be exercised in August, but it cannot be exercised in October after it has expired.
- An intermediate variety also exists: **Bermuda options** may be exercised either at maturity or, irreversibly, upon a small number of specified dates prior to maturity.

When a contract is exercised by its long holder, a market participant who sold a contract is selected at random and obligated to take the other side of the exercise. This process is called **assignment**. For example, if a trader is short two in-the-money QRS May 30 calls, and QRS stock closes at $22 on the May expiration, that trader may be assigned and obligated to sell 200 QRS shares at a price $8 below the last trade price.

Depending on the contract specifications, settlement style may vary. An option exercise may involve a **physical settlement** of funds in exchange for the underlying asset, or it may be a **cash settlement** whereby the in-the-money amount of the contract is paid to the option holder.

Standards and customs around settlement style differ depending upon the asset involved. Exchange-listed equity options in the US are physically settled by delivering shares in exchange for payment, whereas many index options are cash settled with a transfer of the in-the-money amount to the option's long holder.

The **Options Clearing Corporation (OCC)** determines the criteria and characteristics for adjustments to option contracts and releases an information memo to explain each contract adjustment to participants in the options market. For example, the strike of an option contract may be adjusted downward on the ex-dividend date of a large special cash dividend.

The OCC maintains a document titled "Characteristics and Risks of Standardized Options," often called the **options disclosure document (ODD)**. It is more than 180 pages long and must be provided to a customer before the customer may buy or sell an option contract. The ODD explains the risks and attributes of listed options.

> **DID YOU KNOW?**
> The Options Disclosure Document is available for download, and printed copies are sold at a low price by the OCC.

QUICK REVIEW QUESTIONS

28. ABC stock is trading at $88. Is the ABC Feb 90-strike put in-the-money, or out-of-the-money?

29. What settlement style delivers stock to the long holder of a call option?

30. What option style only allows exercise of an option upon maturity and at no point prior?

Packaged Products

Types of Investment Companies

Open-end funds create shares when a new investment is made and those shares are taken out of circulation when an investor sells the shares. Many exchange-traded funds, mutual funds, and hedge funds operate in this way:

- The price of an open-end fund is based on its **net asset value (NAV)**, the total value of assets minus liabilities divided by the number of shares.
- With every new investment in an open-ended fund, money enters the fund and shares are created.

In addition to paying the NAV, investors in mutual funds often pay a sales fee as a percent of the NAV:

- This fee is called a **front-end load** if it is charged at the time that shares are purchased.
- It is called a back-end load or **contingent deferred sales charge** if it is charged when shares are sold.
- **FINRA Rule 2341** imposes a cap on these fees at 8.5%.

Front-end sales loads may be discounted when an investment in a mutual fund or fund family exceeds a threshold amount known as a **breakpoint**.

An investor who owns holdings in a mutual fund and wants to buy more shares may receive discounted pricing if the sum of the existing holdings and the new investment exceeds a **rights of accumulation** breakpoint.

Similarly, an investor who plans to buy a large stake in a mutual fund through multiple smaller purchases can sign a **letter of intent** to receive a volume discount corresponding to the breakpoint for the total stake.

Breakpoint sales are restricted by **FINRA Rule 2342** (Breakpoint Sales). According to the rule, broker-dealers are obligated to inform customers about breakpoint discounts. If the investor loses out on a breakpoint discount due to a broker-dealer's recommendations, this is a violation of the rule.

Mutual funds are often categorized into **classes** that roughly correspond to their fee type, as described in Table 5.2.

HELPFUL HINT

Rights of accumulation may take holdings of immediate family members into consideration, as well as holdings of companies controlled by the investor.

TABLE 5.2. Mutual Fund Fees

TYPE OF SHARE	TYPE OF FEE
Class A	front-end load
Class B	contingent deferred sales charge • may be reduced or waived if the mutual fund shares are held for a long time
Class C	annual expenses • may have no front-end or back-end load

Mutual funds may charge other fees, including an annual **12b-1 fee** to be used for marketing the mutual fund. (See Chapter 6 for more on the 12b-1 and other fees.)

Information about every mutual fund's expenses, performance, risks, and objectives is disclosed in its prospectus (see Chapter 1 for more information about prospectuses).

Closed-end funds have shares that can be neither created nor redeemed. Like stocks, those shares are traded on an exchange or over the counter:

- The price of a closed-end fund can deviate from its NAV because it is based on the supply of, and demand for, its outstanding shares.
- When an investor purchases a share of a closed-end fund in the secondary market, no new money enters the fund.
- A closed-end fund may or may not have a termination date upon which shareholders receive a cash payout equal to the NAV.

A **unit investment trust (UIT)** maintains a set portfolio of securities, designed around a stated investment objective, in a buy-and-hold strategy.

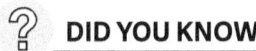 **DID YOU KNOW?**

The oldest exchange-traded fund in the United States, SPY is a UIT. SPY was first introduced in 1993 and tracks the S&P 500 index.

QUICK REVIEW QUESTIONS

31. What kind of sales charge is to be expected with a class A mutual fund?

32. How can an investor reduce the sales charge when buying a large mutual fund stake via small transactions over the course of a year?

33. What kind of investment company has shares that can be neither created nor redeemed?

Variable Contracts/Annuities

Variable annuities are tax-deferred investment products offered by insurance companies. They provide periodic payments over a long span of time and offer a guaranteed payout to a beneficiary in case the policyholder passes away, making them useful for retirement-related financial planning. A variable annuity operates in two phases: the accumulation phase and the payout phase.

During the **accumulation phase**, the investor makes purchase payments and allocates them to various investment offerings available within the annuity:

- These offerings are mainly mutual funds but also include fixed accounts that pay a guaranteed rate of return.
- The performance of those investments affects the value of the annuity.

The second phase of the annuity's operation is the **payout phase**, during which the annuity begins to provide periodic payments:

- The transition between the accumulation phase and payout phase is called the annuitization period.
- The payout phase can last for life or for a set duration.

Also, some annuities penalize the investor with **surrender charges** for making large withdrawals during a certain period of time, known as the surrender period, after having invested.

HELPFUL HINT

Rather than deferring payments until the payout phase, some annuity contracts have no accumulation phase and make payments immediately within the first year.

QUICK REVIEW QUESTIONS

34. During what period would an investor be penalized for making withdrawals from a variable annuity?

35. What term describes the period when a deferred annuity transitions from the accumulation phase to the payout phase?

36. What kind of investment offering within a mutual fund guarantees a set rate of return?

Municipal Fund Securities

529 (Qualified Tuition) Plans

Section 529 of the Internal Revenue Code establishes special tax advantages for qualified tuition plans, so they are also known as **529 plans**. These investment vehicles allow people to save money for tuition and other higher education costs:

- 529 plan accounts are established by an account **owner**—often a parent—to help pay for a named **beneficiary** to go to school:
- 529 plans are transferable.
  - Under certain circumstances, the named beneficiary can be changed without penalty.
- 529 plans vary from state to state; various options may be offered in any one state.
- 529 plans may be sold by an investment advisor, or they may be sold directly by a fund company.

Prepaid tuition plans are generally sponsored by state governments for residents of their state. Prepaid tuition plans

- allow the beneficiary to purchase credits at participating colleges and universities (usually in-state, public institutions); and
- promise the beneficiary an economic benefit versus out-of-pocket tuition.

HELPFUL HINT

Direct-sold 529 plans often, but not always, have lower expenses than advisor-sold plans, but they may not offer access to the same investment products.

Prepaid tuition plans have some drawbacks. Their deposits are not guaranteed by the federal government and may not be guaranteed by the state government. Furthermore, if the beneficiary chooses to attend a non-participating institution, the economic benefit may be substantially reduced. Prepaid tuition plans cannot pay for room, board, or secondary school tuition.

Education savings plans offer greater flexibility and apply to qualified higher education expenses. In addition to the tuition and mandatory fees covered by prepaid tuition plans, education savings plans may cover room and board, books, software, and computers.

Broadly speaking, withdrawals from education savings plans may be used at any college or university. In contrast to the restrictions upon prepaid tuition plans, education savings plans permit $10,000 per year to be allocated toward elementary or secondary school costs.

QUICK REVIEW QUESTIONS

37. A grandfather opens a 529 plan for his grandson's education. Who is the beneficiary of the plan?

38. What kind of 529 plan would be the best way to save for tuition at a private high school?

39. What kind of 529 plan would cover costs for room and board?

Other Securities

ABLE accounts are also known as 529 A savings plans. They are similar to 529 qualified tuition plans, but instead of being targeted toward education, they apply to individuals who became disabled before turning twenty-six:

- The person with the disability is the owner and beneficiary of the ABLE account.
- An ABLE account can receive up to $16,000 in total investments annually.
- Anybody (e.g., friends and family) can make post-tax contributions up to the annual maximum.

If the account owner is employed but does not have an employer-sponsored retirement account, the account owner can further contribute all employment proceeds up to the poverty line amount ($13,590 in 2022 within the continental US, slightly more in Alaska and Hawaii).

Earnings in an ABLE account are tax-deferred, and withdrawals are not taxed when used for a qualified disability-related purpose. The first $100,000 saved in an ABLE account is also exempted from the asset limit for Supplemental Security Income (SSI) benefits and Medicaid.

HELPFUL HINT

ABLE stands for **A**chieving a **B**etter **L**ife **E**xperience.

HELPFUL HINT

Because LGIPs are exclusively governmental, they are not required to register with the SEC.

Local government investment pools (LGIPs) are funds that accept and invest money from municipalities, school districts, counties, special purpose districts, community colleges, universities, and other nonfederal public entities.

LGIPs are established by state governments or, if permitted by the state of jurisdiction, through joint powers agreements between local governments. Some LGIPs focus on liquidity and invest in money market assets while others aim for investment performance.

QUICK REVIEW QUESTIONS

40. What is the maximum amount that a disabled person with no employer-sponsored retirement plan can contribute to an ABLE account this year, if earnings total $8,000?

41. Who makes the rules that determine the conditions by which municipalities can invest in LGIPs?

42. What is the threshold age for disability onset, beyond which a disabled person is not eligible to be the beneficiary of an ABLE account?

Direct Participation Programs

A **direct participation program (DPP)** is a pooled investment entity where profits are taxed at the individual level but receive **pass-through tax treatment** at the entity level, so double taxation is avoided:

- Units of a DPP are not typically listed on an exchange, so investors cannot easily trade or liquidate their holdings.
- Real estate and petroleum exploration are two business activities that are commonly financed via DPPs.
- Other business activities (e.g., agriculture and cattle ranching) may be structured in this way as well.

DPPs are generally organized as limited partnerships, general partnerships, limited liability companies (LLCs), or subchapter S corporations. Individuals who lack a certain level of wealth or investment proficiency may be prohibited from investing in a DPP.

In practice, DPPs operate as **limited partnerships** where limited partners invest in the entity without taking on the personal liability assumed by general partners who manage its business operations. Management benefits from this because they can access capital provided by limited partners to support the operations of the company. Limited partners benefit because they can protect their downside while choosing to invest in risky or otherwise complicated businesses that they do not directly manage.

Structuring a business venture as a DPP may not be necessary or useful for small investor pools or business activities where investors are expected to have input in day-to-day operations. **Tenancy in common (TIC)** is a form of concurrent estate that allows up to thirty-five persons to co-own property and is one alternative arrangement for real estate.

Tenants in common must unanimously approve certain decisions, including the hiring of a property manager and the sale of the property. Tenancy in common does not include rights of survivorship, so if a part-owner passes away, that person's estate retains the ownership stake. In contrast, **joint tenancy** would allow the deceased person's ownership stake to be absorbed by the remaining owners.

QUICK REVIEW QUESTIONS

43. At what level are the profits of a DPP taxed?

44. Persons A and B own a rental property as tenants in common. Person A dies. Who receives Person A's ownership stake in the rental property?

45. Who bears personal liability in a limited partnership?

Real Estate Investment Trusts (REITs)

Types of REITs

Real estate investment trusts (REITs) are required to pass through almost all income from real estate operations to their holders. REITs are required

- to operate under the same rules as public companies, and
- to have a minimum of 100 shareholders after the first year of inception.
  - Shares must be transferable.
  - A board of directors or trustees must manage the REIT.

REITs must distribute 90% or more of their taxable income to shareholders as dividends. They must also invest 75% or more of their total assets in real estate or cash and derive 75% or more of their gross income from real estate or associated sources—including rent and mortgage interest.

Tower REITs pass income from radio tower leases to shareholders. These REITs aggregate and pass along revenue streams within the wireless networking

DID YOU KNOW?

No five shareholders are permitted to hold more than 50% of the ownership interest of a REIT.

industry. Tower REITs may have some geographic diversification, but they are not diversified across business segments.

Many REITs are listed on equity exchanges, allowing their shares to be bought and sold with ease, but this is not always the case:

- **Public non-listed REITs (PNLRs)** are registered with the SEC but lack the liquidity of listed stocks.
- **Private REITs** are exempt from SEC registration, but there are limitations on the investors to whom they may be offered.

QUICK REVIEW QUESTIONS

46. By law, how much of a REIT's taxable income must be distributed to shareholders?

_____

47. By law, how much of a REIT's gross income must come from real estate?

_____

48. At what level are the profits of a REIT taxed?

_____

REIT Issues

Equity REITs directly own a portfolio of real estate holdings, such as shopping malls and office buildings. **Mortgage REITs** do not own real estate directly but instead purchase and/or originate mortgages and mortgage-backed securities to collect interest income.

REITs receive preferential tax treatment because they pass earnings along to the shareholders without paying corporate income tax. In this way, REIT income avoids double taxation. REITs benefit the shareholder by allowing greater effective yield due to reduced taxes on profits from real estate holdings that the shareholder never needs to personally acquire or manage.

Like REITs, **Business Development Companies (BDCs)** are a form of regulated investment company that receives preferential tax treatment in exchange for meeting certain regulatory requirements and distributing at least 90% of the taxable income to shareholders.

Under the Investment Company Act of 1940, a BDC must satisfy a variety of requirements, including investment of 70% or more of its holdings in "eligible" assets. For a public company to be considered an "eligible portfolio company," the market capitalization of the company's equity must be below $250 million. A BDC is not permitted to invest more than 25% of its assets in any one holding.

QUICK REVIEW QUESTIONS

49. What kind of REIT would own nothing but agency pass-through securities and pay dividends to shareholders with the resulting interest income?

_____

50. How much of a BDC's taxable income must be distributed to shareholders as ordinary dividends to avoid corporate income tax at the entity level?

_____

51. At what level are the profits of a BDC taxed?

_____

Hedge Funds

Wealthy and/or professional investors may invest in **hedge funds**, where money managers pool assets in order to actively target particular investment ideas. Hedge funds have greater regulatory freedom than mutual funds. Their risk profiles can vary: some funds may be tailored to outperform market index returns while others are designed to outperform in volatile market conditions.

Investors pay a **management fee** on the amount that they invest, as well as a **performance fee** in case the fund's returns are good. The management fee is generally much smaller than the performance fee; traditionally, a 2% and 20% fee structure (respectively) is common.

Hedge funds tend to be structured as a limited partnership between the fund managers and their investors, and managers often invest a substantial amount of their own capital alongside the capital of their investors.

From the investor's perspective, hedge funds are not liquid investment vehicles. Participation in a hedge fund often requires a minimum investment of $100,000 or more, and investors may be required to meet a certain standard for wealth, income, or professional experience, such as being considered "accredited investors" as defined by the SEC (see Chapter 3 for more on accredited investors).

Those investors who wish to take money out of a hedge fund must typically request their withdrawal, also known as a **redemption**, well in advance. A redemption may take weeks or months due to restrictions imposed by the hedge fund.

Investors may be subject to a **lockup** whereby they cannot withdraw funds for a certain amount of time after investing (or are required to pay a penalty fee to do so). The hedge fund may not allow more than a limited amount to be redeemed at any given time, either overall across the fund's investor pool or by any individual investor. This restriction is called a **gate**. Redemptions may be entirely suspended in extreme market conditions.

Hedge funds use various strategies to generate returns, and they are often categorized by the overall strategy that they employ:

- Long-only and short-only funds do precisely what those terms suggest: buy or short-sell securities, respectively.
- Long/short funds will buy stocks they believe to be a good value and short-sell stocks that they believe to be overvalued.
  - Some of these funds are market-neutral, meaning that they short-sell enough shares (or achieve the same by using derivatives) to counteract the overall price sensitivity of their long holdings, but many long/short funds maintain a net-long exposure.
- Relative value arbitrage is another approach whereby a hedge fund attempts to trade related securities, such as different parts of an issuer's capital structure, against one another in expectations that a dislocation in their market prices will converge.
- Event-driven strategies are common; for example, a hedge fund may buy shares of one participant in a merger and sell shares of the other.

Hedge funds are similar—but distinct from—**private equity firms**, which use investor capital for leveraged buyouts, the expansion or restructuring of operations, and provide venture funding to early-stage companies. Private equity investments often have a far longer time horizon than those of hedge funds.

> **HELPFUL HINT**
> Global macro hedge funds take positions around large-scale political and economic expectations.

QUICK REVIEW QUESTIONS

52. What is the term for a withdrawal from a hedge fund?

53. How liquid is an investment in a hedge fund?

54. What sort of investment firm might provide venture funding and engage in leveraged buyouts?

Exchange-Traded Products

Stock exchanges provide investors and issuers with several benefits. Continuous double auctions make it easy to observe the current price of a security. Transacting in a single and centralized place simplifies brokerage and settlement and reduces concerns about counterparty risk. Market access improves liquidity. In addition to the stock of single companies, to reap these benefits, some funds and notes are also listed on exchanges. Some of these **exchange-traded products (ETPs)** are discussed next.

Types of ETPs

Exchange-traded funds (ETFs) are investment funds whose shares are listed on a stock exchange. Those shares represent holdings in an asset or basket of assets. An ETF must be structured as an investment company registered under the Investment Company Act of 1940, either as a UIT or an open-end fund, except when the ETF's underlying asset is a currency, physical commodity, or a derivative thereof.

Exchange-traded notes (ETNs) are issued by financial institutions specifically to track particular indices or benchmarks. They are unsecured bonds, so they carry credit risk. Unlike their ETF counterparts, exchange-traded notes may not own any of the underlying assets that they track, and they make no dividend or interest payments.

HELPFUL HINT

Both ETFs and ETNs can have listed options.

QUICK REVIEW QUESTIONS

55. Who insures an ETN in case the issuer goes bankrupt?

56. An exchange-traded product is based on the value of underlying holdings of short-term government bonds and passes interest income along to the shareholder. Is it an ETN or an ETF?

57. Is an ETF with underlying currency assets required to be structured as an investment company?

Considerations

In combination with closed-end funds, ETFs and ETNs provide investors with sophisticated and versatile alternatives to mutual fund investments. Investors use these ETPs to target returns of equity indices or volatility futures and gain cross-asset exposure to commodities, debt, and currencies. They can participate in actively managed strategies without the complexity and cost of mutual fund sales charges and breakpoints. Fees for exchange-traded products are included in the share price.

Many ETFs permit the **creation** or **redemption** of shares in exchange for the fund's underlying asset(s). Consider an ETF whose underlying asset is physical gold. If this ETF's market price rallies and substantially dislocates from the spot price of gold bullion in the metals market, a commodities trader can short-sell the ETF and buy an equivalent amount of gold bullion to lock in the price difference, then create shares of the ETF to close the position for a profit.

FINANCIAL PRODUCTS 113

> **DID YOU KNOW?**
>
> ETNs typically have inferior liquidity to ETFs.

Whether the underlying asset is a physical metal or an assortment of stocks that replicate an index, this arbitrage condition serves two functions that benefit the market:

- It keeps the price of the ETF in line with its NAV.
- It allows traders of the ETF to access liquidity in the market for the underlying asset.

Exchange-traded funds that are designed to track a benchmark index can have a **tracking error** that results from the difference between the performance of that benchmark and the performance of the fund's actual holdings. Exchange-traded notes have no tracking error.

QUICK REVIEW QUESTIONS

58. What kind of exchange-traded product has no tracking error?

_____

59. What is the impact of arbitrage on ETF markets?

_____

60. What is the name for a conversion of ETF shares into the underlying assets of the fund, as facilitated by the ETF trustee or sponsor?

_____

Answer Key

1. Common stock allows the shareholder to vote and receive dividends.

2. Cumulative preferred stock must receive all past unpaid dividend payments before a new dividend can be distributed to common stockholders.

3. An American Depositary Receipt (ADR) is listed on a US stock exchange.

4. Common stockholders are last in line to receive a payout when a company goes bankrupt and gets liquidated.

5. Creditors with the earliest claim to secured debt are first in line to receive a payout when a company goes bankrupt and is liquidated.

6. Convertible equity is preferred stock.

7. An affiliate of the issuer can never make a sale of more than 1% of the outstanding shares of a restricted stock that does not trade on any exchange.

8. A restricted security from a company that is not subject to the reporting requirements of the Securities Exchange Act of 1934 must be held for at least one year before it can be sold.

9. The issuer of the restricted security decides whether a restrictive legend can be removed.

10. The current yield of the bond is 4%/0.5 = 8%.

11. An on-the-run Treasury security that matures in seven years is a Treasury note.

12. In this case the market price of the bond will go down since market price and current yield have an inverse relationship.

13. An asset-backed security (ABS) is backed by credit card receivables.

14. A collateralized mortgage obligation (CMO) groups mortgage principal repayments by tranche.

15. The US federal government owns the Government National Mortgage Association (GNMA)—Ginnie Mae.

16. This type of bond is a revenue bond, which is backed by cash flows from a specific project or activity.

17. The interest income of a tax-exempt municipal bond is exempt from federal tax.

18. A city can use a grant anticipation note when it is expecting federal grant money.

19. The least-risky instrument traded in the money market is a Treasury bill.

20. The maximum time to maturity for most commercial paper is 270 days.

21. The maximum time to maturity for most banker's acceptances is six months.

22. A bond rated BB- by Fitch is a high-yield bond.

23. A noncallable bond is worth more to a bondholder.

24. The bond yield of a rising star falls because interest rates go down as credit quality improves.

25. The premium of the option (also called the price) is $2.

26. A put option gives the holder a right to sell the underlying asset at the strike price.

27. The ABC May 45-strike put is worth more because it allows more time for the option holder to make an exercise decision.

28. The ABC Feb 90-strike put is in-the-money.

29. A physical settlement delivers stock to the long holder of a call option.

30. The European style only allows exercise of an option upon maturity.

31. A front-end load sales charge is to be expected with a class A mutual fund.

32. By signing a letter of intent an investor can reduce the sales charge when buying a large mutual fund stake via small transactions over the course of a year.

33. A closed-end fund has shares that can be neither created nor redeemed.

34. An investor would be penalized for making withdrawals from a variable annuity during the surrender period.

35. The annuitization period is when a deferred annuity transitions from the accumulation phase to the payout phase.

36. A fixed account guarantees a set rate of return.

37. The grandson is the named beneficiary of the plan.

38. An education savings plan would be the best way to save for tuition at a private high school.

39. An education savings plan would cover costs for room and board.

40. The maximum amount that a disabled person with no employer-sponsored retirement plan can contribute to an ABLE account this year is $16,000 + $8,000 = $24,000.

41. State governments make the rules that determine the conditions by which municipalities can invest in Local Government Investment Pools (LGIPs).

42. A disabled person is not eligible to be the beneficiary of an ABLE account if disability onset occurs after turning twenty-six.

43. Profits of a direct participation program (DPP) are taxed at the investor level, not the entity level.

44. Person A's estate receives person A's ownership stake in the rental property.

45. The general partner(s) bear personal liability in a limited partnership.

46. By law, 90% of a real estate investment trust's (REIT's) taxable income must be distributed to shareholders.

47. By law, 75% of a real estate investment trust's (REIT's) gross income must come from real estate.

48. The profits of a real estate investment trust (REIT) are taxed at the investor level—not the entity level.

49. A mortgage real estate investment trust (REIT) would own nothing but agency pass-through securities and pay dividends to shareholders with the resulting interest income.

50. At least 90% of a Business Development Company's (BDC's) taxable income must be distributed to shareholders as ordinary dividends to avoid corporate income tax at the entity level.

51. The profits of a Business Development Company (BDC) are taxed at the investor level, not the entity level.

52. A withdrawal from a hedge fund is known as a redemption.

53. Generally, an investment in a hedge fund is illiquid.

54. A private equity firm might provide venture funding and engage in leveraged buyouts.

55. Nobody insures exchange-traded notes (ETNs); they are unsecured bonds and carry counterparty risk.

56. This is an exchange-traded fund (ETF) because it has holdings and pays dividends.

57. No, an exchange-traded fund (ETF) with underlying currency assets is not required to be structured as an investment company.

58. Exchange-traded notes (ETNs) have no tracking error.

59. Arbitrage on exchange-traded fund (ETF) markets maintains price accuracy to net asset value (NAV) and allows traders of the ETF to access liquidity in the market for the underlying asset.

60. A conversion of exchange-traded fund (ETF) shares into the underlying assets of the fund is called redemption.

6   Investment Risks and Rules

Investment Risks

Types of Risk

Financial risk is the chance that making a financial commitment will result in an outcome negatively different from the investor's expectations. There are several types of financial risk discussed in this section:

- capital risk
- credit risk
- currency risk
- inflationary/purchasing power risk
- interest rate risk
- systematic risk
- unsystematic risk
- political risk
- prepayment risk

Capital risk refers to the possibility of losing all or part of the money (capital) that the investor injects into securing or establishing a project position that is unsecured by a reliable third-party guarantee. In most cases, projects involve the utilization of tangible or intangible assets:

- For example, a homeowner invests $300,000 in a house but personally assumes the risk of it burning down by deciding not to insure it with an insurance provider.
- A fire destroys all or part of the homeowner's capital.
- By guaranteeing the real estate's protection from natural hazards through purchasing insurance, the investor shifts the capital risk of fire to the insurance provider.

Credit risk arises when lenders advance money or assets to borrowers (debtors) who fail to pay interest on the loan, or worse, default in returning the asset value of the loan when it runs its course.

Sometimes, lenders assume legal security over debtor assets in case of default. For example, a mortgage lender holds a lien over the property for a loan until the borrower returns the original advance plus all the accrued interest.

Currency risk occurs when businesses trade across international borders. For example, a US company sells goods invoiced at US $100,000 to an Australian company on December 1. The parties agreed that payment in Australian dollars (AUD) would be calculated at the USD/AUD currency exchange rate on the transaction date (December 1)—0.70 USD for 1.00 AUD, with payment execution on December 20:

- On December 20, the US supplier will receive AUD 143,000 (USD100,000/0.7 = $142,857).
- The AUD 143,000 will be converted back to USD when it enters the bank account.
- The Australian customer submits the agreed AUD 143,000 on the payment date.
- Unfortunately for the US company, the AUD has weakened against the USD by December 20—to 0.65 USD for 1.00 AUD.
- On December 20, the bank converts the AUD to USD: AUD 143,000 × 0.65 = $92,950.
- The US company receives USD 7,050 less than the expected $100,000 ($100,000 - $92,950 = $7,050).
- Sometimes the opposite occurs: if the value of the AUD had strengthened against the USD, the US company would have received more money than expected.

US citizens holding cash assets face **inflationary/purchasing power risk**; they are risking these resources to the extent of the inflationary rate. The inflationary rate defines how much buying power the USD is losing annually.

For example, if bread prices are inflating by 10% per annum from January to December 2022, a $4 loaf at the beginning of the year costs consumers $4.40 by the year's end. Therefore, $400 set aside to buy ten loaves of bread twelve months earlier must expand in the budget to $440 to buy the identical ten loaves.

The same goes for any product—gas, cars, industrial equipment, raw materials, and so forth. Therefore, holding cash without earning after-tax interest that is at least equal to the inflation rate (determined by the Fed) means that cash reserves risk losing purchasing power due to inflation.

Interest rates fluctuate depending on the Fed's discount rate adjustments; therefore, borrowers and lenders assume **interest rate risk** every time they make the decision to either fix the rate for a term going forward or let it float. One example is home buying. Most homebuyers take out mortgages. In 2020 and 2021, mortgage interest rates were low but began increasing significantly in 2022:

HELPFUL HINT

Credit cards are typically unsecured loans, leaving companies like American Express with credit risk.

DID YOU KNOW?

Currency risk can be reduced by hedging it with a market-maker or currency dealer under a futures contract. It involves selling AUD 143,000 at 0.70 USD on the payment date. All that would be lost in that event is the cost of the hedge (i.e., relatively less than USD 7,050).

- **Borrowers** in 2020 and 2021 who never fixed their mortgage rates could pay close to double in monthly mortgage costs by the end of 2022:
  - Not freezing the interest rate meant taking on the risk of rates going up, which they did.
  - Conversely, borrowers who fixed their rates in 2018 believed mortgage rates would rise.
  - Interest rates actually went down from 2018 – 2021, resulting in a losing position in the opposite direction.
- **Lenders** are on the opposite end of a financial transaction with borrowers:
  - Lenders lose the difference if they fix rates only to see interest rates go up.
  - Likewise, if rates stay variable and go down, freezing the interest rate earlier would have been the right decision.

Overall, any interest rate decision means taking on the risk that interest rates will move conversely to expectations.

The well-known sayings, "cash is king" and the related "asset rich, cash poor" describe **liquidity risk**. Everyone requires some flexibility to invest when the opportunity arises; however, liquidity risk arises when investors invest all their cash in illiquid assets—those that cannot be sold quickly when money is urgently needed. Illiquid assets may include

- property,
- automobiles, and
- artwork.

Investors making decisions that create liquid cash pressures are taking on liquidity risk. The inability to meet interest or repayment of loan obligations at agreed dates because resources are tied up in illiquid assets creates liquidity risk.

Systematic risk is a pervasive risk that impacts macro markets or economies, not just sectors like stocks, companies, or an industry:

- Systematic risk is often measured by the Cboe Volatility Index (VIX).
- When the VIX is high, it signifies significant fear in the economy and markets in general.
- People who are frightened produce irrational reactions with unpredictable outcomes.

Overall, high systematic risk is impossible to hedge against or diversify to avoid. Moreover, this type of risk affects the entire economy—the totality of markets, no matter how diversified one is.

The opposite of systematic risk is unsystematic risk. **Unsystematic risk** is the risk one takes by investing in a company, product, or small sector of a larger market.

HELPFUL HINT

The risk of the COVID-19 fallout on the total market can be considered systematic risk.

HELPFUL HINT

total risk = systematic + unsystematic risk.

For example, instead of investing in a few stocks, an investor selects a Dow 500 Index to lessen unsystematic risk. However, no matter how diversified a portfolio is, if systematic risk—like COVID-19—impacts the marketplace, diversification will not deflect it. Unsystematic risk is also known as diversifiable risk.

Investors must account for **political risk** as well. Politics play a role in investment decisions and carry a degree of uncertainty. For example, state and federal governments make laws that

- affect energy production,
- generate gun sales,
- encourage (or discourage) legally growing marijuana,
- impose, sustain, or release tariffs,
- tax specific industries and relax taxes on others, and
- promote or discourage immigration.

Investing in an industry, company, product, or market entry based on potential political initiatives may or may not pay off—it is a political risk.

Finally, investors must account for **prepayment risk**. Anyone who makes a deposit or prepays suppliers to deliver services or goods may be disappointed. Suppliers may fail to either meet the terms of the sales contract, return the money to the customers, or both. Prepayment risk can be anything from a partial to a total loss. Customers carry prepayment risk when they pay ahead of time for a project.

QUICK REVIEW QUESTIONS

1. When lenders advance money or assets to borrowers who may fail to pay interest on the loan, what kind of risk are they assuming?

   _____

2. A pervasive risk that impacts macro markets or economies is what kind of risk?

   _____

Risk Mitigation Strategies

Diversification in finance has two profiles:

1. **Asset class diversification** involves spreading funds over numerous assets in the same class (e.g., the S&P 500) to reduce exposure.
2. **Portfolio diversification** is broader and involves spreading funds over different asset classes (e.g., stocks, bonds, real estate) to reduce exposure to any one class in the portfolio.

There are degrees of diversification. The S&P 500 is an effective stock diversification within one asset class. For example, Microsoft may be one stock in the S&P 500 index; however, owning the index means the 499 other stocks completing the index significantly reduce the impact of a drop in Microsoft price. The S&P 500 is a reliable option for anyone who is investing in stocks and wants maximum stock diversification.

However, if stock prices decline, even an index fund like the S&P 500 will not protect investors. For protection, investors can diversify away from stocks by adding bonds and real estate investment trusts (REITs) to the portfolio or alternative assets like art, gold, or cryptocurrencies. These other asset categories may still prop the portfolio up if stocks crash.

HELPFUL HINT

In plain language, diversification means "not putting all your eggs in one basket." Instead, diversification is putting a few eggs in several baskets. If one basket falls and the eggs break, other eggs remain in secure containers.

When structuring investment portfolios, broker-dealers must account for the risk tolerances of clients and apply the principles of diversification to deliver favorable returns while simultaneously protecting against unexpected volatility. For example, an investor may invest 100% of funds by dividing them into three equally valued categories: stocks, bonds, and REITs. Over time, however, those percentages deviate from the intended ratios. A broker may then **rebalance** the portfolio by selling and buying assets in order to return to the original percentage allocations.

The initial distribution of funds may also change over time, or new asset classes may be added. In such cases, rebalancing refers to market activities—buying and selling—to match the newly structured asset allocations.

Hedging is a focused type of diversification where the investor takes an opposite position to a trade as a hedge against the trade losing money. In other words, hedging is a risk management strategy that investors deploy to minimize or offset losses if a core asset acts up.

For example, an investor goes long on a stock with the expectation that the price will rise in the future. That investor could hedge the position by placing a preemptive short on the stock if the price goes against expectations and travels 5% below the purchase price.

So, while the investor hopes to profit and never need the hedge, paying a little of the expected profits to position it is prudent to cut the loss down to 5% (plus the hedge cost) if the plan goes wrong. If the hedge is never used, the only debit against profits is the unused hedge's cost.

QUICK REVIEW QUESTIONS

3. Spreading funds over different asset classes to reduce exposure to any one class in the portfolio is called what?

4. What is it called when an investor diversifies by taking an opposing position to a trade?

Investment Rules

Trading risk is also mitigated by SRO rules and federal law. Traders should be aware of the relevant laws and rules.

FINRA Rules

FINRA rules address how to reduce investor risks. **FINRA Rule 2261** (Disclosure of Financial Condition) aims for enhanced transparency and requires FINRA members to provide their latest balance sheet—directly or electronically—for inspection at the request of any customer who deposits cash or securities with the member. It also applies to any member (Member A) through industry interaction who deposits securities or money with another (Member B):

- On request, Member B will allow Member A to inspect its latest balance sheet for compliance with the same regulations in the same way as the customer described above.
- In both cases, Member A and the customer must agree that electronic delivery is acceptable.

FINRA Rule 2262 (Disclosure of Financial Relationship with Issuer) applies when the securities issuer controls a member:

- The member must disclose the relationship to any customer transacting the security through the member before the transaction occurs, or at the very latest, before the transaction concludes.
- The disclosure must be in writing.

FINRA Rule 2310 (Direct Participation Programs) restricts FINRA members' participation in direct participation programs (DPPs) and REITs:

- Essentially, members may not participate in DPPs unless the general partner discloses certain information.
- Annual reports must show the estimated value per share of the DPP.

FINRA Rule 2330 (Members' Responsibilities Regarding Deferred Variable Annuities) tightens the compliance and supervisory systems of brokerage firms in order to protect the deferred variable annuities of investors. Essentially, FINRA members who recommend deferred variable annuities can only do so if the investor demonstrates a good understanding of the features of these, which include

- fees and charges that emerge with early surrender,
- tax penalties that align with early surrender,
- various fees and costs involved, and
- upside limits and downside possibilities.

Moreover, the member must understand vital aspects of the client's profile and, therefore, suitability for deferred variable annuities. This includes age, investment goals, level of investment experience, risk tolerance, and more.

HELPFUL HINT

Direct participation programs are covered in depth in Chapter 5.

FINRA Rule 2360 (Options) provides in-depth guidance concerning options and the restrictions around them. Key points include

- position limits,
- exercise limits, and
- restrictions on option transactions and exercises.

Position limits and **exercise limits** restrict the latitude for market manipulation and unethical practices. Section (b)(3) (Position Limits) of Rule 2360 outlines the maximum number of option contracts in each class or category.

Section (b)(4) (Exercise Limits) of Rule 2360 sets the maximum number of option contracts, in clearly identified categories, that trading parties cannot exceed within a given time. A time factor of five consecutive business days is attached to the stated contract limits, requiring compliance from all FINRA members or associated persons.

Neither these limitations nor the five days are set in stone. Section (b)(8) (Restrictions on Option Transactions and Exercises) of Rule 2360 allows FINRA some latitude. With reasonable notice, FINRA can change limitations to maintain undistorted market operations in option contracts or the underlying securities covered by such option contracts. FINRA would do this in order to

- act in the public interest, and
- protect investors.

Ten days before an option's expiration date, all restrictions fall away to allow traders to protect or take advantage of previously traded contracts without fear of watching trading limitations.

HELPFUL HINT

Options are covered in more detail in Chapter 5.

QUICK REVIEW QUESTIONS

5. Which FINRA Rule encourages transparency?

   _____

6. Which FINRA Rule addresses participation in direct participation programs (DPPs)?

   _____

MSRB and Cboe Rules

Both the Municipal Securities Rulemaking Board (MSRB) and the Cboe lay out definitions for securities. The Cboe defines important investment terms in its lengthy **Cboe Rule 1.1 (Definitions)**. Likewise, in **MSRB Rule D-12** (Definition of Municipal Fund Securities) the MSRB defines municipal fund securities as securities issued by entities considered investment companies under the Investment Company Act of 1940. The MSRB also regulates broker-dealers and municipal advisors:

- **MSRB Rule G-17** (Conduct of Municipal Securities and Municipal Advisory Activities) requires broker-dealers to act with honesty and integrity.

- **MSRB Rule G-30** (Pricing and Commissions) requires that broker-dealers be reasonable in their commissions and strive to get reasonable prices for customers.
- **MSRB Rule G-45** (Reporting of Information on Municipal Fund Securities) requires broker-dealers to periodically report data to the MSRB when underwriting 529 savings plans or ABLE programs.

QUICK REVIEW QUESTIONS

7. Which Rule requires dealers to be reasonable in pricing?

8. Which Rule requires periodic data reporting for 529 savings plans and ABLE programs?

SEC Rules and Regulations

SEC Rule 3a11-1 defines the term *equity security*, which covers interests in ventures structured under limited partnerships, joint ventures, and business trusts. It also extends to voting trust certificates and American Depositary Receipts.

The purchase price and transaction date are required information for securities transaction reports under **Rule 10b-10** of the Securities Exchange Act of 1934 (Purchases of Certain Equity Securities by the Issuer and Others). The Rule also requires the disclosure of early redemption features of debt securities.

Yield to maturity is difficult to calculate without a fixed maturity date. Accordingly, in such cases, Rule 10b-10 waives the usual requirement for transaction confirmations to disclose the yield to maturity for debt security.

QUICK REVIEW QUESTIONS

9. Which SEC Rule requires the disclosure of early redemption features of debt securities?

10. When does Rule 10b-10 waive the usual requirement for transaction confirmations to disclose the yield to maturity for debt security?

Investment Company Act of 1940

The Investment Company Act of 1940 defines **investment companies** in Section 3(a)—Definitions. According to Section 3(a), the term *investment company* refers to securities issuers whose primary business is engaging in

- investing, reinvesting, owning, holding, or trading securities;
- issuing face-amount, installment type certificates; or

- acquiring investment securities that will bring the company's value over 40% of its total assets.

The Investment Company Act defines **investment securities** as

- securities other than government securities,
- those issued by employees' securities companies, and
- certain other majority-owned subsidiaries of the owner.

Section 4 of the Investment Company Act explains how investment companies are classified. There are three types of companies to know:

- a face-amount certificate company (an investment company currently issuing installment-type face-amount certificates)
- a unit investment trust (see Chapter 5 for more on UITs)
- a management company (any investment company other than the two described above)

Section 5 of the Investment Company Act (Subclassification of Management Companies) defines different types of management companies:

- An **open-end company** is a fund management entity under a corporate structure that issues and sells securities and is willing to redeem them from investors at net asset value (NAV).
- A **closed-end company** is a similar entity that issues shares but
  - is unable to enter any secondary market activities (i.e., redemption of investors' units), and
  - leaves only stock exchanges as exit and entry platforms for investors after the IPO.

Closed- and open-end companies get their names from their fund management specialties, namely, managing open-end funds (OEFs) and closed-end funds (CEFs). In the US, CEFs are equivalent to closed-end companies, and OEFs are equivalent to open-end companies.

When a management company presents itself as **diversified**, it indicates to investors that there is less risk when investing with the company. In other words, it takes countercyclical positions across various assets so that no single one can significantly downgrade the portfolio's value. Recalling the plain language analogy described earlier, a diversified company does not keep all its eggs in one basket.

According to the SEA, a registered diversified company is one where a minimum of 75% of its total assets consists of

- liquid assets (cash or instruments easily convertible to cash),
- government securities,
- other investment company securities, and/or
- certain other securities.

A company loses its status as a diversified company when it purchases or sells an asset that throws the formula into imbalance due to that transaction.

A registered diversified company meets these standards and ratios; however, if discrepancies appear over time due to market volatility or influences other than portfolio adjustments, its diversification status will not dissolve.

Rule 12b-1 of the Investment Company Act of 1940 (Distribution of Shares by Registered Open-end Management Investment Company) permits mutual funds to use fund assets for the purposes of marketing and distribution. A **12b-1 fee** is an annual marketing or distribution fee on a mutual fund.

QUICK REVIEW QUESTIONS

11. What kind of management company issues and sells securities and redeems them from investors at NAV?

12. What is an annual marketing or distribution fee on a mutual fund called?

Answer Key

1. Lenders assume a credit risk when they advance money or assets to borrowers who may fail to pay interest on the loan.

2. A systematic risk is a pervasive risk that impacts macro markets or economies.

3. Diversification (or portfolio diversification) is spreading funds over different asset classes to reduce exposure to any one class in the portfolio.

4. Hedging is when an investor diversifies by taking an opposing position to a trade.

5. FINRA Rule 2261 encourages transparency.

6. FINRA Rule 2310 addresses participation in direct participation programs (DPPs).

7. MSRB Rule G-30 requires dealers to be reasonable in pricing.

8. MSRB Rule G-45 requires periodic data reporting for 529 savings plans and ABLE programs.

9. Rule 10b-10 requires the disclosure of early redemption features of debt securities.

10. Rule 10b-10 waives the usual requirement for transaction confirmations to disclose the yield to maturity for debt security when a fixed maturity date is absent.

11. An open-end company is a management company that issues and sells securities and redeems them from investors at net asset value (NAV).

12. An annual marketing or distribution fee on a mutual fund is called a 12b-1 fee.

7 Trading, Settlement, and Corporate Actions

Orders and Strategies

There are several different types of orders that customers issue when trading equities. Brokers should also know common trading strategies.

Types of Orders

Customers place **market orders** when they want to purchase or sell a stock for the best price possible at the time of execution. Most orders are market orders, which are typically executed immediately. However, market orders can still be risky since the price may fluctuate. There are generally three reasons for market orders:

1. Prices are fluctuating quickly and are expected to continue fluctuating.
2. The customer is confident in the transaction regardless of price.
3. The trade must be executed quickly for whatever reason.

Generally, market orders end up with sellers getting the lowest bid price and buyers securing the highest ask price when everything concludes. See more below under "Bid and Ask" strategies.

Stock quotes typically reflect the highest bid price (from buyers) to attract sellers' attention or the lowest offer price (from sellers) to capture buyers' attention. However, prices may not be current—they could have occurred minutes or hours before.

Therefore, a market order should only be placed during trading hours. Placing a market order after closing, to be executed when the markets open, risks price change. Many factors can affect a closing price from one day to the next.

A **stop order** is a trigger order. Dealers must buy or sell the order the moment the current market price trades at or goes through the specified stop price.

Once the stock reaches the stop price, a market order is triggered to fill as fast and as close to the stop price as possible. If the stock fails to reach or breach the stop price, no order occurs.

Stock owners use stop orders to function as a "stop loss" to protect potential unrealized gains or to minimize a loss. It works by setting the stop order at a point below the current price to achieve these objectives, as described in the examples below:

- An investor group buys a stock at $5.00. It goes up quickly to $6.00. At this point, the investor puts in a stop order at $5.80. The aim is to lock in most of the gains in the event of a price reversal.
- On the day of buying the stock at $5.00, the same investor group might put in a stop order at $4.80 to minimize losses if the price decreases immediately.
- When a price move up occurs (i.e., to $6.00), the investor removes the $4.80 stop order and replaces it with a stop order at $5.80.
- If the stock price moves up more, from $6.00 to $6.50, the investor cancels the $5.80 stop and replaces it with a stop order at $6.30.

These examples show how the investor uses a series of stops to protect growing profits. There is no guarantee that the stop order fills at the stop price with a price drop; however, most of the profit is likely protected even if the order fills lower than the stop.

Investors who want to buy a stock might expect that the price will rise and may therefore place a stop order at $5.20 when the price is $5.00, believing it will rise to $6.00. They use the stop order to get in early enough to capture most of the gain.

The order may fill at a higher price because hitting the $5.20 converts the stop order into a market order where there are no guarantees.

A **limit order** is an order to

- buy stocks by establishing the maximum price the investor is ready to pay, or
- sell stocks with the minimum price a stock owner is prepared to receive.

Limit orders set a "limit price" to restrict the buy or sell order. Filling the order means it is at the limit price or better. If the dealer transacting on behalf of the investor cannot abide by the limits set, the order will remain unfilled. There are critical differences between a limit order and a stop order:

- A limit order, once placed, must fill at the specified limit or better, or not at all.
- A stop order triggers at the specified stop price and sets off a market order. This means it can fill at the prevailing market price (which could be at the stop price or—as is frequently the case—worse).

Setting a time limit for expiration is a key aspect of placing orders. Sometimes an order is not executed for various reasons.

HELPFUL HINT

A stop order is sometimes referred to as a stop-loss order.

A **good-till-canceled (GTC)** order to buy or sell a stock means it remains active until filled; however, FINRA member firms have their own rules regarding the maximum time expiration of GTCs, which differ from firm to firm. Investors should inquire about the applicable time frame when placing a GTC order.

Investors may open non-discretionary or discretionary accounts at a brokerage firm. Few brokers clarify the differences between these types of accounts:

- In a **non-discretionary** account, brokers must contact the investor for permission to place a buy or sell order that is considered to be in the client's best interests.
- In a **discretionary account** brokers exercise their own discretion and are allowed to place buy or sell orders without discussing the reasons with the client.
  - An essential requirement is that the investment must be in the client's best interests.
  - Discretionary accounts should connect to signed paperwork or e-documents in the brokerage firm's records.

In both types of accounts, brokers must always act or make recommendations that consider a client's unique circumstances, goals, and risk tolerance.

Some brokers routinely regard non-discretionary accounts as if they were discretionary—even without customer authority to do so. In other situations, brokers may not act in the client's best interest. Both situations create fertile ground for clients to claim dealer misconduct, such as

- unauthorized trading,
- purchasing or recommending unsuitable investments, and/or
- breach of fiduciary duty.

When brokers make trades on behalf of clients, trades are either solicited or unsolicited:

- **Solicited** trades are broker-recommended transactions and influence client decisions.
- **Unsolicited** trades are transactions that result from a client's suggestion that financial advisors execute on behalf of their client.

Under **FINRA Rule 2010** (Standards of Commercial Honor and Principles of Trade) registered members must accurately report and mark all transactions.

The "2018 Report on FINRA Examination Findings" reflects significant grounds for investor claims of improper marking, noting that numerous brokers were guilty of misconduct in this category. Therefore, client claims along these lines can lead to arbitration.

FINRA Rule 2111 (Suitability) addresses whether a trade is suitable for a client's investing profile and risk tolerance level. Even solicited transactions deemed unsuitable (given a client's profile) can trigger damages awards as compensation for losses.

QUICK REVIEW QUESTIONS

1. What kind of order is executed as soon as possible?
   _____

2. An order that is broker-recommended is called what?
   _____

Strategies

Buy-and-sell strategies really mean "buy low, sell high"; otherwise, there is no purpose in buying and selling. It takes unique skills to buy at a price that will soon rise. Traders should understand

- trading patterns,
- moving averages,
- business cycles, and
- consumer sentiment.

In many cases, even with astute predictions, stocks that follow an irrational herd mentality overshoot on both the downside and the upside. It can be extremely challenging to see through these circumstances.

Bid-ask spread strategies begin when the ask price is more than the bid price for securities traded in the financial markets. Bid-ask is the difference between the highest price a buyer will pay and the lowest price a seller will accept.

Sellers receive the bid price; buyers pay the ask price. This bid price is how much the buyer is willing to pay for a stock; the ask price is how much the seller is willing to sell the same stock.

Stock market quotes reflect a higher ask price than the bid price. The brokers' role is to control the auction by getting buyers to accept a higher ask price than their bid price and, vice versa, convincing sellers to sell at a bid price lower than their ask price.

Brokers facilitate and coordinate the "auction" to consolidate an agreement between buyers and sellers while playing by set rules the moment bids and asks enter the system. The broker's commission delivered by the spread is not the retail commission investors pay to their FINRA member representatives. Instead, the retail commission pays transaction expenses and contributes extra profits to the participating dealers.

Brokers earning spread profits generally do best from market orders because investors placing the orders want fast trades and are most likely to receive either the lowest or pay the highest possible market price emerging on the spreads' extreme ends. Avoidance of market orders whenever possible is sound advice; however, trying to buck the spread activities of seasoned professionals is severely challenging even for veteran traders.

Massive brokerage houses function as market makers, thus establishing bid-ask spreads by actively bidding and asking simultaneously with a readiness to act accordingly. As a result, the spread automatically becomes the firm's profit, notwithstanding that it leaves the entity with a committed investment in the transacted stock or a hole where investment previously existed. Thus, market makers with the capital power to retain securities holdings take on risk alongside these "arbitration" transactions.

Long and short strategies imply taking a time management approach to the market:

- In a **long trade**, investors buy securities in the hope that they rise in value, thus creating the opportunity to sell them and make a profit; the term *going long* implies buying.
- Conversely, in a **short trade**, investors sell an asset at the current price for delivery in the future, believing it will drop before the future term expires.
  - Investors can deliver the stock from inventory and realize a profit on the closing date when they can refill stock at a lower price.

 HELPFUL HINT
In the trading arena, the terms *short* and *long* are standard for the terms *sell* and *buy*. "Shorting securities" is synonymous with selling them, just as "going long" means buying securities.

Naked and covered strategies traditionally occur in the futures arena. The term *naked* refers to taking on abnormal risk in short and long trading situations for future payment or securities delivery when traders do not effectively own the stock when initiating a trade. Naked strategies leverage (i.e., borrow) stock or money from another investor; the traders do not own the securities free and clear. Maximum potential loss is associated with unprotected (naked) trades if things go against expectations.

A stop order offers some protection. By placing a stop order, the investor instructs the broker or agent to sell a security when it reaches a pre-set price limit. This tactic allows traders to **cover** their positions, knowing the worst-case result if things do not go to plan. Without the stop order, the damage could be much worse.

Market makers keep track of stop orders covered in the market and, through their power in the markets, push the prices up or down for short spikes and dips to trigger the precautionary trades. They then reverse the trends and go through the covered side without having to execute. The market makers then make the profit rather than the traders.

Naked trades carry substantial risk, but there is also some uncertainty with covered strategies, although it is significantly less. Many brokers will not accept naked transactions under any circumstances:

- Naked positions can take investors outside the borders of their resources.
- If clients fail to deliver on their obligations, the acting broker-dealers are responsible for making the counteracting parties whole.

A **bearish strategy** is a trader's plan executed to succeed in a marketplace where securities prices are expected to drop in the well-defined future. Short traders thrive in bearish markets.

Conversely, a **bullish strategy** involves transactions with the mindset that securities prices will rise within a defined period. Long traders typically function well in bullish markets.

QUICK REVIEW QUESTIONS

3. How do broker-dealers earn extra commission?

   _____

4. What is the market outlook of a short securities trader?

   _____

Investment Returns

Components of Return

The term *interest* describes the reward a lender receives for loans to a borrower. Interest can be expressed in dollar terms or as a percentage, known as the interest rate. Examples of loans that qualify for interest payments from borrowers include

- mortgages,
- credit card balances,
- debentures, and
- microloans to small businesses.

Loans to borrowers can be secured or unsecured: mortgages are secured by real estate; credit card debt is unsecured.

Traditionally, secured loans carry lower interest rates than unsecured loans. For example, mortgage rates have been as low as 3% annually; rates were as high as 6% in 2022. This is because the mortgage rates align with the federal discount rate set by the Federal Reserve (the Fed; see Chapter 4). However, credit card interest rates can go as high as 29% per annum.

Interest rates on loans can be calculated simply or on a compound basis. Generally, **simple interest** is a system where the borrower submits the interest accrual on time before the next year. For example: Suppose a loan of $100,000 charges an interest rate of 10% annually. As a simple interest calculation, interest in year one is $10,000 (i.e., interest earned on $100,000 at a 10% rate), which repeats in years two, three, and so on until the loan is repaid.

However, if after year one the borrower fails to submit the 10% interest, or the lender doesn't require interest submissions (i.e., it accumulates, adding to the loan), the loan amount at the end of year one equals $110,000 and then year two interest is calculated as 10% of $110,000 equaling $11,000. This is called **compounding interest** at the same 10% interest rate. Depending on the loan terms compounding could occur daily, weekly, monthly, or yearly.

Dividends describe the portion of bottom-line profits a commercial entity distributes to its shareholders. In most cases, dividends are net income after tax (NIAT):

- Revenue - operating expenses (including cost of sales for trading businesses) = net income before tax (NIBT) - tax paid = NIAT.

Some exceptions exist: The IRS allows certain entities, like limited liability partnerships (LLPs), real estate investment trusts (REITs), and S Corporations, to declare dividends before taxing NIBT in what is referred to as a "flow-through profit system." In these cases, the investors in the entity receive the dividend without a tax deduction in the entity. Dividends, however—no matter when or how received—are fully taxable at the investors' tax rate in their own hands.

Gains are terms connected to appreciation in securities or asset values. For example, a home acquired several years ago for $500,000 that is now marketable at $800,000 registers an **unrealized gain**. Why? Because the homeowner has not actually sold the real estate. Between recognizing an unrealized gain, entering the selling process, and closing the deal, the realized profit may be higher or lower than the unrealized number.

HELPFUL HINT

The SEC requires REITs to declare a minimum of 90% NIBT yearly as dividends.

Similarly, securities owned but not transacted out of the portfolio may register various unrealized gains (or losses) as their prices fluctuate. The only time investors realize a profit (i.e., a gain) is when they sell.

Return on capital (ROC) is a ratio that relates realized gain to the investors' securities commitment before making the sale. ROC is a metric that signifies the profitability level and value creation of an investment. It is applied to

- financial transactions,
- business performance, and
- accounting.

ROC reveals an investor's acumen and succeeds in creating value from committing capital to an opportunity in a company's stock, responding to debt requirements, or backing any other asset class.

HELPFUL HINT

ROC can apply to lenders and direct ownership in assets like real estate, cryptocurrencies, or art.

Like dividends, ROC can be calculated:

- ROC = (NIAT)/invested capital (IC) + net taxed realized gain/invested capital.

However, for the metric to relate to time (e.g., ROC per annum), the ROC formula gets more technical. In all cases, ROC refers to realized gains, not those that are unrealized.

QUICK REVIEW QUESTIONS

5. The portion of bottom-line profits a commercial entity distributes to its shareholders is called what?

_____

6. What are the two types of interest a lender can earn?

_____

Types of Dividends

A **cash dividend** is the traditional method of profit distribution to shareholders. It enters the income statement (i.e., the profit and loss [P&L] statement) once the company calculates its bottom line and generally uses the following format:

- Revenue − operating cost (including cost of goods sold for a trading company or cost of production for a factory) = NIBT − tax = NIAT.

The board of directors decides what percentage of NIAT to retain to invest back in company assets for future growth and distribute to the shareholders. Some profit distribution exceptions relating to different company categories do exist, as described in Table 7.1.

TABLE 7.1. Profit Distribution Exceptions

REITS	PASS-THROUGH ENTITIES
• must declare at least 90% of NIAT in dividends • can skip the taxation expense in the company, so NIBT = NIAT • treated by REIT equity holders like any other dividend receiver	• include S-corporations and LLPs • can skip the taxation expense in the company, so NIBT = NIAT

DID YOU KNOW?

The Tax Cuts and Jobs Act (TCJA) provided an additional 20% tax deduction in profit distribution.

Stock dividends are a percentage of shares offered instead of a cash NIAT distribution. Notably, the equity pool grows, but the stakes of equity holders are not diluted (e.g., a 20% equity holder stays at 20%). Stock dividends are offered for the following reasons:

- High-growth businesses frequently need 100% of their NIAT, which means zero cash dividends; however, putting all the after-tax profits into the company should energize the share price down the line.
- Stock dividends are not taxable until the shareholder sells them.

QUICK REVIEW QUESTIONS

7. What is the traditional method of profit distribution to shareholders?

8. What dividend offers shares instead of a cash NIAT distribution?

Dividend Payment Dates

Dividends declaration is a simple concept compared to understanding the timing behind the activity. Various dates and dividend declarations go hand in hand to ensure a seamless process.

Trading is a continuous activity. These are the dates to remember:

- The **record date** is when the company confirms a list of shareholders eligible for the latest dividend declaration.

- Investors must own the shares at the latest close of trading two days earlier to get on the list at the record date.
- An **ex-dividend date** is the day on and after which the dividend is not payable to a new stock buyer.
  - It falls one day before the record date.
- The company announces a **dividend payment date** (generally a week or so after the record date) when it mails out the dividend checks.

QUICK REVIEW QUESTIONS

9. On what date does a company confirm a list of shareholders eligible for the latest dividend declaration?

10. What falls one day before the record date?

Measurement Concepts

An understanding of certain measurement concepts is essential in securities.

Yield measures returns as a percentage of the investment and could include the interest earned on a loan or the dividend earned on a stock. Yield is the projected annualized earnings for the coming year, assuming the last declared interest/dividend dollar value will continue the following year. The subsequent dividend declaration may be different. At that point, it becomes the forward factor for the next year. The investment value used in calculating yield includes

- the investor's commitment, and
- the current market value of the security.

As an example, imagine an investor buys Microsoft shares for $256 and Microsoft's price on the date of calculating the yield is $300. Even though the investor has not sold, an unrelated profit of $44 may be recognized.

Face value applies to the initial cost of the stock or bond on the issuer's certificate. In the case of a bond, face value is the dollar value paid to the investor on maturity, also referred to as the coupon or par value:

- Market forces almost certainly guarantee that the cost of the investment or current price is different from its face value.
- Calculating yield excludes capital gains.

Yield to maturity (YTM) refers to bonds and fixed-interest securities:

- YTM is essentially long-term bond yield, assuming the investor holds the bond until maturity.
- YTM is expressed as an annual percentage rate (APR).
- The lower the bond price, the higher the YTM, and vice versa.

A similar metric, **yield to call (YTC)** also refers to bonds and fixed-interest securities:

- YTC is also expressed as an annual percentage rate (APR).
- Some bonds have call dates (i.e., redemption dates earlier than maturity), which determine how long an investor may hold them.

All interest payments, plus the call value the investor will receive if the bond is held until the call, equal the bond's cost (market value) to the investor. Professionals in the bond trading business rely on YTC as being more accurate than YTM.

Total return (TR) is the combination of dividends and appreciation of the asset. TR on investment for one year can be calculated as follows:

- Current value of the investment (CV) − cost to the investor (IC) + dividend D for the year (D)/IC = TR or return on investment (ROI).

Basis points (BPS) are a broadly used preferred measure of both loan and investment performance:

- Analysts traditionally reflect moves in loan rates or investment returns using BPS.
  - For example, statements like, "The stock price increased by 100 basis points," mean that the price increased by 1%.

Basis points are calculated as follows: 1 BPS = (1%)/100 = (0.01/100) = (0.0001) = 0.01%

QUICK REVIEW QUESTIONS

11. What measures returns as a percentage of the investment?

_____

12. What securities use a yield-to-call metric?

_____

Other Concepts

Whenever investors sell a stock or a bond, they must consider tax consequences. Investors must understand the **cost basis requirements** to see what, if any, taxes they owe. These are the elements that count:

- the price that the investor originally committed to the securities purchase
- increments to the investment created by stock dividends or capital gain distributions
- commissions and other fees involved in consolidating the transaction

Broker-dealers can help investors by outlining the items on structured statements. To avoid IRS queries, it is crucial to include all of the contributing factors to the cost basis of a sold security in a comprehensible manner.

A **benchmark index** is a grouping of selected securities that becomes the performance yardstick (or gauge) for individual securities an investor may consider. Financial institutions assemble the benchmark collection of equities into a structured fund (e.g., an index fund). Structured funds carry significantly less risk than acquiring just one or two securities within that fund.

A good example is any one of the many S&P 500 index funds. These represent the five hundred top-ranked companies on the primary US stock exchanges:

- Without the index fund, an investor would have to buy around fifty shares of every equity in the group (i.e., 50 × 500 stocks), requiring a significant investment.
- One dollar invested in the S&P 500 ties into a piece of every security in the grouping.
  - Fifty units bought in the S&P 500 is still an investment in all of the most reputable publicly traded stocks.
- The S&P 500 offers diversification to small investment commitments.
  - Even if a few stocks in the group experience price drops, others may counteract them by rising.
  - An investor owning individual stocks that perform poorly has no such protection.
- Once compiled, index funds essentially manage themselves. As a result, investors enjoy minimal management fees, low internal turnover (making them tax-efficient), and the average return of 500 stocks.

For single equities to be a compelling buy versus the index, they must

- offer considerably higher performance potential, which is possible, especially with high-growth opportunities, and
- have less risk, which can be challenging to find.

The marketplace has developed along sophisticated lines offering numerous index fund categories that benefit investors by reflecting the benchmark performance of multiple stocks grouped together plus exceptional diversification. Knowledgeable investors respect index funds such as

- the Dow Jones Industrial Average,
- the Russell 2000,
- Barclays Capital US Aggregate Bond Index,
- Barclays Capital US Treasury Bond Index, and
- Lipper indexes surrounding mutual funds.

Thus, all asset classes (e.g., large-cap, mid-cap, small-cap, bonds, mutual funds) with distinct profiles are accessible to investors to either invest in for automatic diversification or use as a benchmark for single securities they are considering.

QUICK REVIEW QUESTIONS

13. Why is an accurate accounting of a "sold" security's cost basis crucial?

_____

14. What is the primary benefit of investing in an index fund?

_____

Trade Settlement and Corporate Actions

Settlement

Settlement describes when securities are officially transferred into the buyer's account and cash is transferred to the seller's account. Unless otherwise specified, trades in stocks and bonds settle based on a **regular-way** settlement, which is trade date plus 2 business days (T + 2).

TABLE 7.2. Settlement Timing

PRODUCT	SETTLEMENT TIME FRAME
common stock	regular way (T + 2)
exchange-traded fund (ETF)	regular way (T + 2)
corporate and municipal bonds	regular way (T + 2)
stock option exercises	regular way (T + 2)
cash	same day
US Treasury bonds and notes	trade date plus 1 business day (T + 1)
municipal bond (new issuance)	2 days to 2 weeks
forward-delivery municipal bond	6 weeks or more

> **DID YOU KNOW?**
>
> Buyers of forward-delivery municipal bonds are subject to the bond's price risk, but neither party receives interest accrual nor makes a cash outlay until settlement occurs.

A standard T + 2 settlement timeline applies to stocks and ETFs whether a round lot of SPY trades directly on an exchange or via the exercise of an option. This settlement time was shortened from T + 3 in 2017.

The settlement time frame for government securities and options transactions is T + 1, but an option exercise is a transaction of the underlier, not a transaction of the option.

Listed stock options in the US are physically settled. This involves delivery of shares rather than delivery of a cash amount. The risk characteristics and margin requirements for physical settlement are different from those for cash settlement. Cash settlement is used for certain index options and other instruments but not for options on single names or ETFs. Note that settlement style is different from exercise style; a physically settled option can be American or European (see Chapter 5).

Entry refers to ownership of securities. **Physical** entry refers to issuing the buyer a physical stock certificate or bond. Today, most settlement occurs as book entry. **Book entry** applies when securities are transacted electronically. The process is electronic, and no physical certificate or bond is issued. The Depository Trust Company (DTC) settles book-entry securities.

Delivery versus payment is a method that is either triggered by payment or implemented to transact simultaneously. The purpose of this method is to minimize settlement-related counterparty risk by quickly executing both sides of the transaction after both have been guaranteed.

In **delivery versus free**, delivery is made before payment with no guarantee of immediacy. That is, payment may occur on a different business day.

Despite meeting the immediacy requirement, the method of **delivery versus delivery** exchanges physical for physical.

QUICK REVIEW QUESTIONS

15. How long does regular-way settlement take?

_____

16. What is the meaning of physical entry?

_____

Splits and Reverse Splits

Companies can take actions to boost the liquidity of their stock. **Splits** are a way to issue additional shares without reducing the value of the company. An example follows:

- Microsoft's (MSFT) price on a particular day is $256. That means that in order to buy 1,000 shares, investors must pay $256,000.
- However, the board decides to open the market for MSFT to smaller investors with budgets of around $10,000 who want to buy parcels of 1,000 shares or more.
- So, they split it twenty to one, meaning
  - each new share price changes to $12.80, and
  - existing stockholders now own 20 shares for every one share they previously owned.

Company capitalization (i.e., the aggregate value of the shares issued) does not change, only the number of tradable units in circulation. Now, $13,000 is more than enough to buy 1,000 new MSFT shares. After shares split, the increase in market appeal often drives the price up.

When the price of a stock rises to a level that requires significant investment to buy a few shares, it becomes disconnected from the average investor's budget. A stock split allows the company to provide shareholders with multiple shares for each one held. In so doing, it makes no difference to the capitalization of the business, nor does it alter an individual investor's stake in the company.

Reverse splits are the opposite of a split. A company's share price is perhaps sitting at $1.50, and the board wants to remove the "penny stock" stigma from

HELPFUL HINT

Splits broaden the market for equity investors by making the price more affordable.

its reputation. So, it decides to apply a reverse split by consolidating 20 shares held into one:

- Equity holders' stakes stay the same in dollar value.
- The number of shares in issue drops to one-twentieth of the previous quantity.
- The stock price rises to $30.00 (twenty times higher).

Sometimes, a company generating significant cash profits cannot deploy the money for internal growth. Traditionally it declares dividends to the stockholders, or the company may conduct buybacks (see below) to enhance investor value instead of a profits distribution.

QUICK REVIEW QUESTIONS

17. How do companies issue additional shares of their stock without reducing the value of the company?

    _____

18. When a company consolidates shares to increase the price, what is this called?

    _____

Buybacks, Tender Offers, and Equity Offers

In **buybacks**, the company enters the open market to purchase shares as they emerge, reducing the issued shares in circulation. As an example, suppose a company with $25 million earnings after tax (EAT) reflects 5 million issued shares before a buyback—earnings per share (EPS) of $5.00.

The market rates the stock at a ten-times EPS multiple, or $50.00, capitalizing the company at $50.00 × 5 million equaling $250 million.

The company has a $5 million cash buildup from the current and past year's EAT (i.e., retained earnings) to deploy in a buyback. In the buyback, the company purchases 100,000 shares × $50.00. That brings the issued stock down to 4.9 million shares and takes the EPS to $5.10 (i.e., $25 million/4.9 million).

An investor with 100,000 shares (still with the same number) who previously owned 2% of the company now owns 2.04 percent. The $250 million capitalization remains the same:

- The buyback increases the percentage stake of all shareholders proportionately without touching their holdings.
- Investors should see their share price upgraded to $5.10 × 10 (the same multiple) = $51.00, a 2% capital appreciation.

The alternative to the buyback is to issue the shareholders (5 million shares in total) a $1.00 dividend per share (also 2%), but fully taxable.

 DID YOU KNOW?

Buyback capital gain is taxed differently: As long as investors do not sell the stock, no tax accrues. If the investor sells after holding the stock for at least a year, the $1 stock gain will be taxed at 20% capital gains tax—a massive discount on regular IRS rates.

Buyback actions frequently cause stock prices to increase, resulting in substantial equity holder after-tax gains—comparatively higher than a straightforward dividend.

A **tender offer** emerges when an investor wants a significant number of shares, making all stockholders in the company eligible to fill the requirement. As an enticement, the tender price is almost always higher than the ruling stock exchange pricing.

In most cases, tenders are designed to assume control. The logic behind a tender offer is to capture a significant minority share, perhaps enough to achieve one or more of the following:

- to demand a board seat
- to induce management to follow specific strategies
- to secure a controlling interest in the business

Exchange offers are used when the company wants to tender to its equity holders for a buyback. Instead of cash, they offer another type of security (e.g., a bond or preference share). It requires moving the number of issued shares down by taking on more debt (with more interest charge obligations).

While this moves the share numbers down, the analysts will assess the simultaneous effect of adding debt. The counteractive activity (i.e., fewer shares, thus potentially higher EPS but increased interest charges) comes into the equation.

Company directors may initiate a **rights offering** when a company wants to raise capital for expansion and simultaneously

- exclude adding debt as a viable option, and
- retain the current body of shareholders.

Suppose there are 500,000 issued shares with a current price of $50. The company wants to raise another $5 million, using the current share price as a yardstick:

- Therefore, it sends the existing shareholders an offer to add to their holdings by subscribing for 125,000 rights at $40 each (i.e., offering a $10 discount on the current share price as an incentive) based on 25 rights for every 100 shares held.
- If fully subscribed, the company raises the funds, and the shareholders remain undiluted because they added to their stake in proportion to their holdings.
- For example, a shareholder with 10,000 shares of 500,000 issued before the rights issue (2%) owns 12,500 shares of 625,000 in issue after the rights issue (still 2%).

In many cases, where the shareholders cannot take up their rights for whatever reason, a rights market opens where they can sell them to interested investors on the exchanges as long as the rights are transferable and not officially stamped as "non-renounceable." They can therefore recoup cash and be compensated for equity percentage dilution after the rights offering concludes.

> **DID YOU KNOW?**
> A publicly traded company may resort to issuing a tender offer to reach a buyback objective (i.e., a tender offer to its own shareholders).

In situations where less than 100% of the rights are taken up, the non-subscribing stakeholders will dilute down without compensation, assuming two possibilities:

- They were not successful in getting third-party takers for their rights.
- They were caught in a non-renounceable rights dilemma (i.e., unable to take up the rights or sell them).

Companies resort to rights issues when there is positive sentiment surrounding their projections, robust analyst comments, and overall enthusiasm to own the stock. Conversely, negative sentiment is not a good precursor for a rights issue.

QUICK REVIEW QUESTIONS

19. How can companies reduce the issued shares in circulation?

20. An investor who wants to capture a significant number of shares to demand a board seat may offer what?

Mergers and Acquisitions

Hedge funds and investment bankers are prolific participants in **mergers and acquisitions (M&As)**. Buying competitors or disruptive start-ups can accelerate growth goals significantly.

When one company buys another in a merger, the complexities which emerge can be severely challenging. As a result, the initiating CEO (or CEOs) will contract an investment bank to carry out the following:

- assess the equity values of all corporate participants
- evaluate and recommend the acquisition methodology (e.g., share swap, cash buyout, a combination of both)
- schedule the timing of the deal
- verify the accuracy of audited statements (i.e., financial due diligence)
- outline the synergies
- present a cost/reward analysis

Most crucially, investment banks analyze the companies' cultures and assess accordingly. Sometimes it can be a case of oil mixing with water, which is a tremendous deterrent—no matter how good the numbers look. With mergers in particular, investment banks also advise on management structuring and responsibilities after everything settles.

Mergers and acquisitions can energize a share price to new heights; however, poorly handled M&As can be disastrous to valuations and damage a company's operations over the long term.

QUICK REVIEW QUESTION

21. What is a major reason behind M&As?

_____

Notices and Proxies

The exchanges are responsible for **delivery of notices** on behalf of any company trading on its platform and initiating corporate actions, such as rights offerings, buybacks, etc. Investors will find the information relating to all aspects of the actions, including **corporate action deadlines**, on the relevant exchange's website.

For **over-the-counter companies (OTC)** involved in corporate actions, investors should check FINRA's "Daily List." The "Daily List" provides everything an investor needs to know about OTC announcements, covering things like

- ex-dividend dates,
- new issues,
- deleted issues, and
- previously announced changes that have been updated or canceled.

Any time a corporate action is in the cards, it likely requires a shareholder vote. When shareholders cannot attend a vote in person, they may use a proxy vote. In a **proxy vote**, a ballot is cast on behalf of the shareholder who cannot attend physically.

Eligible voters (i.e., shareholders) receive a mailed proxy ballot alongside detailed information about what goes into the voting process, commonly referred to as a proxy statement. The **proxy statement** explains that the shareholder can vote by proxy if unable to attend and describes the steps for doing so.

 DID YOU KNOW?

Companies themselves may issue a notice, implying that the corporate action has been approved by the announcing exchange or FINRA's "Daily List." Be aware that this is not necessarily the case. The go-to confirmations of validated corporate actions are the "Daily List" itself or exchange websites.

QUICK REVIEW QUESTION

22. When shareholders cannot physically attend shareholders' meetings to vote on corporate actions, what do they use?

_____

Answer Key

1. A market order is executed as soon as possible.
2. A solicited order is an order that is broker-recommended.
3. Broker-dealers earn extra commission by using different trading strategies.
4. The market outlook of a short securities trader is bearish.
5. The portion of bottom-line profits that a commercial entity distributes to its shareholders is called a dividend.
6. The two types of interest a lender can earn are compound interest and simple interest.
7. A cash dividend is the traditional method of profit distribution to shareholders.
8. Stock dividends offer shares instead of a cash net income after tax (NIAT) distribution.
9. A company confirms a list of shareholders eligible for the latest dividend declaration on the record date.
10. An ex-dividend date falls one day before the record date.
11. The yield measures returns as a percentage of the investment.
12. Bonds and fixed-interest securities use a yield-to-call (YTC) metric.
13. To satisfy IRS requirements in assessing profit or loss, an accurate accounting of a "sold" security's cost basis is crucial.
14. Superior diversification is the primary benefit of investing in an index fund.
15. A regular-way settlement takes the trade date plus two business days (T + 2).
16. Physical entry means issuing the buyer a physical stock certificate or bond.
17. By issuing stock splits, companies issue additional shares of their stock without reducing the value of the company.
18. A reverse split is when a company consolidates shares to increase the price.
19. Companies can reduce the issued shares in circulation through stock buybacks.
20. An investor may make a tender offer to capture a significant number of shares to demand a board seat.
21. A major reason for mergers and acquisitions (M&As) is to accelerate growth goals.
22. Shareholders use a proxy vote when they cannot physically attend shareholders' meetings to vote on corporate actions.

8 Customer Accounts and Compliance Considerations

Account Types and Characteristics

Types of Accounts

Investors require a brokerage account before purchasing securities. There are three primary categories of accounts: cash accounts, margin accounts, and options accounts.

Cash accounts require clients to only transact with the cash value in the account and take long (i.e., buy) positions. There are limited, straightforward options for cash account holders: they can deposit cash to settle transactions or sell securities to create liquidity on the same day to resolve new buy orders.

With specific customer permission, broker-dealers can lend securities in a cash account to other investors, including traders involved in short selling and hedge fund transactions:

- This can be an additional income stream for investors in this category on a quote-by-quote system under broker management. Notably, the broker takes a cut of the "lending fee," which in no way disturbs the investor's long position and any price appreciation resulting from it.
- The percentage commission for lending securities to other investors depends on their demand level (the highest generally being illiquid stocks, thinly traded).
- Not all brokers offer security lending addendums alongside their traditional services; if they do, there is generally a minimum share and dollar requirement.

Margin accounts allow investors to borrow money against the securities' value on an arranged basis, as follows:

- Margin account holders can trade long or short (i.e., sell) positions, and investors can make cash withdrawals within the leverage limits.
- Aggressive traders use margin facilities to their maximum advantage, notwithstanding that borrowing rates can be high.

- Broker-dealers do not require permission to lend securities from a margin account or compensate the account holder if the latter reflects a debit balance.
- When it comes to margin accounts still in credit balance—not making use of leveraging at that point—dealers must treat them as cash accounts for lending purposes (see above).
- Dealers strictly monitor margin accounts to maintain an agreed-upon ratio. Going below this results in a margin call to the investors, notifying them of the position and demanding they bring it back to level with a cash or securities (i.e., long position) input.
- Margin-type facilities exclude retirement accounts from the margin transaction arena because they have annual contribution limits.

Options accounts allow for options trading:

- Brokers must approve every account for options trading before investors can enter the arena.
- Customers must have a working knowledge of options and trading strategies.
- Customers must understand and be able to take on the risks of options trading.
- Brokers structure the account to accommodate a set level of options trading, usually with margin facilities.

Hedge funds are prolific users of options trading strategies, as are individuals trading futures in currency, stock, and commodity markets. Margin accounts will inevitably overlap the options circle of trading, although not all margin account holders are necessarily options traders.

QUICK REVIEW QUESTIONS

1. What type of accounts allow investors to borrow money against the value of the securities?

2. What type of accounts are generally used for long positions?

Characteristics of Accounts

A **discretionary account** allows the investment advisor to execute trades on the investors' behalf without first requesting client consent:

- The investor trusts the dealer to make transactional decisions without pre-discussions.
- All dealer decisions must be in the investors' best interests and consistent with their goals.

Conversely, a **nondiscretionary account** is where the client decides whether to execute a trade.

- The dealer is responsible for closing the requested transaction at the best price.
- The broker may interact with the client as an advisor to recommend asset entries or exits.

HELPFUL HINT

There is a dividing line between advising and implementing trades without express client approval.

TABLE 8.1. Discretionary Versus Nondiscretionary Accounts

WHEN DISCRETIONARY ACCOUNTS WORK BEST	WHEN NONDISCRETIONARY ACCOUNTS WORK BEST
• Passive investors are too preoccupied to monitor market dynamics. • The customer and the dealer are on the same page about a strategy. • Investors want to keep their accounts in balance. (e.g., a client wants the account to reflect consistent stock/bond ratios of 60/40; the broker can implement trades without pre-authorization to maintain the ratio). • It is essential to access the best pricing as it emerges (e.g., delays due to pre-authorization cause opportunities to disappear).	• Investors want hands-on management and involvement in the process, even with dealer guidance. • Investors believe they have the insight to assess dealer advice and the time to listen to it at relevant junctures. • Investors cannot rise to the minimum requirement of a discretionary account (typically six digits).

Broker clients may go from discretionary to nondiscretionary and back again in agreement with the dealer. In such cases, it is advisable to record change dates.

Educational accounts, like 529 plans, allow families to invest in their children's education. (See Chapter 5 for more on 529 plans.)

Investment advisors must choose between a flat fee or a commission calculated on a percentage of the transactional value. **Fee-based financial advisors** collect a pre-stated retainer for their services in agreement with the client:

- If the dealer actively transacts for the clients, the fee will likely align with assets under management (AUM).
  - In cases like this, the fee may be a combination of payment directly from the client and commissions generated from the trades.
- Brokers traditionally structure fee arrangements hourly, monthly, quarterly, or annually.

Alternatively, a broker-client relationship may ride on fixed fees and commissions. A crucial aspect of a fee-based advisor relationship is that in every instance, the advisors must put the client's interests before their own, and there can be no conflict of interest.

Commission brokers earn based on transactional activity:

- The more they transact, the more they make.
- Their actions must align with the client's best interests and objectives.

However, unlike fee-based financial advisors, the legal obligations for commission brokers are to the member firms that employ them. Commission brokers have no obligation to declare or observe conflicts of interest before transacting.

QUICK REVIEW QUESTIONS

3. What kind of account allows investment advisors to execute trades on an investor's behalf without first requesting client consent?

   _____

4. In what kind of accounts do clients decide to execute a trade?

   _____

Requirements for Broker-Dealers

Broker-dealers must abide by certain rules in customer accounts. **SEC Rule 15c2-12** (Municipal Securities Disclosure) prohibits an underwriter from transacting municipal securities if the issuer cannot, will not, or is unsure about annually providing the financial information and operating data outlined in a written continuing disclosure agreement.

Similarly, **MSRB Rule G-47** (Time of Trade Disclosure) requires broker-dealers to disclose to the customer everything they know about a municipal securities transaction (including accessibility) that can impact its result. This information must coincide with the transaction—preferably before it.

The Federal Reserve Board's **Regulation T** and **SEC Rule 15c3-3** (Customer Protection) address broker-dealers who grant investors credit extensions outside of promptly settling their securities obligations.

According to Regulation T, investors must deposit at least 50% of the value of the securities purchased on margin. The broker-dealer lends the rest of the value. As long as payments due exceed $1,000, Regulation T gives investors up to four business days to meet their responsibility, irrespective of whether it is a cash or margin account. Failing to do so leaves the broker no choice but to

- liquidate the position, or
- apply for and receive an extension from an SRO like FINRA.

FINRA Rule 2264 (Margin Disclosure Statement) restricts accounts opened under Regulation T (on margin). **MSRB Rule G-18** (Best Execution) requires dealers representing clients' interests to investigate where and how to transact municipal securities to get the clients the best possible results (given different volatility levels). Rule G-18 asks dealers to document their findings covering

- price,
- volatility,
- relative liquidity,

- transaction scale,
- category,
- the number of markets reviewed,
- the source of information relied on, and
- accessing quotes.

Broker-dealers must evaluate how all of the described factors relate to the customer's order, inquiry, and terms and conditions as communicated to the dealers involved in the transaction.

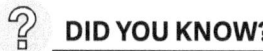 **DID YOU KNOW?**

Rule G-18 applies to any municipal security transaction involving a customer (even if it is another dealer's customer), but not to inter-dealer trades.

QUICK REVIEW QUESTIONS

5. Which rule requires an underwriter to provide financial information and operating data when transacting municipal securities?

6. According to Regulation T, at least how much must an investor deposit in a margin account?

Customer Account Registrations

Customer Accounts

Before transacting securities through registered broker-dealers, investors must open an account (cash, margin, or option). The simplest type is an **individual account** with one person's name (i.e., one account owner).

On the other end of the spectrum, a company owns the assets in a corporate account, which is identified with a company name. Institutions invest this way, and many individual investors or families have their assets organized under company structures.

Partnerships (e.g., limited liability partnerships) are managed by a general partner or a nominated shareholder who conducts business with the brokerage. Both options are acceptable to broker-dealers acting for investing syndicates.

In between the individual and company account types are **joint accounts**. The most crucial consideration with this type of account is what occurs if the parties do not agree on decisions, or if one of the parties dies. Brokerages try to cover these eventualities by offering the following options:

- joint tenants with rights of survivorship
  - The account owners (i.e., the names on the account) own the assets equally.
  - When one of the partners dies, the other partner owns all the assets in the account—including the decedent's share.

- tenancy in common (TIC)
    - There is no right of survivorship in this account.
    - The deceased partner's share goes automatically to the decedent's estate.
- community property
    - This represents a 50/50 split and is only applicable to married couples in certain states.
    - Community property functions similarly to TIC except that the share is always 50%.

Broker-dealers must seek clarity on transactional instructions for joint brokerage accounts. For example, must all parties sign off on joint arrangements, or may one party act for the rest? The more cumbersome the sign-off process, the less likely it is that a timing advantage will play a role in getting the best price. Furthermore, when the partnership dissolves, accounts must be closed and replaced.

Corporate/LLC/LLP accounts are generally better in the long term than joint accounts because they do not depend on personalities other than the general partners, which the investing entity can easily alter. Individual accounts also become somewhat complicated when a person dies since the assets fall into an estate.

Broker-dealers must follow **SEC Rule 15c3-3** (Customer Protection) when they take custody of client assets. Although brokers traditionally comingle clients' assets as part of their operations, broker-dealers still have certain obligations:

- Clients' securities are physically or digitally held free of liens and obligations.
- Clients' securities experience zero comingling with the member firm's affairs.
- Clients' assets are identifiable and immune from paying off the member firm's debts.

Rule 15c3-3 aims to protect customers from monetary losses and delays in case the broker firm goes into bankruptcy. As an adjunct to the Rule, every FINRA member must undergo independent CPA-administered audits.

In addition, brokerage firms must comply with **SEC Rule 15c3-1** (Net Capital Requirements). This rule requires firms to maintain a 1:1 ratio of cash and T-bills to liabilities. The measure establishes the firm's standing to meet liabilities without any possibility of incursion into clients' assets held in brokerage accounts.

Still, many broker firms create custodian divisions as an extra layer of protection within the business to segregate assets. These are specifically aimed at high-net-worth clients; the member firms provide this service for a separate fee. Custodian-held assets are not part of a broker's balance sheet and will therefore remain outside any litigation proceedings against the brokerage house.

QUICK REVIEW QUESTIONS

7. Which rules protect client assets when clients transact through registered brokers?

8. What are the three primary joint account options at brokerages?

Trusts and Custodial Accounts

Trusts are accounts managed by a trustee for the benefit of another person. **Custodial accounts** are established specifically for minors who are too young to open their own accounts. In custodial accounts, an adult custodian makes investment decisions on behalf of the beneficiary minor.

The **Uniform Transfers to Minors Act (UTMA)** covers custodial accounts. Under the UTMA, cash, securities, real estate, and other assets may be given to minors via custodial accounts:

- An UTMA account may have only one adult custodian and one minor.
- Anyone may provide gifts for a beneficiary through an UTMA account.
- Gifts through UTMA accounts are irrevocable.
- In UTMA accounts, securities may not be traded on margin or sold short.
- UTMA accounts are registered in the name of the custodian, but the minor is responsible for taxes.

> **DID YOU KNOW?**
> Custodians are not required to be related to the minor—although in many cases custodians include a parent.

QUICK REVIEW QUESTIONS

9. Who makes investment decisions in custodial accounts?

10. Who may give gifts via an UTMA account to a minor?

Retirement Accounts

An **individual retirement account (IRA)** is a great way to build savings in preparation for retirement. IRAs offer special tax breaks and, for many, can be a

→ CONTINUE

foundation for building wealth. Both traditional IRAs and Roth IRAs are available.

TABLE 8.2. Comparing Roth and Traditional IRAs

ROTH IRAS	TRADITIONAL IRAS
• Contributions are after-tax. • Contributions grow tax-free. • Withdrawals are permitted once the contributor reaches the age of 59 years and 6 months. • Withdrawals are NOT taxed.	• Contributions are pretax. • Contributions grow on a tax-deferred basis. • Withdrawals are permitted once the contributor reaches 59 years and 6 months. • Withdrawals ARE taxed.

Individuals can initiate Roth and traditional IRAs. On the other hand, **qualified plans** (e.g., 401(k), 403(b), and profit-share plans) are provided by corporate employers to attract staff. There are three main types of qualified plans:

- defined contributions, which are managed by the employee
- defined benefit plans, which give employees guaranteed returns and are operated by the employer
- combined plans, which are a mix of defined contributions and defined benefit plans

In all situations, registered broker-dealers have the resources and skills to open the accounts and offer aligned services to optimize the investments within these accounts. Customers connect with them to manage their plans from end to end on a discretionary or nondiscretionary basis.

Investors should consider how much they can contribute to the various retirement plans available. These **contribution caps** can change annually. For 2023, the IRS has established updated contribution limits as follows:

- Roth and traditional IRAs are capped at $6,500 per year.
  - Individuals aged 50 and over are entitled to a catch-up contribution of $1,000 that is not subject to a yearly cost-of-living adjustment.
- Qualified plans are capped at $22,500 per year.
  - Individuals aged 50 and over are entitled to a catch-up contribution of $7,500.

Required minimum distributions (RMDs) are the amount of money that contributors must begin taking from their retirement accounts after they reach the age of 72. RMDs apply to all employer-sponsored retirement plans, traditional IRAs, and Roth 401(k) accounts. However, RMDs do NOT affect Roth IRAs while the contributor is alive.

The latest any retirement fund contributor (as described above) can make the first withdrawal is age 72 (if the investor's seventieth birthday is on or after July 1, 2019). For contributors withdrawing in earlier years, RMDs are not

> **HELPFUL HINT**
> Stocks, mutual funds, REITs, and money market funds are all acceptable investment assets for any IRA or qualified plan.

applicable. To calculate the RMD for an account, the last year-end balance is divided by a life expectancy factor determined by the IRS.

QUICK REVIEW QUESTIONS

11. What are the main differences between Roth and traditional IRAs?

12. What is the maximum annual contribution to an IRA (as of 2023)?

Privacy Requirements

Broker-dealers are required to safeguard certain consumer financial and personal information. **SEC Regulation S-P** (Privacy of Consumer Financial Information and Safeguarding Personal Information) requires privacy policies and practices to be communicated to customers initially and annually. **Privacy notifications** inform customers about their rights and how information is shared.

Specifically, Regulation S-P restricts firms from providing **nonpublic personal information** to third parties. Nonpublic personal information is any personally identifiable information, such as name, address, and Social Security number.

The regulation distinguishes among "consumers," "customers," and "former customers." Apart from stipulating that policy notices be provided to customers annually, Regulation S-P establishes opt-out policies, limits on information sharing, and exceptions thereof.

QUICK REVIEW QUESTIONS

13. Which SEC Regulation requires firms to explain privacy practices to customers?

14. How often must customers be informed of their privacy rights?

Communicating with the Public

Broker-dealers are bound by law and rules in their communications with the public. **FINRA Rule 2210** (Communications with the Public) sets certain requirements for the approval, review, and recordkeeping of institutional communications:

- Rule 2210 establishes a different standard for institutional communications than for retail communications.
- Institutional standards are generally looser because of the greater level of awareness and sophistication expected of securities professionals.

Similarly, **FINRA Rule 2251** (Processing and Forwarding of Proxy and Other Issuer-Related Materials) requires firms to transmit proxy materials to owners of securities (see Chapter 7 for more on proxy voting).

Broker-dealers are restricted in using the telephone to solicit business or advertise services. **Telemarketing** refers to promotional telephone calls to solicit interest in services or request charitable donations:

- The **Federal Trade Commission (FTC) Telemarketing Sales Rule** requires all telemarketers to obtain clear authorization from customers before accepting any payment or billing and forbids advance payments for services.
- The **National Do Not Call Registry**, initiated by the FTC, aims to stop unwanted sales calls; anyone can register.

FINRA Rule 3230 (Telemarketing) restricts telemarketing. While there are some exceptions, Rule 3230 prohibits members and associated persons from deploying a telemarketing strategy that makes outbound telephone calls. There are three classifications:

- during restricted times
- to individuals on the firm-specific do-not-call list
- to anyone on the National Do Not Call Registry

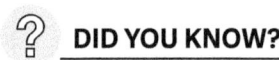

DID YOU KNOW?

Rule 3230 aligns closely with NYSE Rule 440A(h) caller identification information provisions; however, it excludes provisions regarding recorded messages and using fax or computer advertisements covered by NYSE Rule 440A(h).

Rule 3230 does not affect members involved in telemarketing activities that are in compliance with relevant state/federal laws and regulations, including FCC rules relating to telemarketing practices and the rights of telephone consumers. Similarly, **MSRB Rule G-39** (Telemarketing) covers much of the same ground as FINRA Rule 3230, except it focuses specifically on municipal securities traders (including banks).

Taping firms are member firms with a prevalent number of registered persons who are linked—either directly or by having worked at a disciplined member firm—with disciplinary history over the past three years:

- FINRA requires these firms to tape record the telemarketing activities of their registered persons.
- For a firm employing more than 20,000 persons, the taping threshold is crossed when 20% or more of the registered persons are associated with disciplinary history.

DID YOU KNOW?

If a firm is designated as a taping firm for the first time, it has options to remove the designation: It may cut its staff to fall below the taping threshold. The firm must tell FINRA who the terminated persons are, and it may not rehire any of the terminated persons for 180 days.

QUICK REVIEW QUESTIONS

15. Which rule requires that any telemarketer obtain authorization from customers before accepting any payment or billing?

16. Firms with several registered persons who are linked in the past three years with disciplinary history are called what?

Documentation Requirements and Prohibitions

Broker-dealers are prohibited from falsifying or withholding documents and must follow certain requirements regarding documentation. According to the Securities Exchange Act of 1934:

- Rule 10b-10 (Confirmation of Transactions) requires the purchase price and transaction date to be included information for securities transaction reports.
- Rule 10b-10 also requires the disclosure of early redemption features of debt securities.

Several FINRA and MSRB rules cover the transmission of information and documentation (see Table 8.3.).

TABLE 8.3. Documentation Requirements and Prohibitions

REQUIRED OR RESTRICTED ACTIVITY	FINRA OR MSRB RULE
Account statements must be issued at least quarterly.	FINRA Rule 2231 (Customer Account Statements)
Written confirmations must be offered to customers when broker-dealers transact on their behalves.	• FINRA Rule 2232 (Customer Confirmations) • MSRB Rule G-15 (Confirmation, Clearance, Settlement and Other Uniform Practice Requirements with Respect to Transactions with Customers)
Broker-dealers involved with municipal securities must communicate with customers at least once annually in writing or electronically.	MSRB Rule G-10 (Investor and Municipal Advisory Client Education and Protection)
Members may only publish information about transactions if they are certain that the transaction occurred in real time and within SEA protocols.	FINRA Rule 5210 (Publication of Transactions and Quotations)
Broker-dealers must fulfill their offers at a stated quote. (They may only make buy or sell offers when they are prepared to purchase or sell the security at the stated price.)	FINRA Rule 5220 (Offers at Stated Prices)
Members may not use gifts or other rewards in exchange for the publication of communications that can influence a security's value.	FINRA Rule 5230 (Payments Involving Publications that Influence the Market Price of a Security)
Members may hold mail for up to 90 days for customers unable to receive mail at their usual address.	FINRA Rule 3150 (Holding of Customer Mail)

> **? DID YOU KNOW?**
> Markup disclosure is NOT required as part of the transaction confirmation when a broker-dealer acquires securities as part of a fixed-price offering and sells them at the public offering price on the same day.

Signatures of convenience are also prohibited. Signatures of convenience are when a customer's signature is forged (even with their permission). Authorized signatures should always be used.

FINRA and other government agencies periodically make requests of broker-dealers across a broad range of subjects. Members are responsible for responding to regulatory requests in a timely manner. Failure to respond could result in suspension from the securities business.

QUICK REVIEW QUESTIONS

17. According to FINRA, how frequently should account statements be issued?

_____

18. How frequently should broker-dealers involved with municipal securities communicate with customers?

_____

Best Interest Obligations and Suitability Requirements

FINRA expects every member firm to know all the essential facts about their customers' goals and risk tolerances. **FINRA Rule 2090** (Know Your Customer) outlines these requirements:

- FINRA uses the term *reasonable due diligence*, which implies asking enough questions to give the member the insight it needs to conduct business for its customers.
- Moreover, staying in touch with clients' needs must include
  - recording the derived information guiding the investment strategies, and
  - updating it as needs change.

In other words, due diligence is a continuing process for the entire life cycle of the member/customer relationship.

Members must also adhere to guidance regarding accounts at other institutions. **FINRA Rule 3210** (Accounts at Other Broker-Dealers and Financial Institutions) lays out the details:

- Members working within an employer member firm (EMF) and associated persons (EMF employees) can only open their securities transactional accounts at the EMF.
  - All outside members and financial institutions are excluded from consideration.
  - The only exception is if the EMF gives prior consent in writing.
- In the case of exceptions, the EMF employees opening the accounts will inform the relevant outside members or financial institutions of their relationship with the EMF.

- The relevant outside members and financial institutions, if requested by the EMF, will reveal transactional data on statements and confirmations executed on behalf of the EMF employees holding the outside accounts.

Rule 15l-1 of the SEA (Regulation Best Interest) also requires that broker-dealers act in the client's best interest. Broker-dealer recommendations to retail customers should be driven by reasonable diligence, care, and skill. Broker-dealers should not let their advice be influenced by any benefit they may derive from the customer's responsive actions.

QUICK REVIEW QUESTIONS

19. Which FINRA rule requires broker-dealers to exercise reasonable due diligence in determining client needs?

_____

20. Which law requires that broker-dealer recommendations to retail customers are driven by reasonable diligence, care, and skill?

_____

Recordkeeping Requirements

Broker-dealers are required by law—the Securities Exchange Act of 1934—to create certain records and follow recordkeeping guidelines:

- **Rule 17a-3** of the SEA (Records to be Made by Certain Exchange Members, Brokers, and Dealers) requires broker-dealers to create records of transactions.
- **Rule 17a-4** of the SEA (Records to be Preserved by Certain Exchange Members, Brokers, and Dealers) lays out rules for methods and types of preservation, including electronic archiving.

In addition to following the SEA, broker-dealers must follow FINRA and the MSRB rules on books and records retention requirements. **FINRA Rule 4511** (General Requirements) requires members to follow the SEA in maintaining updated books and records:

- Members should maintain most records for at least **six years**.
- In some cases, records may be kept for a shorter period—usually three years.

MSRB Rule G-8 (Books and Records to be Made by Brokers, Dealers, and Municipal Securities Dealers and Municipal Advisors) mandates recordkeeping by municipal securities dealers and advisors. According to Rule G-8, records must be accurately updated to satisfy regulatory inspections by the MSRB or when disputes occur. Typical records covered by Rule G-8 include

- original entry,
- customer accounts,

- securities,
- municipal securities in different stages of transactional transition,
- put options and repurchase agreements,
- transactions, and
- primary offerings.

MSRB Rule G-9 (Preservation of Records) outlines how long records must be retained. It covers the recording of all trades, customer account statements (settlement dates), general ledgers, and account records.

Like FINRA Rule 4511, MSRB Rule G-9 requires that most information be kept for six years (e.g., closed accounts, customer complaints, suitability, and gifts). Unlike FINRA, the MSRB requires retention of transaction and employment records for only four years. These include

- trade confirmations,
- order tickets,
- U4 and U5 forms, and
- compensation documentation.

In most cases, articles of incorporation, charters, partnerships, and similar records require indefinite maintenance.

FINRA also lays out requirements for keeping certain information regarding customer accounts. According to **FINRA Rule 4512** (Customer Account Information) **customer account information** covers

- individual accounts,
- institutional accounts,
- underage persons,
- company accounts, and
- discretionary accounts.

FINRA requires names, addresses, and contact details of account holders. When associated persons act with authority (or in a trust capacity), the SRO requests that the accounts record social security numbers, tax ID numbers, names of employers and addresses, occupation, and more. Finally, the relevant signatures driving transactions must appear in the account information in all cases.

Falsifying records means fraudulently creating or altering records. It is unethical and potentially criminal. Similarly, **improper maintenance or retention of records** may be unethical or illegal. It may violate FINRA or MSRB rules as outlined above, or even the Securities Exchange Act of 1934. Improper signatures, as mentioned earlier, can result in severe consequences.

FINRA and MSRB rules and regulations consistently state their requirements for recording transaction information (written and electronic), authorizations, complaints, and "know your customer" details. They also emphasize that members must ensure they attach the correct signatures in every relevant situation.

HELPFUL HINT

Most documents should be retained for six years. In cases where a shorter period is allowed, the MSRB calls for four years, whereas FINRA usually requires three years of record retention.

The recordkeeping as described above is critical because disputes and client/broker disagreements frequently occur. Both SROs depend on the official records going back up to six years (at minimum three) to unravel the rights and wrongs that are driving the conflicts. Consequently, non-compliant content will count heavily against the members' counterarguments.

FINRA Rule 4370 (Business Continuity Plans and Emergency Contact Information) requires firms to develop and maintain business continuity plans. A **business continuity plan (BCP)** outlines asset recovery, employee mobilization, and operations continuity in case of an emergency. The recovery plan should address all of the logistics necessary to mitigate losses to the business:

- Who is responsible for notifying the authorities?
- How will first responders obtain access to the facilities?
- How will employees be evacuated?
- What will the company do to help employees find medical attention and safety if necessary?
- Where will employees work? Where will they stay? How will the company keep track of where employees are?
- How will employees be paid?
- What resources do employees need to continue doing their jobs (e.g., mobile workstations or personal protective equipment), and how will the company provide these resources?
- How will the company's data, files, and information be protected to prevent disaster and recover from disaster?
- Are backup copies maintained remotely?

The BCP should identify the resources available to the firm to overcome emergencies. A BCP helps a firm maintain transparency and drives the business forward.

DID YOU KNOW?

As a good example to its members, FINRA updates and tests its own BCP regularly and submits it to the SEC.

QUICK REVIEW QUESTIONS

21. At a minimum, how long should most records be maintained?

22. What necessary document outlines how a business will handle an emergency?

Anti-Money Laundering

Money laundering is a criminal activity in which people hide the origins of illegally obtained money. Broker-dealers, institutions, and all financial professionals are essential partners with the federal government in combating money laundering.

Stages of Money Laundering

There are three main stages of money laundering:

- placement
- layering
- integration

Figure 8.1. Stages of Money Laundering

Placement refers to introducing illegally obtained money into the legitimate financial system. This may occur by adding illegally obtained cash to the legal funds of a legitimate business. For instance, Al Capone placed money from criminal activity into legitimate cash businesses. False invoicing—another illegal and fraudulent activity—is usually required to accomplish this.

Placement can also involve buying monetary instruments, such as checks or money orders, and depositing them into various other reciprocals or credit card accounts in other locations. Placement strategies also cover actions related to hiding the beneficial owner's identification behind trusts, offshore shell companies, and/or foreign bank accounts.

Placement is often accomplished through **structuring**, which means depositing funds into a bank account by unreasonably exploiting the rules. For example, a drug trafficker has $100,000 of illegally obtained funds and wants to avoid the reporting protocol banks have when deposits of $10,000 or more pass through the system:

- The trafficker makes ten deposits of $9,990 and one deposit of $100.
- The trafficker has manipulated the system by structuring multiple smaller deposits to bypass reporting protocols.

Money launderers feel that the more convoluted the trail between the money source and the final bank deposit, the harder it is to prove criminality. Thus, they use **layering** to disconnect the illegal money from the unlawful activity it emerged from with layer after layer of intermediaries:

- In many cases, the bank or company whose accounts the money passes through en route to its final destination are outside the US, with no obligation to be transparent.
- Layering can also involve changing assets from cash to commodities, cryptocurrencies, casino chips, and other hard assets.
- To further complicate layering, criminals may also deploy bank wires, Automated Clearing House (ACH) transactions, paper transactions, and even manually move funds between geographic locations.

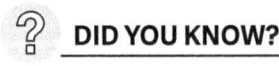 **DID YOU KNOW?**

Al Capone originally used cash laundromat businesses for the placement of cash from criminal enterprises. Some believe this is the origin of the term *money laundering*.

The goal of money laundering is to integrate illegitimate funds into the legitimate financial system. In integration, money launderers disguise the illegitimate funds using tactics that give them legitimacy. They may also use fake employees or loans to disguise funds.

QUICK REVIEW QUESTIONS

23. What are the three main stages of money laundering?

24. What is the goal of money laundering?

Preventing Money Laundering

The United States government uses anti-money laundering (AML) to combat foreign adversaries, fight terrorism, and control international narcotics trafficking. The US Department of the Treasury actively combats money laundering through several units:

- The **Financial Crimes Enforcement Network (FinCEN)** reviews financial transactions to combat money laundering and terrorist financing.
- The **Office of Foreign Asset Control (OFAC)** enacts foreign policy by enforcing sanctions against threats to national security (terrorists, certain foreign regimes, drug traffickers).

OFAC publishes the Specially Designated Nationals and Blocked Persons (SDNs) List. SDNs include

- people and entities controlled by certain countries,
- terrorists, and
- international drug traffickers.

Cooperation to fight money laundering and connected criminal or terrorist enterprises is encouraged by the USA PATRIOT Act. **Section 314** (Cooperative Efforts to Deter Money Laundering) facilitates information sharing between law enforcement and financial institutions.

Firms are required by law and by SROs to combat money laundering. Under the **USA PATRIOT Act Section 352** (Anti-Money Laundering Programs), all financial institutions must develop anti-money laundering programs.

- **FINRA Rule 3310** (Anti-Money Laundering Compliance Program) also requires members to develop AML compliance programs.
- The MSRB also requires such programs under **MSRB Rule G-41** (Anti-Money Laundering Compliance Program).

AML compliance programs must ensure the firm looks for signs of suspicious activity that may suggest money laundering. AML compliance programs must be tested to ensure their efficacy, offer ongoing training to personnel, and ensure the identity of customers through due diligence.

Section 326 of the USA PATRIOT Act (Verification of Identification) requires financial institutions to fight money laundering by following minimum standards in confirming the identification of customers. Section 326 applies when individuals or entities open accounts.

US-registered financial institutions and associates file **suspicious activity reports (SARs)** whenever they suspect customers or employees are laundering money via placement, structuring, or integration methods. SARs are filed with FinCEN.

US banks use **currency transaction reports (CTRs)** to stop money launderers. CTRs are integral to the banking industry's AML protocols and responsibilities:

- Whenever more than $10,000 enters an account, the bank reports it in a CTR.
- In such instances, the relevant banking institution fills in the identities and Social Security Numbers of large money depositors (no matter how legitimate the transaction may be).
- Banks are not obliged to divulge their CTR to those involved unless the perpetrators request it.
- Canceling the questionable deposit may, in turn, generate the submission of an SAR.

QUICK REVIEW QUESTIONS

25. What are three laws and rules that require institutions to implement AML compliance programs?

26. Which US government entity reviews financial transactions to combat money laundering?

Answer Key

1. Margin accounts allow investors to borrow money against the value of the securities.

2. Cash accounts are generally used for long positions.

3. A discretionary account allows investment advisors to execute trades on an investor's behalf without first requesting client consent.

4. Clients decide to execute a trade in nondiscretionary accounts.

5. SEC Rule 15c2-12 requires an underwriter to provide financial information and operating data when transacting municipal securities.

6. Regulation T requires the investor to deposit at least 50% of the value of the securities purchased on margin.

7. Rule 15c3-1 and Rule 15c3-3 protect client assets.

8. The three primary joint account options at brokerages are joint tenants with rights of survivorship, tenancy in common (TIC), and community property.

9. An adult custodian makes investment decisions in custodial accounts.

10. Anyone can provide gifts through a Uniform Transfers to Minors Act (UTMA) account.

11. Contributions to Roth individual retirement accounts (IRAs) rely on after-tax earnings and withdrawals are not taxed; traditional IRAs rely on pretax contributions and withdrawals are taxed.

12. As of 2023, the maximum annual contribution to a traditional or Roth individual retirement account (IRA) is $6,500. Individuals aged 50 and over are entitled to a catch-up contribution of $1,000 that is not subject to a yearly cost-of living adjustment.

13. SEC Regulation S-P (Privacy of Consumer Financial Information and Safeguarding Personal Information) requires firms to explain privacy practices to customers.

14. Customers must be informed of their privacy rights initially and every year thereafter.

15. The Federal Trade Commission (FTC) Telemarketing Sales Rule requires telemarketers to obtain authorization from customers before accepting payment.

16. Taping firms are member firms with many registered persons who have been linked to disciplinary history in the past three years.

17. Per FINRA Rule 2231 (Customer Account Statements), account statements must be issued at least quarterly.

18. Broker-dealers involved with municipal securities must communicate with customers at least once annually in writing or electronically, per MSRB Rule G-10 (Delivery of Investment Brochure).

19. FINRA Rule 2090 (Know Your Customer) requires that broker-dealers use reasonable due diligence to meet client needs.

20. Rule 15l-1 of the Securities and Exchange Act (Regulation Best Interest) requires broker-dealers to act in the client's best interest.

21. Most records should be maintained for at least six years.

22. A business continuity plan (BCP) outlines asset recovery, employee mobilization, and operations continuity in case of an emergency.

23. Placement, layering, and integration are the three main stages of money laundering.

24. Money launderers seek to integrate funds into the legitimate financial system.

25. Section 352 of the PATRIOT Act, FINRA Rule 3310, and MSRB Rule G-41 all require institutions to implement anti-money laundering (AML) compliance programs.

26. Financial Crimes Enforcement Network (FinCEN) reviews financial transactions to combat money laundering.

9 Prohibited Activities

Market Manipulation

Types of Market Manipulation

Financial Industry Regulatory Authority **(FINRA) Rule 2010** (Standards of Commercial Honor and Principles of Trade) calls for members to show integrity, honesty, and fairness in business. Similarly, **FINRA Rule 2020** (Use of Manipulative, Deceptive or Other Fraudulent Devices) prohibits manipulation, deception, and fraud in buying and selling securities. These Rules prohibit deceptive practices, such as market manipulation. Certain forms of market manipulation are described below.

Market rumors are securities information suspected or known to contain inaccuracies that are likely to mislead investors, and thus likely to move prices. Members who originate or circulate market rumors are guilty of committing a prohibited activity. Members who suspect—and fail to report to FINRA—activities that are designed to initiate and spread false information are also committing a prohibited activity.

Pump and dump schemes typically consist of distributing (verbally or via text) false or exaggerated content that misleads investors by unrealistically "pumping up" the value of a security. Pump and dump schemes refer to situations where FINRA members

- are involved in plots (schemes) to artificially increase security prices;
- are aware of a scheme, even if they are not a direct participant, and fail to report it; and
- innocently promote pump and dump schemes without doing reasonable due diligence.

The ultimate sign of a pump and dump is a sudden and sharp drop to the launch price after it rises to an impressively high level. Investors who fall for the hype built up around the security end up taking significant losses. The sellers who unload their holdings as the launch price increases are on the winning end.

Excessive trading is a problem because buying and selling securities generates commission earnings for members and other expenses that negatively impact investors' net returns. Excessive trading can be challenging to pin down; however, FINRA believes that the turnover rate is the most reliable gauge as to whether a member is excessively trading a client's portfolio. **Turnover rate** represents the number of times a broker swaps a securities portfolio for another.

FINRA communicates portfolio turnover standards and cost-to-equity ratios it expects members to follow. For example, in a prominent case, FINRA determined that a portfolio turnover rate above six, or a cost-to-equity ratio above 20% taints member activities as falling into the "excessively traded" arena. Any member directly initiating excessive trading—or connected to another member involved in the practice—by exceeding the metrics described is guilty of a prohibited activity.

Marking the close is a method of window dressing that members deploy when they (or members they are associated with) represent a significant holding in a thinly traded security. In **marking the close**, members collude to enter orders that result in prices at the close of an exchange session, which favors the held position.

Similarly, **marking the open** is a ploy by a member or members to enter security trades at an exchange opening to influence the price of that security. Since market openings and closings are closely followed by investors, they are crucial focal points for regulations.

In investor cash accounts, the Securities and Exchange Commission (SEC) and FINRA mandate that holders pay for securities bought before they are eligible to sell them. **Freeriding** is when investors fail to comply with this rule.

FINRA members must stop freeriding by freezing delinquent accounts for 90 days and requiring the investor to remit funds for the relevant security purchases. Failure to reel in the freeriding investors as described is a member-prohibited activity.

In **backing away**, the market maker fails to honor the quoted price. **FINRA Rule 5220** (Offers at Stated Prices) prohibits the bond trader from "backing away" from a firm offer.

A registered representative may not trade stock for his firm's benefit ahead of a customer's market order for the same stock in the same direction. This is known as **front running**, and it harms the customer by both impacting the market price ahead of the customer execution and delaying the customer's market access. Front running is unlawful and violates **FINRA Rule 5270** (Front Running of Block Transactions) as well as FINRA Rules 2010, 5310, and 5320.

QUICK REVIEW QUESTIONS

1. What term describes the number of times a broker swaps a securities portfolio for another?

2. Which violation occurs when the market maker fails to honor the quoted price?

_____

Preventing Market Manipulation

Preventing market manipulation is not just part of good conduct for members of SROs: the Securities Exchange Act of 1934 (SEA) and the SEC legally bind broker-dealers to exercise honesty and fairness in buying and selling securities.

The SEA has rules that encourage transparency and fight market manipulation. All offerings must be registered with the SEC:

- According to **Section 15** of the SEA broker-dealers must register with the SEC.
- Section 15 also requires broker-dealers to file periodic reports.

Section 11d of the SEA (Prohibition on Extension of Credit by Broker-Dealer) prohibits broker-dealers who were part of the new issue of a security from extending credit to customers to finance that security.

Regulation M prohibits market manipulation and restricts the behavior of market makers who could benefit from an offering. Regulation M restricts activity before offerings are priced.

In general, Regulation M defines the restricted period as beginning five days prior to the pricing of the offering. However, for securities where the average daily trading volume exceeds $100,000 and the issuer has a public float beyond $25 million, the restricted period begins one business day prior to the pricing of the offering.

The Municipal Securities Rulemaking Board (MSRB) also has guidelines to limit manipulation and encourage ethical behavior:

- According to **MSRB Rule G-13** (Quotations Relating to Municipal Securities) quotations of municipal securities must represent real bids; furthermore, dealers may not misrepresent quotations from competitors.
- Per **MSRB Rule G-25** (Improper Use of Assets), broker-dealers are prohibited from **misusing** customer assets.

 HELPFUL HINT

FINRA strictly prohibits threatening conduct, intimidation, and the coordination with others to determine prices, trades, or reports in **FINRA Rule 5240** (Anti-intimidation/Coordination).

QUICK REVIEW QUESTIONS

3. Which law prohibits broker-dealers who were part of the new issue of a security from extending credit to customers to finance that security?

_____

4. What is the typical restricted period under Regulation M?

_____

Insider Trading

Definitions

Insider trading is taking advantage of another investor's lack of information to secure monetary gain. Insider trading is a breach of fiduciary duty and is against the law:

- **Material nonpublic information (MNPI)** pertains to data and information that can impact a security's price but is not yet public knowledge.
- Anyone with access to MNPI who uses it to profit at the expense of others without access to the MNPI is guilty of insider trading.

Corporate officers, directors, shareholders controlling at least 10% of the equity, or company members with significant access to MNPI are under constant scrutiny. Companies must report their transactions to the SEC.

Someone using MNPI to make a profit may or may not be employed by the company. Company employees might pass MNPI to family, friends, and associates to act as their transactional proxy or for their own benefit. This is just as unacceptable as an employee using MNPI directly to earn a profit. Both cases are considered insider trading.

Section 10b of the SEA addresses prohibited and manipulative behavior, such as insider trading. **Section 10b5-1** of the SEA (Trading "On the Basis Of" Material Nonpublic Information in Insider Trading Cases) specifically forbids using MNPI in trading securities.

Similarly, **Section 10b5-2** (Duties of Trust or Confidence in Misappropriation Insider Trading Cases) explains the level of trust required for a trade. Information communicated in confidence, and in certain family relationships, should not be used for trading purposes.

QUICK REVIEW QUESTIONS

5. Information that can impact a security's price but is not yet public knowledge is called what?

6. Which section of the SEA forbids using MNPI in trading?

Prevention

Several laws and FINRA rules work to prevent insider trading:

- The **Insider Trading and Securities Fraud Enforcement Act (ITSFEA)** was passed in 1988 to amend the Securities and Exchange Act of 1934.
    - ITSFEA increased the SEC's enforcement power against participants in insider trading.

- **FINRA Rule 5280** (Trading Ahead of Research Reports) prohibits FINRA members from trading based on nonpublic research reporting.
- **FINRA Rule 6438** (Displaying Priced Quotations in Multiple Quotation Mediums) requires members to offer the same quotes in all media they use (e.g., electronic, paper).
- Similarly, **FINRA Rule 5320** (Prohibition Against Trading Ahead of Customer Orders) enforces integrity in trades by prohibiting trading ahead.

Section 17 of the **Investment Company Act of 1940** regulates who may transact securities. Some of the rules to know include the following:

- **Rule 17a-6** (Exemption for Transactions with Portfolio Affiliates) allows a registered investment company to transact with its portfolio affiliates when such interactions would usually be prohibited.
  - The board of directors must be satisfied that the affiliate represents material financial interests in the company's activities.
  - The board must post its findings in the board minutes maintained under proper regulatory protocols.
  - The affiliate generally has a controlling interest in the fund or exercises more than 5% of the vote on issues involving the fund.
- **Rule 17a-7** (Exemption of Certain Purchase or Sale Transactions Between an Investment Company and Certain Affiliated Persons Thereof) addresses investment company cross trading.
  - **Cross trading** refers to securities transactions between an investment company and certain affiliated persons.
  - Rule 17a-7 permits some cross trading under certain circumstances.

 HELPFUL HINT

Trading ahead is when a market maker uses its own account to fulfill a customer's trade instead of soliciting bids on the market.

QUICK REVIEW QUESTIONS

7. What law amended the SEA to increase the SEC's power against participants in insider trading?

8. What term describes when a market maker uses its own account to fulfill a customer's trade instead of soliciting bids on the market, and what rule forbids this practice?

Penalties

The SEA lays out the penalties for insider trading. These penalties include
- fines,
- expulsion, and/or
- incarceration.

A **contemporaneous trader** in insider trading is someone who trades at the same time as an inside trader. Contemporaneous traders are excluded from the information that benefits the inside trader and have recourse under the law: they may sue inside traders under **Section 20A** (Liability to Contemporaneous Traders for Insider Trading).

Section 21A of the SEA (Civil Penalties for Insider Trading) specifies penalties for insider trading:

- People found guilty of insider trading must pay the government an amount equal to however much they profited (or lost) due to the insider trading.
- Additional penalties of up to three times the amount profited or lost may be imposed.
- Insider traders may not be able to hold certain positions (e.g., officer or director of public companies).

The SEA was amended by the **Sarbanes-Oxley Act** in 2002, which put harsher criminal penalties on insider trading, including

- fines of up to $5 million per violation (for individuals),
- fines of up to $25 million for corporations, and
- imprisonment of up to twenty years.

QUICK REVIEW QUESTIONS

9. What are three possible penalties for insider trading?

10. What 2002 law amended the SEA to punish insider trading more harshly?

Other Prohibited Activities

Initial Public Offerings (IPOs)

Certain restrictions prevent associated persons from purchasing initial public offerings (IPOs). **FINRA Rule 5130** (Restrictions on the Purchase and Sale of Initial Equity Public Offerings) lays out the guidelines.

Rule 5130 prohibits members from transacting new security issues with accounts connected to restricted persons who have a beneficial interest. **Restricted persons** include

- portfolio managers (except for advisors to family investment vehicles),
- executive officers or directors of public companies with whom the members materially support or have an investment relationship, and
- executive officers or directors of certain non-public companies.

QUICK REVIEW QUESTION

11. When are restricted persons prohibited from transacting new security issues?

Manipulative, Deceptive, and Other Fraudulent Devices

The use of manipulative, deceptive or other fraudulent devices is prohibited by the Securities and Exchange Act of 1934. **Section 10** of the Act (Regulation of the Use of Manipulative and Deceptive Devices) outlines and prohibits fraudulent schemes, plans, and activities in general. Specific rules are as follows:

- **Section 10b-1** (Prohibition of Use of Manipulative or Deceptive Devices or Contrivances with Respect to Certain Securities Exempted from Registration) prohibits fraud in general.
- **Section 10b-3** (Employment of Manipulative and Deceptive Devices by Brokers or Dealers) prohibits broker-dealers and municipal dealers from engaging in any fraudulent or manipulative practices.
- **Section 10b-5** (Employment of Manipulative and Deceptive Devices) forbids broker-dealers from using manipulative or fraudulent programs, systems, or schemes.

SEC Rule 35d-1, also known as the **Names Rule**, stipulates that investment companies may not have deceptive or misleading names. Investment companies whose names state a particular investment focus must maintain 80% or more of their assets invested in the stated area of focus.

Section 15 of the SEA addresses **fraud** and **misrepresentation. Section 15c1-2** (Fraud and Misrepresentation) defines fraud and misrepresentation as

- any activity intended to deceive, and
- purposely lying about facts or omitting facts.

Section 15c1-3 of the SEA (Misrepresentation by Brokers, Dealers and Municipal Securities Dealers as to Registration) addresses fraud and misrepresentation when registering with the SEC. Per Section 15c1-3, just because a broker-dealer is registered does not mean the SEC or SROs approve of the broker-dealer's conduct, financial standing, or business.

Again, the MSRB also has rules prohibiting manipulative, deceptive, or fraudulent activities. According to MSRB **Rule G-14** (Reports of Sales or Purchases), municipal securities dealers must be honest in reporting transactions. They are forbidden from issuing fraudulent reports (e.g., creating reports about transactions that have not happened).

In addition, municipal securities dealers must be transparent and honest in **advertising**. Per MSRB **Rule G-21** (Advertising):

- Advertising of new issues of municipal securities must follow certain guidelines.
- A principal must approve advertisements in writing prior to first use.

PROHIBITED ACTIVITIES   **175**

QUICK REVIEW QUESTIONS

12. What law prohibits broker-dealers from using deception or fraud?

    _____

13. What rule stipulates that investment companies may not have deceptive or misleading names?

    _____

14. When transacting municipal securities, must a principal approve advertisements?

    _____

Customer Protections

Numerous customer protections exist regarding every aspect of securities trading. There are several customer protections to know, which are discussed in this section.

FINRA and the MSRB have stringent rules regarding interaction with customers. Under certain circumstances, broker-dealers and associated persons may **borrow** from or lend to customers. FINRA **Rule 3240** (Borrowing from or Lending to Customers) lays out the parameters. Borrowing/lending between registered members and customers is only allowed when the following are met:

- The member has a written policy outlining when registered representatives may borrow or lend money from customers.
- The customer is part of the member's immediate family.
- The customer is a financial lending institution.
- The borrower and lender already have a personal relationship beyond the broker-dealer relationship.

FINRA Rule 2150 (Improper Use of Customers' Securities or Funds; Prohibition Against Guarantees and Sharing in Accounts) forbids the misuse of customer funds. The Rule also addresses **sharing** in customer accounts. Members and associated persons may not share in profits or losses in customer accounts. One exception is that it is only allowed with written authorization and is proportionate to investments made into that account by the member or associated person.

Long and detailed protocols are attached to **margin requirements** applied to securities transactions. **FINRA Rule 4210** (Margin Requirements) mandates that customers' equity in their accounts must not fall below 25% of the portfolio's current market value.

Failure of the customer to increase equity to 25% (should it fall below that level) requires the member to liquidate securities until that level emerges or the entire portfolio converts to cash. Moreover, FINRA details that some securities do not qualify for margin assistance, and no member can lend more than half the purchase value of IPOs, new, or initial security issues.

Member firms must also get written authorization from customers when obtaining negotiable instruments (e.g., checks). That is, customers must knowingly affirm that they are handing over money to the firm. **FINRA Rule 4514** (Authorization Records for Negotiable Instruments Drawn From a Customer's Account) lays out specifics.

Firms must also follow rules regarding account **designation**. Firms must designate customer accounts using the customer's name (or another symbol that the customer has agreed to in writing) per **FINRA Rule 3250** (Designation of Accounts).

Broker-dealers must also adhere to guidance regarding the value of commissions, markups, and charges. **FINRA Rule 2120** (Commissions, Mark Ups and Charges) explains what is allowed:

- Overall, members must adhere to fair prices when buying or selling securities on behalf of customers.
- Members should not overcharge for commissions or service charges.

According to FINRA's **5% markup policy**, broker-dealers should not charge more than 5% for commissions or markups/markdowns. Though sometimes called the "five percent rule," the policy is a guideline, not a true rule; in some cases, firms may charge more (or less).

FINRA also restricts what a broker-dealer can charge beyond the commission. Certain chargeable services are permitted, but the costs must be reasonable. According to **FINRA Rule 2122** (Charges for Services Performed), these include

- amounts due for interest, principal, or dividends;
- costs for transfer, exchange, safekeeping, or the custody of securities; and
- other services.

Per the Securities and Exchange Act of 1934, brokers must deliver a form to customers outlining their relationship. **Section 17a-14** (Form CRS, for Preparation, Filing and Delivery of Form CRS) addresses this form—Form CRS. **Form CRS** is a relationship summary that explains important information for investors to know including

- fees and costs,
- any conflicts of interest,
- disciplinary history of any firm members, and
- how to get more information on the firm.

Accuracy is also legally required in statements and proxies sent to investors. **Section 14** of the SEA (Proxies) requires that proxies be accurate and that important information is not omitted.

QUICK REVIEW QUESTIONS

15. What percentage of margin are customers required to keep in their accounts?

16. What percentage may broker-dealers charge for commissions or markups/markdowns?

Best Execution, Suitability, and Discretion

FINRA Rule 5310 (Best Execution and Interpositioning) requires broker-dealers to get the best price possible for their customers. This rule also forbids **interpositioning**, a deceptive and illegal practice of using a third party to generate extra commissions. Similarly, **FINRA Rule 5290** (Order Entry and Execution Practices) prohibits members from **splitting** orders in such a way that they incur extra commissions.

A broker-dealer should make recommendations that are suitable for the customer who receives them. If broker-dealers tailor smart and suitable recommendations for their customers, there is no problem with a customer benefiting from this effort and transacting every such recommendation. However, FINRA views **suitability** as a three-part question:

- Per **FINRA Rule 2111** (Suitability), there must be a reasonable basis for the recommendation.
- The recommendation must fit the customer's specific investment profile, risk tolerance, and objectives.
- The recommendation must be quantitatively contextualized within the broader picture of the customer's existing positions, transaction costs, and other recommendations being made by the broker-dealer.

Time and price discretion is a stipulation of **FINRA Rule 3260** (Discretionary Accounts), which addresses just that—**discretion**. If a written authorization is not available, a customer may give the broker time and price discretion for a trade on the same day to buy or sell a specific amount of a security.

QUICK REVIEW QUESTIONS

17. What term describes the illegal practice of using a third party to generate extra commissions?

18. What FINRA rule addresses suitability by requiring a reasonable basis for an investment recommendation?

Activities of Unregistered Persons and the Protection of Seniors

FINRA Rule 2040 (Payments to Unregistered Persons) stipulates that, in certain cases, registered representatives can receive continuing commissions after they retire. In some cases under Rule 2040, nonregistered foreign persons may receive commissions; otherwise, it is generally prohibited to pay commissions to unregistered persons.

Finally, FINRA offers protections for vulnerable populations. Per **FINRA Rule 2165** (Financial Exploitation of Specified Adults), for customers aged 65 or older, as well as customers aged 18 or older who are reasonably believed to have a mental or physical impairment that renders them unable to protect their own interests, FINRA provides a **safe harbor** for members to pause disbursements and account transfers.

This intervention must be based on a reasonable belief that exploitation has taken place, will take place, or is taking place, and it must be immediately investigated. Notification must be given within two business days. The hold cannot persist beyond fifteen business days unless the facts and circumstances of the situation justify the member's initial belief about the occurrence of exploitation.

QUICK REVIEW QUESTIONS

19. For which customers does FINRA provide a safe harbor to pause disbursements in cases of possible exploitation?

20. Can registered representatives receive continuing commissions after they retire?

Answer Key

1. The term *turnover rate* describes the number of times a broker swaps a securities portfolio for another.

2. Backing away is the violation that occurs when the market maker fails to honor the quoted price.

3. Section 11d of the Securities Exchange Act of 1934 (SEA) prohibits broker-dealers who were part of the new issue of a security from extending credit to customers to finance that security.

4. In most cases, Regulation M defines the restricted period as beginning five days prior to the pricing of the offering.

5. Material nonpublic information (MNPI) refers to information that can impact a security's price but is not yet public knowledge.

6. Section 10b5-1 of the Securities Exchange Act of 1934 (SEA) specifically forbids using MNPI in trading securities.

7. The Insider Trading and Securities Fraud Enforcement Act (ITSFEA) increased the SEC's enforcement power against participants in insider trading.

8. The term *trading ahead* describes when a market maker uses its own account to fulfill a customer's trade instead of soliciting bids on the market. Trading ahead is prohibited by FINRA Rule 5320.

9. Fines, expulsion, and incarceration are all possible penalties for insider trading.

10. The Sarbanes-Oxley Act of 2002 amended the Securities Exchange Act of 1934 (SEA) and enhanced penalties for insider trading.

11. Members may not transact new security issues with restricted persons who will have a beneficial interest.

12. Section 10 of the Securities Exchange Act of 1934 (SEA) forbids using deception or fraud in the securities arena.

13. The Names Rule (SEC Rule 35d-1) stipulates that investment companies may not have deceptive or misleading names.

14. Yes, prior to first use, a principal must approve advertisements in writing per Municipal Securities Rulemaking Board (MSRB) Rule G-21 (Advertising).

15. FINRA Rule 4210 requires customers to keep at least 25% of equity in their accounts.

16. Per FINRA's 5% markup policy, broker-dealers should not charge more than 5% for commissions or markups/markdowns.

17. Interpositioning is the deceptive and illegal practice of using a third party to generate extra commissions.

18. Per FINRA Rule 2111, there must be a reasonable basis for the recommendation.

19. Customers aged 65 or older and customers aged 18 or older who have certain impairments are protected by the safe harbor rule (FINRA Rule 2165).

20. Yes, in certain cases, registered representatives can receive continuing commissions after they retire.

10 SIE Practice Test

Practice Test

1. Which of the following is NOT a characteristic of preferred stock?
   A) company ownership
   B) a fixed and guaranteed rate of return
   C) perpetuity
   D) priority over common stock for dividends

2. A company is calling the preferred stock it issued for $102. The preferred stock is convertible into 4 shares of common stock, which is trading at $20 per share. What should the holder of the preferred stock do?
   A) allow the preferred stock to be called by the company
   B) do nothing because the company cannot force shareholders to sell the preferred stock
   C) convert the preferred stock into shares of common stock
   D) sell the preferred stock to someone else at $100

3. General Manufacturing Corp has a $6 preferred stock that is outstanding. Which of the following statements is true?
   A) Par value is $100 per share.
   B) There is no par value.
   C) The issue is considered prior preferred.
   D) The issue can be converted into common stock at $6 per share.

4. An individual investor looking to receive a pro rata share of company dividends and the ability to vote for members of the board of directors should purchase what type of stock?
   A) common stock
   B) preferred stock
   C) prior preferred stock
   D) convertible preferred stock

5. Fixed-maturity securities are typically BEST described as which of the following?
   A) They provide fixed, periodic payments.
   B) They do not return the principal upon maturity.
   C) They are typically stocks or preferred stocks.
   D) They have payments that vary according to prime rate fluctuations.

6. All else being equal, which of the following types of municipal bonds issued by the City of Smallton is backed by the full faith and credit of Smallton?
   A) general obligation bond to build a schoolhouse in West Smallton
   B) revenue bond to build an Olympic-sized swimming pool in North Smallton
   C) moral obligation bond to buy salt trucks and snowplows for areas near Mount Smallton
   D) none of the above

7. Which of the following purchases has the LOWEST degree of risk to capital?
   A) common stocks
   B) options
   C) corporate bonds
   D) warrants

8. If the opening transaction in a customer's account is the purchase of $10,000 ABC convertible bonds at par, under Regulation T, how much cash must be deposited?
   A) $2,000
   B) $2,500
   C) $5,000
   D) $10,000

9. A stock's tangible NAV per share is the same as its
   A) book value.
   B) market value.
   C) par value.
   D) stated value.

10. A mutual fund invests almost entirely in short-term commercial paper and original issues of 6-month Treasury debt. How can its core asset class BEST be described?
    A) high yield
    B) equities
    C) money market
    D) commodities

11. From the perspective of a bond buyer, which of the following ratings by S&P Global is high yield for a bond issue?
    A) A+
    B) B+
    C) BBB−
    D) BBB+

12. Which of the following BEST characterizes REITs?
    A) They are investment vehicles that offer diversification.
    B) REITs are trusts, so they are not required to operate under the same rules as other public companies.
    C) They are only required to have fifty shareholders at a minimum.
    D) They are typically traded through Series A investments.

13. A UIT is characterized by which of the following?
    A) a managed portfolio of only Treasury bills and Treasury notes
    B) an unmanaged portfolio of stocks and bonds
    C) a managed portfolio of ETFs
    D) a portfolio that provides a basket of options so the investor can write calls when he wants to

14. Radio Mast Corporation is a REIT. This year, the corporation earned taxable income of $20 million, and it has 5 million shares outstanding. It declares a dividend in December to be paid in January of next year. What is the minimum amount of the per-share dividend?
    A) $4.00
    B) $3.80
    C) $3.60
    D) $3.40

15. SEC and FINRA rules require securities brokers to deliver an options disclosure document to customers before they do which of the following?
    A) open an option account
    B) effect an options trade
    C) sell an option contract
    D) sell an option contract short

16. A young professional decides to roll over her entire Roth 401(k) to a Roth IRA that she has set up specifically for this purpose. She chooses to set up this transaction in the form of a trustee-to-trustee transfer. How much of the balance will be withheld for taxes and penalties?
    A) 0%
    B) 10%
    C) 20%
    D) 25%

17. From its date of issuance, how long might a Treasury note take to mature?
    A) 1 year
    B) 7 years
    C) 20 years
    D) 30 years

18. After a registration statement is filed for an initial public offering, the SEC mandates a 20-day waiting period wherein certain activities relating to the IPO are prohibited. Which activity is permitted during the waiting period?
    A) sale of the offered security
    B) solicitation of indications of interest
    C) disclosure of new information about the company
    D) acceptance of deposits for a future sale of the security

19. A FINRA member requests information from a prospective customer who seeks to open a brokerage account. What information must be received and recorded before opening the new account?
    A) whether the customer is an associated person of another member firm
    B) the customer's social security number
    C) the customer's occupation
    D) the customer's residence

20. Which of the following transactions would NOT need to be registered with the Securities and Exchange Commission?
    A) initial public offering
    B) shelf offering
    C) intrastate offering
    D) Regulation A offering

21. A FINRA member firm files Form U4 after hiring a salesperson. Three days later, the member firm learns that the salesperson's residential history includes one address that the firm spelled incorrectly in its filing. Assuming no statutory disqualifications are involved, within how much time (from the date of learning of the error) must the FINRA member firm update its Form U4 filing?
    A) 7 days
    B) 10 days
    C) 30 days
    D) 60 days

22. Which of the following Treasury securities pays NO coupons?
    A) Treasury note
    B) Treasury bond
    C) Treasury bill
    D) TIPS

23. For an investment company to lawfully operate under the name *XYZ Cruelty-Free Cosmetics Equity Fund*, at LEAST what percent of its investments must consist of equity in cruelty-free cosmetics companies?
    A) 60%
    B) 70%
    C) 80%
    D) 90%

24. The content of an investment company's sales literature may include which of the following?
    A) inferences about future returns based on past performance
    B) charts and analysis based only on past performance
    C) commentary about future returns without discussion of risks and limitations
    D) assurances that the fund manager will not lose an investor's money

25. Of the following, which is a federally taxable, federally subsidized municipal bond?
    A) Treasury note
    B) general obligation bond
    C) Revenue Anticipation Note
    D) Build America Bonds

CONTINUE

26. PQR Corporation, an aircraft manufacturer based in the United States, raises $90 million via a 30-year bond sold exclusively to individual investors outside the United States. PQR Corporation does not register the issuance with the SEC. Which of the following Securities Act safe-harbor provisions is most applicable to this bond?
    A) Regulation S
    B) Rule 144a
    C) Rule 504 of Regulation D
    D) Section 3(a)(2)

27. Which of the following can be described as a blank-check company?
    A) unit investment trust company
    B) special purpose acquisition company
    C) direct participation program
    D) Depository Trust & Clearing Corporation

28. A noninstitutional customer buys a corporate bond on the day of a fixed-price offering at the public offering price from a broker-dealer who acquired the security as part of the offering. Which of the following must be included in the customer's transaction confirmation?
    A) National Best Bid at the time of the transaction
    B) National Best Offer at the time of the transaction
    C) the execution time of the transaction, expressed to the second
    D) the broker's markup, expressed as a dollar amount and percentage

29. Up to how many years after an alleged violation of FINRA rules may a complaint seeking arbitration be submitted?
    A) 3
    B) 4
    C) 6
    D) 9

30. A salesperson wants to drum up business by sending a letter to retail customers about opportunities presented by a multi-class agency debt instrument backed by a pool of mortgage pass-through securities or mortgage loans. All of the following must be included in this letter, EXCEPT
    A) the term *collateralized mortgage obligation* in the name of the product.
    B) a disclosure that agency backing applies to the product's face value, not to any premium paid.
    C) a comparison between this product and a bank certificate of deposit.
    D) a disclosure that yield will fluctuate with the prepayment rate of the underlying mortgages.

31. Which of the following is exempt from disclosure on the FINRA's BrokerCheck website?
    A) the full name of an associated person
    B) the reason for termination of an associated person as reported by a member on Form U5
    C) registration history of associated persons before their present employment with a member
    D) information about a Final Regulatory Action where an associated person was the subject

32. For a person other than the customer to exercise discretionary power in a particular customer account, a member firm must acquire and document all of the following EXCEPT
    A) written authorization from the customer.
    B) the date discretionary power shall expire.
    C) the date discretionary power is granted.
    D) the signature(s) of the person(s) authorized to exercise discretionary power in the account.

33. A FINRA member sells software that enables investors to perform analysis of various securities. This software (and any related retail communications) must
    A) come with a written disclosure of its limitations and assumptions.
    B) be fully functional with all securities in the selected asset class.
    C) reflect actual future investment results.
    D) provide the same results consistently when used repeatedly.

34. When can a registered principal supervise their own activities?
    A) never
    B) only on principal transactions
    C) only on agency transactions
    D) only when unavoidable

35. A customer has $10,000 to invest and wants to buy a government security at a discount, with a maturity in 3 months. Which government security should the investor purchase?
    A) Treasury bills
    B) Treasury notes
    C) Treasury bonds
    D) Treasury receipts

36. An individual investor looking to receive a pro rata share of company dividends and the ability to vote for members of the board of directors should purchase what type of stock?
    A) common stock
    B) preferred stock
    C) prior preferred stock
    D) convertible preferred stock

37. What is the difference between an open-end investment company and a closed-end investment company?
    A) investment objective
    B) fund management
    C) fund capitalization
    D) method used to calculate the NAV

38. What is the most important suitability consideration for a client who chooses to purchase a variable annuity?
    A) Monthly payments will remain fixed.
    B) There will be a penalty for the early withdrawal of funds.
    C) Assumed interest rate (AIR) will vary.
    D) Benefit payments will vary.

39. What risk is associated with a security that may lose value due to a drop in stock prices?
    A) credit risk
    B) market risk
    C) capital risk
    D) call risk

40. Who is responsible for ensuring that dividends and proxy information are distributed to the correct party after a shareholder sells his shares to another investor?
    A) officers of the issuing corporation
    B) brokerages of the buyer and seller
    C) the exchange where the shares traded
    D) the transfer agent and registrar

41. A 12b-1 fee is which of the following?
    A) a fee on a buy or sell transaction, charged by the broker to the investor
    B) an annual marketing or distribution fee on a mutual fund
    C) an annual fee assessed to a mutual fund's director, unless the director has less than $1 million in investable assets
    D) any fee on a mutual fund that is over 1% of the fund's net assets

42. A customer's first transaction in a margin account is a purchase of 100 shares of ABC for $50 per share. Under Regulation T, what is the customer's initial equity requirement?
    A) $1,000
    B) $1,500
    C) $2,500
    D) $5,000

43. Why is arbitration preferred over litigation to settle disputes in the securities industry?
    A) It is often less costly than litigation.
    B) It results in decisions that are more binding than those of local courts.
    C) It excludes those arguments from personnel of firms outside the industry.
    D) It allows the parties more opportunity to present their cases.

44. Which of the following groups establishes blue sky laws to protect investors from fraud?
    A) Congress
    B) states
    C) municipalities
    D) FINRA

45. A customer receiving interest income from holding a qualified private activity bond would MOST likely pay which of the following taxes?
    A) ordinary income tax
    B) alternative minimum tax
    C) capital gains tax
    D) excise taxes

46. A broker who extends credit for the purpose of purchasing or carrying margin stocks must comply with what rules?
    A) Regulation G
    B) Regulation T
    C) Regulation D
    D) Regulation X

47. Which of the following is true for individuals, regardless of their income level, who are active participants in an employer-sponsored qualified retirement plan?
    A) Contributions are allowed for Roth IRAs but not for traditional IRAs.
    B) Contributions to a Roth or traditional IRA are allowed.
    C) Contributions to an IRA are allowed but can never be deducted from gross income.
    D) Contributions to an IRA are allowed and can always be deducted from gross income.

48. Fixed-maturity securities are typically BEST described as which of the following?
    A) They provide fixed, periodic payments.
    B) They do not return the principal upon maturity.
    C) They are typically stocks or preferred stocks.
    D) They have payments that vary according to prime rate fluctuations.

49. A customer gave a registered representative $15,000 with instructions to "buy whatever tech stock you think is best and let me know when you're done." The registered representative must
    A) follow the customer's verbal instructions.
    B) ask the customer to repeat the verbal authorization to the representative's branch manager.
    C) accept the customer's verbal instructions only if the registered representative is registered as an investment advisor.
    D) obtain a signed and firm-approved discretionary disclosure from the customer before executing the instructions.

50. A market maker is asked by a customer for a firm offer on 1,000 shares of XYZ Corp stock. The market maker provides a quote of $15.46. The customer promptly responds by placing a limit order to buy 1,000 shares of XYZ Corp stock for $15.46 or better, but the market maker does not fill the order before the closing bell. Which term BEST describes the action of the firm holding XYZ Corp stock?
    A) interpositioning
    B) hypothecation
    C) disintermediation
    D) backing away

51. An increase in the price of open-end investment shares from the initial purchase is called what?
    A) accretion
    B) amortization
    C) appreciation
    D) capital gain

52. An investor owns a US government security with a 20-year maturity and interest coupons attached. What type of security does the investor own?
    A) Treasury bills
    B) Treasury notes
    C) Treasury bonds
    D) Treasury receipts

53. To create a limited partnership, which of the following must be filed with the state?
    A) limited partnership agreement
    B) limited partnership certificate
    C) subscription agreement
    D) underwriting agreement

54. The fees that a firm charges for services must adhere to what standard?
    A) They must be first approved by FINRA.
    B) They must represent a fair and reasonable charge.
    C) They may not exceed 5%.
    D) They must be based on what the market can bear.

55. Which of the following is the LOWEST investment-grade bond rating?
    A) AA
    B) BBB
    C) A
    D) C

56. Which statement applies to warrants?
    A) Warrants generally have voting rights.
    B) Warrants are the same as short-term options.
    C) Warrants cover 10 shares of the underlying stock.
    D) Warrants do not pay dividends.

57. Who would execute an order from a member firm to buy 100 XYZ stock?
    A) registered representatives
    B) floor brokers
    C) specialists
    D) competitive traders

58. Which of the following entities guarantees a listed option contract?
    A) the Options Clearing Corporation
    B) broker-dealer firms
    C) the seller of the option
    D) the exchange where the option was traded

59. A group of investors is interested in the purchase of a new-issue municipal bond of Ironworks City. Where would the investors go for information about the issue?
    A) bond registration statement
    B) new issue prospectus
    C) preliminary official statement
    D) Moody's or S&P bond-rating service

60. Which of the following is NOT a responsibility of a designated market maker?
    A) to communicate with NYSE-listed companies to let them know how their stock is trading
    B) to provide liquidity to ease large market imbalances
    C) to oversee opening and closing auctions
    D) to approve floor brokers for trading of individual securities

61. A customer enters an order for the purchase of XYZ stock at the best available price without specifying the price but expecting execution. What type of order is this?
    A) market order
    B) limit order
    C) stop order
    D) stop limit order

62. Atlantic Railroad Corp wants to sell 500,000 shares to the public. Of these, 200,000 are coming from the company's treasury shares and 300,000 are new shares. What is this offering considered?
    A) initial public offering
    B) primary distribution
    C) secondary distribution
    D) split offering

63. An associated person writes a retail communication recommending LMN stock as an attractive buy at $2.20. Three months later, LMN stock trades at an all-time high of $55.95. In what case may the associated person write follow-up correspondence that lists this extremely profitable recommendation without mentioning any other past recommendations?
    A) This is always permitted.
    B) This is permitted only if the firm has made no other recommendation for similar securities in the past year.
    C) This is permitted only if the firm has made no other recommendations in the past year at all.
    D) This is never permitted.

64. When can a FINRA member firm sell collateralized mortgage obligations (CMOs) to a first-time customer without providing educational materials about CMO characteristics and risks?
    A) never
    B) when the customer affirms in writing that she understands CMOs and their risks
    C) when the customer is an institutional investor
    D) any time

65. When is a member permitted to temporarily prevent disbursements from an account in good standing that belongs to an adult customer believed to have no mental or physical impairment?
    A) when the customer is 65 or older
    B) under no circumstances
    C) upon reasonable belief that exploitation has happened, will happen, or is happening
    D) when A and C are both true

66. Which of the following constitutes backing away by a member firm?
    A) placing an offer to tighten a market, then canceling it and buying from other offers at that price
    B) providing a firm quotation to a customer and then refusing to trade promptly at that level
    C) buying and selling a large amount of the same penny stock to create an illusion of activity
    D) trading for a principal account before effecting a same-way agency transaction for a customer

67. A broker-dealer establishes a monthly list of trade recommendations based on extensive analysis of risk and reward and sends them only to retail customers whose specific investment profiles and risk appetites are a match for all of the recommended trades. One of those customers receives the list and asks if he should trade all of the recommendations simultaneously in his portfolio. Based on the suitability standard, is there a reason for the broker-dealer to recommend against this course of action?

    A) No; customers bear the burden of determining the suitability of a recommendation.
    B) No; the suitability of each recommendation is considered separate from other recommendations.
    C) Yes; all of the individual recommendations may be good, but they may be dangerously correlated.
    D) Yes; a customer should never trade every recommendation provided by a broker-dealer.

68. A registered representative in New York City is prohibited from cold-calling a prospective customer's residence at 10:30 a.m. EST if that customer
    A) has not specifically requested a cold call.
    B) has published their phone number in a public directory.
    C) resides in San Francisco, California.
    D) is not listed in the FTC's do-not-call registry.

69. A member firm files Form U4 to register a new hire as an associated person, but the member is unable to review a copy of the new hire's most recent Form U5. What must the member do if it is unable to review Form U5 within 60 days of filing Form U4?
    A) No additional action is required.
    B) The member must demonstrate to FINRA that it took steps to review the most recent Form U5.
    C) The member must withdraw the Form U4 filing until it can review the most recent Form U5.
    D) The member must terminate the employment of the new hire.

70. Which of the following is necessarily true of a Treasury note that trades roughly at par?
    A) Its current yield roughly equals its nominal yield.
    B) Its nominal yield roughly equals zero.
    C) Its current yield roughly equals zero.
    D) It is an on-the-run Treasury security.

71. Which of the following methods for holding securities allows investors to maintain stock ownership in book entry form with the issuer?
    A) physical certificates
    B) direct registration
    C) street-name registration
    D) treasury stock

72. Of the following account types, which may a broker liquidate due to a decline in market value?
    A) cash
    B) margin
    C) traditional IRA
    D) Roth IRA

73. Which of the following debt products is NOT secured with collateral?
    A) equipment trust certificate
    B) senior debenture
    C) residential mortgage-backed security
    D) credit card asset–backed security

74. Select the true statement.
    A) Hedge funds are not subject to any disclosure requirements.
    B) Hedge funds are subject to more stringent disclosure requirements than mutual funds.
    C) Hedge funds are subject to the same disclosure requirements as mutual funds.
    D) Hedge funds are subject to less stringent disclosure requirements than mutual funds.

75. Robert and Susan have a joint tenancy account with rights of survivorship. Robert designates Thomas as his sole beneficiary in his will. To whom does Robert's stake in the account go if Robert passes away?
    A) Susan only
    B) Thomas only
    C) Robert's estate
    D) Half to Susan and half to Thomas

76. If there is no activity in a client's account, how often must the brokerage firm send a statement to the client?
    A) monthly
    B) quarterly
    C) semiannually
    D) yearly

77. A customer of Retirement Investment Advisers, Inc, signs the required documentation to convert his retirement account into a discretionary account. The registered representative responsible for the account purchases 2,000 shares of a mutual fund offered by his firm for $50.00 without asking the customer for approval first. One week later, the registered representative sells the shares for a small profit at $50.45, again without contacting the customer. A month after that, the registered representative buys another 2,000 shares of the same mutual fund for $50.00 without asking the customer for approval. Is the registered representative breaking the law?
    A) No, because he has generated a profit.
    B) No, because the customer submitted paperwork to make the account discretionary.
    C) Yes, because he is churning.
    D) Yes, because he failed to notify the customer of his trades before executing them.

78. Firm X is a member of a selling group, and Firm Y is not a participant in the offering. Firm X sells a small number of shares to Firm Y at a price that is slightly below the public offering price. This is considered to be what?
    A) illegal
    B) reallowance
    C) retention
    D) undercutting

79. A registered representative who has limited trading authorization in a client's account may do which of the following?
    A) deduct a monthly fee for handling the account
    B) buy and sell stocks, bonds, warrants, and mutual funds
    C) transfer securities in and out of the client's account
    D) pay money to a third party

80. The Securities Act of 1933 pertains to which securities market?
    A) primary
    B) secondary
    C) third
    D) fourth

81. A city issuing bonds would retain the services of what type of attorney to issue a legal opinion?
    A) city attorney
    B) district attorney
    C) trust attorney
    D) bond counsel

82. If someone wants to review the performance of a revenue bond that matures in 30 years, where would that person look?
    A) Bond Buyer 20 Bond Index
    B) Bond Buyer 30 Bond Index
    C) Revenue Bond Index
    D) Visible Supply

83. What is cash flow?
    A) gross income less operating expenses and mortgage costs
    B) gross income less depreciation plus mortgage costs
    C) gross income plus depreciation plus operating expenses
    D) net income less operating expenses, mortgage costs, and depreciation

84. A customer looking to buy a Treasury security directly from the US government that matures in 10 years would choose which of the following?
    A) Treasury bonds
    B) Treasury notes
    C) Treasury bills
    D) Treasury STRIPS

85. A client tells you to buy 340 shares of Company XYZ at $45 per share, with the note "AON." Two hundred shares are bought at $45, but then the price rises to $47. What will happen to the client's order?
    A) He will not be filled with any shares.
    B) He will buy 200 shares at $47 because that is where the stock price is now.
    C) He won't trade with you because you didn't get the order he wanted.
    D) The entire order will be executed at $46 because that is the average price.

Answer Key

Answer Key

1. **B is correct.** Preferred stock does not provide a guaranteed dividend; when dividends are issued and paid, they are based on a fixed (stated) rate.

2. **A is correct.** The parity price of the common stock can be determined by dividing the call price ($102) by the number of shares of common stock into which the preferred stock is convertible (4 shares), equaling $25.50 ($102 ÷ 4 = 25.50). Because the common stock is trading at $20.00 per share, the shareholder should allow the preferred stock to be called, resulting in 4 shares valued higher than the prevailing market value.

3. **B is correct.** The dividend is explicitly stated as a $6 sum rather than as a yield, which means that no par value is necessary to determine the dividend payout.

4. **A is correct.** Common stock allows the shareholder to receive a pro rata share of dividends issued and vote for members of the board of directors.

5. **A is correct.** Fixed-maturity securities, also known as fixed-income securities, provide a known, fixed, periodic payment. At maturity, they return the principal. Bonds are the most common type of fixed-income securities; however, preferred stocks can also be fixed-income securities. Certificates of deposit (CDs) and money markets are other types of fixed-income securities.

6. **A is correct.** General obligation bonds are a common municipal debt instrument that is backed by the full faith and credit of the issuer. In contrast, a revenue bond is backed by cash flows from a specific project or activity, and a moral obligation bond is not technically backed by anything save for the issuer's desire to maintain its credit quality.

7. **C is correct.** Corporate bonds have the lowest risk to capital (as most debt securities do) and would provide the customer with a priority claim on assets upon dissolution of the company during a bankruptcy proceeding.

8. **C is correct.** Under Regulation T, the margin requirement is 50% for convertible corporate bonds.

9. **A is correct.** The tangible net asset value (NAV) of a stock is the same as its book value.

10. **C is correct.** Money market securities are liquid, with minimal credit risk and short-term maturities. Commercial paper, or unsecured short-term promissory notes issued by corporations, represent one example of a money market security; Treasury bills represent another. Money market yields tend to be low, partly because they lack much credit risk and partly because they are short-term investments that reside at the front of the yield curve.

11. **B is correct.** Bond ratings can be divided into "investment grade" and "high yield," with the latter also described as "speculative," "noninvestment grade," or "junk." Of the three major rating agencies, S&P and Fitch use a rating scale that categorizes issues from AAA to D. Bonds categorized as BBB− or better are considered investment-grade securities. Bonds categorized as BB+ or worse are considered high-yield securities. (Moody's uses a slightly different scale, from AAA to C.)

12. **A is correct.** Real estate investment trusts (REITs) offer diversification and are required to operate under the same rules as public companies. REITs must have a minimum of one hundred shareholders, and they are traded on major stock exchanges.

13. **B is correct.** A unit investment trust (UIT) is an unmanaged portfolio of stocks and bonds designed to provide capital appreciation and/or dividend income.

14. **C is correct.** Real estate investment trusts (REITs) must distribute 90% or more of their taxable income to shareholders as dividends. They must also invest three-fourths or more of their assets in real estate and derive three-fourths or more of their gross income from real estate–related sources.

15. **B is correct.** The Options Clearing Corporation (OCC) maintains a document titled "Characteristics and Risks of Standardized Options," often called the options disclosure document (ODD). It is more than 180 pages and must be provided to customers before they buy or sell an option contract. The ODD explains the risks and attributes of listed options. It is available for download, and printed copies are sold at a low price by the OCC.

16. **A is correct.** An early retirement plan distribution would normally be subject to mandatory 20% withholding, and an early IRA distribution would normally be subject to mandatory 10% withholding. However, when the retirement plan distribution is transacted directly into the IRA (as is the case with a trustee-to-trustee transfer or with a distribution check made out to the IRA), the IRS stipulates that no taxes will be withheld.

17. **B is correct.** The US Treasury currently issues Treasury notes in terms of 2, 3, 5, 7, and 10 years. Treasury notes bear coupon interest semiannually until maturity. Longer-term Treasury debt is known as a bond rather than a note and bears coupon interest semiannually as well. Shorter-term Treasury debt is known as a bill and does not bear coupon interest.

18. **B is correct.** During the waiting period, also known as the "cooling-off" period, the issuer may not engage in sales activity, but soliciting and receiving nonbinding indications of interest is permitted. This sometimes helps determine demand for the new issue; however, no new information that is not included in the preliminary prospectus may be provided in the process. Also, no deposits may be accepted during the cooling-off period for the purpose of transacting the security after the cooling-off period has ended.

19. **D is correct.** For every account held by a customer who is a natural person, FINRA requires that members keep records of the customer's name and residence. In addition, the customer's legal age status must be known, and if the customer is under eighteen, the contact information for a trusted guardian of that individual must also be kept. The member must also keep track of any associated persons assigned to monitor or interact with the account, as well as the signature of a principal denoting that the account was opened in accordance with the firm's policies and procedures. For noninstitutional accounts in which investments go beyond the scope of mutual fund shares not recommended by the member or the member's associated persons, a FINRA member is required to make a reasonable effort to obtain the customer's social security number, occupation, employer address, and status as an associated person of another firm. This effort must be made before settlement of the first transaction in the account.

20. **C is correct.** Intrastate offerings are exempt from SEC registration under a safe-harbor provision of Rule 147 of the Securities Act of 1933. To qualify, the issuer must be incorporated in the state of distribution, must conduct a large amount of its business there, and the securities must be offered and sold exclusively to residents of that state.

21. **C is correct.** Form U4 (Uniform Application for Securities Industry Registration or Transfer) is used to establish registration of an associated person. When a member firm must amend Form U4, it has a period of 30 days to do so. In cases where the amendment involves a statutory disqualification, that period is shortened to 10 days.

22. **C is correct.** Treasury bills are issued at a discount to par with maturities of 1 year or less and pay no coupons. Treasury notes have maturities of 2, 3, 5, 7, or 10 years. Treasury bonds have maturities of 20 or 30 years. Both Treasury notes and Treasury bonds pay coupons. Treasury Inflation-Protected Securities (TIPS) are issued with maturities of 5, 10, and 30 years, and TIPS pay coupons.

23. **C is correct.** SEC Rule 35(d)-1, also known as the Names Rule, stipulates that investment companies may not have deceptive or misleading names. Investment companies whose names state a particular investment focus must maintain 80% or more of their assets invested in the stated area of focus.

24. **B is correct.** SEC Rule 156 prohibits false or misleading content in an investment company's sales literature. This includes untrue statements, misleading statements, and omissions of material facts. Assertions that future returns can be inferred from past performance is one example of an untrue statement. Assurances that there is no downside risk is an example of a misleading statement. Failure to describe risks associated with the investment is an example of an omission of material fact.

25. **D is correct.** Build America Bonds were established by the American Recovery and Reinvestment Act of 2009 in response to concerns about reduced confidence in the ability of state and local governments to access capital in debt markets. These bonds came in two versions, one involving direct payments from the federal government to issuers in the amount of 35% of the issuer's interest costs, and another granting tax credits to bondholders for 35% of interest costs. These bonds could not be issued by private institutions, and they could only be used for the same purposes permitted for tax-exempt municipal bonds. By making Build America Bonds federally taxable (unlike other municipal bonds), the federal government gave a broader group of market participants an incentive to buy Build America Bonds.

26. **A is correct.** Regulation S exempts debt issuances that are offered to and bought by non-US-located buyers from registration with the SEC. Rule 144a does not apply when a security is offered to individual investors; a 144a security can be purchased only by Qualified Institutional Buyers (QIBs). Rule 504 of Regulation D is intended for small issuances; it does not apply to issuances that exceed $5 million in a 12-month period. Section 3(a)(2) applies to bank note programs.

27. **B is correct.** Special purpose acquisition companies (SPACs), also known as blank-check companies, are publicly listed companies with no stated business operations. They exist only to merge with or acquire another company. A unit investment trust (UIT) maintains a particular, usually fixed, portfolio of securities designed around a stated investment objective in a buy-and-hold strategy; investors can purchase units of the total portfolio. A direct participation program is a pooled investment whereby limited partners can invest in businesses without taking on the personal liability assumed by the general partners who manage the business operations of the entity. The Depository Trust & Clearing Corporation is the most active clearinghouse and settlement processor for financial markets in the United States.

28. **C is correct.** Noninstitutional customer transactions for corporate or agency debt securities must be accompanied by confirmations that include the exact time of the transaction, so Option C is correct. According to FINRA Rule 2232, markup (or markdown) disclosure is NOT required as part of the transaction confirmation when a broker-dealer acquires securities as part of a fixed-price offering and sells them at the public offering price (POP) on the same day. Finally, a corporate bond is generally not considered a national market system (NMS) security by the SEC. Usually, there is no way to observe a National Best Bid and Offer (NBBO) for these securities.

29. **C is correct.** According to FINRA Rule 12206, claims submitted for arbitration cannot postdate the alleged violation by more than 6 years. However, this limitation does not preclude legal action in court for grievances that took place more than 6 years prior. In fact, a party that succeeds in having a FINRA arbitration claim dismissed using Rule 12206 agrees that the claimant has a right to pursue the grievance (and any related grievances) in court.

30. **C is correct.** The product being pitched is an agency collateralized mortgage obligation (CMO). FINRA Rule 2216 controls the content and presentation of retail communications regarding CMO products. Options A, B, and D describe requirements imposed as part of Rule 2216; however, retail communications regarding CMOs are not permitted to compare the CMO to any other investment product, not even to a bank certificate of deposit (CD).

31. **B is correct.** BrokerCheck is a tool for transparency and a central repository of information about employment history, registration exam history, and disciplinary actions. However, information reported only in Section 3 ("Reason for Termination") of Form U5 is not disclosed through BrokerCheck when an associated person leaves employment with a member.

32. **B is correct.** For a person or group to exercise discretionary power in a customer account, FINRA requires members to receive the customer's written authorization, and also requires members to record the signature(s) of the empowered person or group. This information must be recorded along with the date that discretionary power is granted. A termination date of discretionary power is not required to be set.

33. **A is correct.** FINRA establishes disclosure requirements for investment analysis tools. One such requirement is a description of the methodology and criteria used, including the limitations and assumptions thereof. Software is permitted to exclude or favor certain investments, as long as the reasons are explained in writing. Analysis results may depend on constantly changing factors like market contexts, user-generated inputs, and randomized characteristics, and the fact that results may vary with each use and over time must be disclosed in writing. Software is not expected to predict the future, and the hypothetical nature of its predictive analysis must be clearly disclosed using specific language.

34. **D is correct.** With few exceptions—all of which must be unavoidable, documented, and explained—FINRA rules disallow an associated person who performs a supervisory role from supervising their own activities. Furthermore, no associated person may supervise people who make decisions about their compensation and continued employment.

35. **A is correct.** US government securities issued with a maturity of 1 year or less are called Treasury bills. They are zero-coupon bonds. Treasury receipts are not issued by the US government.

36. **A is correct.** Common stock allows the shareholder to receive a pro rata share of dividends issued and vote for members of the board of directors.

37. **C is correct.** Capitalization is the chief difference between open-end and closed-end investment companies. Open-end funds (referred to as mutual funds) continuously issue new shares for investors; closed-end funds (referred to as publicly traded funds) trade in the secondary market, similar to corporate stocks.

38. **D is correct.** Income from a variable annuity will vary and is not fixed (as with a fixed annuity); this may be a concern for an individual who is dependent on a certain level of monthly income in retirement.

39. **B is correct.** Market risk (also known as systematic risk) is the risk that a security may lose value due to a decline in the market.

40. **D is correct.** Companies use a transfer agent and registrar to log ownership changes, generate and keep shareholder records, cancel and issue share certificates, make dividend distributions, and manage annual meeting services. These functions can be separated from one another, but in practice, they are often combined. Transfer agents must register with regulators.

41. **B is correct.** According to the Investment Company Act of 1940, a 12b-1 fee is an annual marketing or distribution fee on a mutual fund.

42. **C is correct.** Regulation T requires 50% initial equity for margined long stock positions. The total cost of the shares is $5,000, so the customer must have equity of $2,500 for this transaction.

43. **A is correct.** Arbitration is generally less costly than litigation.

44. **B is correct.** States establish blue sky laws. They are separate from, but similar to, federal securities laws insofar as they protect investors from fraudulent exploitation in the securities markets. The term refers to a quote from Supreme Court justice Joseph McKenna about "speculative schemes which have no more basis than so many feet of blue sky."

45. **B is correct.** Qualified private activity bonds are taxable under the alternative minimum tax. These bonds are issued by (or for) a municipal or state government to finance qualified projects, and they are typically exempt from many taxes.

46. **B is correct.** Regulation T deals with the extension of margin credit from broker-dealers and their customers. Regulation G was established to provide transparency regarding a bank's compliance with anti-discrimination lending laws. Regulation D pertains to private placement exemptions. Regulation X protects consumers applying for and securing mortgage loans.

47. **B is correct.** Individuals participating in an employer-sponsored qualified retirement plan may also contribute to an individual retirement account (either traditional or Roth IRA) under the provisions of the Tax Reform Act of 1986. Depending on their income level, they may be able to deduct contributions to a traditional IRA from gross income.

48. **A is correct.** Fixed-maturity securities, also known as fixed-income securities, provide a known, fixed, periodic payment. At maturity, they return the principal. Bonds are the most common type of fixed-income securities; however, preferred stocks can also be fixed-income securities. Certificates of deposit (CDs) and money markets are other types of fixed-income securities.

49. **D is correct.** This situation describes a discretionary transaction. According to FINRA Rule 3260, it requires written authorization from the customer and approval by the registered representative's firm.

50. **D is correct.** Backing away is a prohibited practice whereby market makers do not honor their quoted bids and offers. The market maker has backed away from his firm offer of $15.46 for the stock by failing to execute the customer's limit order. Interpositioning is a deceptive and illegal practice of using a third party to generate extra commissions; hypothecation is involved in lending, so it is irrelevant here; and disintermediation essentially means "cutting out the middleman" in transactions or decision-making processes.

51. **C is correct.** An increase in the share price of an open-end investment, like a US mutual fund, is referred to as a "price appreciation." Capital appreciation is often a stated goal for mutual funds, and it does not turn into a capital gain until a taxable event occurs.

52. **C is correct.** Treasury bonds have a maturity of more than 10 years and provide interest coupon payments. The other options either have shorter maturity rates or do not have coupons attached. Treasury bills are short term with a maturity of 1 year or less; Treasury notes have a maturity between 1 and 10 years. Treasury receipts are a zero-coupon bond, meaning the investor buys the receipt at a deep discount and, when the bond reaches maturity, can receive the full value of the receipt.

53. **B is correct.** A state requires that a certificate of limited partnership be filed to establish a limited partnership.

54. **B is correct.** Fees to a firm's customers must be fair and reasonable and not unfairly discriminatory among its customers.

55. **B is correct.** Bonds that are deemed investment grade have ratings of AAA, AA, A, or BBB. Bonds that are rated C or lower are considered high-yield bonds, or junk bonds.

56. **D is correct.** Warrants represent a right, but not an obligation, to purchase shares of the underlying stock directly from the issuer. Until the warrant is exercised, the stock has not been bought, so there are no dividends paid to the warrant holder. Warrants are often structured like options, but they generally have a longer time to maturity. The number of shares addressed by each warrant can vary; an investor may need several warrants to purchase 1 share.

57. **B is correct.** A floor broker performs order executions for member firms.

58. **A is correct.** Listed options contracts are cleared and guaranteed by the Options Clearing Corporation (OCC).

59. **C is correct.** The bond's official statement would provide investors with information about a new-issue municipal bond, just as a prospectus provides information about a new-issue corporate security. Municipal bonds are exempt from the registration requirements under the Securities Act of 1933.

60. **D is correct.** Designated market makers, formerly called specialists, assume accountability for orderly trading of stocks on the NYSE. They serve as liaisons to issuers listed on the exchange, provide liquidity to offset imbalances, reinforce the National Best Bid and Offer (NBBO) throughout the trading day, oversee the opening and closing auctions, facilitate price discovery, and dampen volatility. They are not, however, responsible for the approval of floor brokers; that is a responsibility that belongs to the exchange itself.

61. **A is correct.** Market orders are the only type of order that guarantees immediate execution. Market orders may trade at a price that is substantially higher or lower than the last trade.

62. **D is correct.** The offering described is a split offering, also known as a combined offering, because it includes a primary distribution of new shares and a secondary distribution of previously issued treasury shares.

63. **B is correct.** FINRA prohibits correspondence or retail communication that cherry-picks specific past recommendations that would have generated a profit. However, lists of all recommendations by a member firm for "the same type, kind, grade or classification of securities" from the past year or longer are permitted. In this case, the associated person may indeed list this profitable recommendation by itself. The statement must include, "it should not be assumed that recommendations made in the future will be profitable or will equal the performance of the securities in this list." The associated person must also include the security name, recommended action, date and price at that time, recommended target entry price, and current price.

64. **C is correct.** Collateralized mortgage obligations (CMOs) are a complicated product with esoteric correlation risks. These risks are generally considered to have been a contributing factor to the Great Recession. Before selling CMOs to any person except an institutional investor, FINRA requires that a member firm provide educational materials about CMO structure, characteristics, risks, terminology, and key facts.

65. **D is correct.** According to FINRA Rule 2165, members have a safe harbor to pause disbursements and account transfers for customers 65 or older. This intervention must be based on a reasonable belief that exploitation has taken place, will take place, or is taking place, and it must be immediately investigated. Notification must be given within 2 business days, and the hold cannot persist beyond 15 business days unless the member's initial belief about the occurrence of exploitation is justified by investigation.

66. **B is correct.** Backing away is the practice of providing ostensibly firm quotations but then qualifying them or refusing to trade when the customer responds with an interest to trade at that level. This is a prohibited practice. Option A describes spoofing; Option C describes "painting the tape"; Option D describes front-running. These three practices are considered manipulative and/or exploitative and are also prohibited.

67. **C is correct.** A broker-dealer should not make recommendations that are unsuitable for a customer who receives them. If a broker-dealer does the work to specifically tailor smart and suitable recommendations for its customers, there is no problem with a customer benefiting from this effort and transacting every such recommendation. However, FINRA views suitability as a three-part question: 1) there must be a reasonable basis for the recommendation; 2) the recommendation must fit the customer's specific investment profile, risk tolerance, and objectives; 3) the recommendation must be quantitatively contextualized within the broader picture of the customer's existing positions, transaction costs, and other recommendations being made by the broker-dealer. Option C correctly touches on this third point of quantitative suitability because while each recommendation may be good, taking them all together would expose the investor to excessive risk.

68. **C is correct.** Cold calls—calls that are not predicated on an existing business or personal relationship—are not permitted before 8:00 a.m. or after 9:00 p.m. in the called party's location.

69. **B is correct.** Each member is responsible for investigating the good character, business reputation, qualifications, and experience of the employees that it sponsors for FINRA registration. Part of this process includes a review of the most recent Form U5 for an employee, which corresponds to the termination of the employee's status as an associated person of a previous employer. However, if this is not possible, the member shall demonstrate to FINRA that it has made a reasonable effort to review the most recent Form U5.

70. **A is correct.** Treasury notes pay coupons, so their nominal yield should never be zero. Long-term interest rates in the United States are positive as a matter of policy, so the current yield of a Treasury note should also never be zero. When a bond trades near par, that means the coupon ("nominal") yield roughly equals the market-determined ("current") yield. This can happen with off-the-run Treasurys (not the most recently auctioned ones) if the market-determined yield hovers near the coupon yield.

71. **B is correct.** The Direct Registration System (DRS) allows assets to be moved electronically and with little effort. This enables a very large volume of stock to change hands without extraordinarily long settlement times. Some shareholders prefer to bear physical stock certificates. Others hold shares in street name, simplifying their interactions with their brokerage firms and allowing their brokers to clear only their net transacted share differences through the National Securities Clearing Corporation (NSCC). Treasury stock is not held in any investor's name; it is stock that was previously outstanding, later reacquired by the issuer.

72. **B is correct.** A customer with a margin account can post equity and borrow funds from the broker to buy and sell securities. If the value of these securities declines beyond a certain threshold, the customer will typically be asked to post additional equity (a "margin call"). Depending on market conditions, the broker sometimes liquidates holdings of an account immediately without contacting the customer first. Liquidation based solely on a decline in market value does not happen in a cash account, which is fully capitalized by the customer. Some IRAs allow what is known as "limited margin." Limited margin in a retirement account typically permits a customer to borrow against impending settlements, but it is not a means for the customer to use additional leverage.

73. **B is correct.** In the United States, a debenture is an unsecured bond that is not collateralized by a claim on specific assets or cash flows thereof. When issued by a corporation, a debenture falls in the more junior portion of the capital structure. Typically, in the event of bankruptcy, holders of a debenture may recover some of their investment after holders of more senior collateralized debt are made whole. An equipment trust certificate (ETC) is a form of debt that is commonly used to purchase commercial aircraft. Residential mortgage-backed securities (RMBSs) are collateralized with homes, and the cash flows of credit card asset–backed securities (ABS) are derived from a pool of credit card debt.

74. **D is correct.** In general, investors in mutual funds have the benefit of greater transparency and stronger federal and state legal protections than investors in hedge funds. Both investment vehicles have a fiduciary duty to investors, and both are prohibited from engaging in fraudulent behavior. Some small hedge funds are not required to file periodic reports with the SEC. For these reasons and others, Rule 506(b) imposes a maximum of thirty-five nonaccredited investors who may invest in a hedge fund offering.

75. **A is correct.** Unlike a tenancy in common arrangement, the ownership stake of a deceased stakeholder in a joint tenancy account stays with the remaining stakeholders. Even though Robert's will leaves his estate to Thomas, Susan retains Robert's stake in the joint tenancy account in the event of Robert's death.

76. **B is correct.** If there is no activity in the account, the client receives quarterly statements. If there is activity, the client receives a monthly statement.

77. **C is correct.** A registered representative is permitted to make trades in a discretionary account without the prior knowledge or instructions of the customer. However, this situation is an example of churning, an unlawful practice whereby a registered representative makes unnecessary trades in a customer account to generate commissions or sales charges (SCs). While churning is sometimes difficult to prove, a rapid series of buys and sells in a discretionary account intended for long-term investment is a clear red flag. These trades may not be profitable after redemption fees are applied, and even if they are, profits may receive inferior tax treatment depending on the context and circumstances of the client's finances.

78. **B is correct.** Selling a small amount of an offering at a discount to a firm that is not a participant in the selling group is considered a reallowance. It is an incentive for Firm Y to sell shares to its customers.

79. **B is correct.** Limited trading authorizations allow the registered representative to buy and sell for the client. The registered representative cannot withdraw money or securities.

80. **A is correct.** The Securities Act of 1933 governs the initial registration and distribution of securities, which is the primary market.

81. **D is correct.** A bond counsel provides legal opinion on the issuance of bonds.

82. **C is correct.** The Revenue Bond Index is composed of 25 revenue bonds with a maturity in 30 years, with a Moody's rating of A1 and an S&P rating of A+. Option A is incorrect, as the 20 Bond Index is an index of general obligation (GO) bonds. Option B is incorrect as there is no 30 Bond Index. Option D is a measurement of the supply of municipal bonds about to be issued within 30 days.

83. **A is correct.** Cash flow is based on the operating expenses and mortgage costs of the program as deducted from gross income.

84. **B is correct.** Treasury notes have a maturity of 10 years. Separate Trading of Registered Interest and Principal of Securities (STRIPS) must be purchased through a financial institution or brokerage firm.

85. **A is correct.** All or none (AON) is a condition in which the broker must fill the order in its entirety or not at all. Here, there is insufficient supply to meet the quantity requested by the client, so the order will be canceled at the close of the market.

www.ingramcontent.com/pod-product-compliance
Lightning Source LLC
Chambersburg PA
CBHW080734300426
44114CB00019B/2585